The Church
and the Latin American
Revolution

The Church
and the Latin American
Revolution

François Houtart and Emile Pin
translated from the French by Gilbert Barth

Sheed and Ward : New York

Acknowledgments

The authors wish to express their thanks to Msgr. Luigi G. Ligutti, Permanent Observer of the Holy See to the Food and Agriculture Organization of the United Nations, and Director for International Affairs of the National Catholic Rural Life Conference. Without his help the research carried on by FERES (International Federation of Institutions for Socio-Religious and Social Research) would not have been possible. We also wish to thank Msgr. Manuel Larrain, president of CELAM, and Msgr. Helder Camara, vice president of CELAM, as an expression of our admiration for their pioneer work. Finally, we express our gratitude to Frédéric Debuyst for his invaluable assistance. Rev. Emile Pin, S.J., assumes responsibility for chapters 13, 14, 15, and Abbé François Houtart for the editing of the entire work.

Contents

I

Historical Introduction

1

The Early Centuries

CONQUEST AND EVANGELIZATION, 1492–1520

At the end of the fifteenth century, Spain had just completed the *reconquista*. The crusading spirit which animated the country did not, however, die out with the expulsion of the Moors. On the contrary, Spain became conscious of her forces, which were young and real and which were to seek beyond the seas an outlet worthy of their vitality. The discovery and conquest of the Indies would prove to be such an outlet.[1]

The work of unification accomplished by the Catholic Kings had marvelously prepared the ground. It would be up to Charles V to justify it. This great monarch felt charged with a mission which was both imperial and Christian, and which was steeped in the waves of humanism then surging over Europe. But the son did not inherit the broad outlook of the father. The intransigent and somber Philip II was to close the windows of Spain to the gusts of the Renaissance. Humanistic universalism was to give way, during the second half of the sixteenth century, to a cultural and religious isolation, and this held heavy consequences for the colonization of the Indies, which was to become the exclusive work of the *Hispanidad.*

What kind of more or less conscious objectives did Spanish colonization pursue? Although it is almost impossible to separate them, so much do they intermingle, complement or even contradict each other, we can distinguish a spiritual, an economic and a humanistic objective.

The spiritual objective of colonization was to enlarge the territory of Christianity. By virtue of the Bull of Alexander VI (1493) this was part of the very mission of the kings. In his *Ordenanzas de Poblaciones* of 1573, Philip II explained it thus: "The principal motive that urges us to make new discoveries is the preaching and diffusion of the Catholic Faith, so that the Indians might be educated and live in peace and order."

The economic objective of the colonization needs little explanation. In the war-ridden sixteenth century, the political power of European countries depended in great measure on monetary possessions. The Indies represented a precious reservoir of raw materials which could feed the coffers of the State, and the State would not hesitate to tap it.

Finally, a humanistic objective was not absent from the colonial venture. In addition to being the fief of a new Christianity, the Indies appeared as the Chosen Land, a utopia for a new golden age of humanity. It would not only slake the thirst of the *conquistadores* for riches and power, but also attract the great educators of the time, the missionaries (principally the Jesuits), who would strive to implant there a humanistic and Christian social order.

As must be evident, these diverse objectives can be understood only against the cultural and political background of the Iberian Peninsula. They merge together or remain distinct depending on the groups which made the conquest or were responsible for the colonization. Keeping this in mind will help toward understanding the paradoxes and contradictions of the "American epic."

The conquest, therefore, was not brought about by a truly objective need, that is, the need for an expanding population to emigrate. It was rather an answer to the subjective aspiration of a few strong personalities who often acted without mandate and outside the control of a colonial administration. These *conquistadores,* these far-seeing adventurers, in some thirty years' time, made themselves masters of an immense continent. They were driven by the lure of profit and the mirage of gold; but also by *la virtud,* an ensemble of qualities expressing courage, the dream of grandeur and renown, and the confidence in invincibility which a militant faith inspires—even though that faith be at the service of material undertakings.[2]

The spirit in which the *conquistadores* operated explains why there was a hasty occupation of the territories and an unimaginative extraction of riches, rather than a truly economic development of the land, as was accomplished in the Anglo-Saxon colonies. As Pierre Chaunu observes, in Anglo-Saxon America colonization preceded conquest, while in Latin America conquest preceded colonization.[3] This resulted in a destructive exploitation not only of natural resources, but of human relationships.[4] The military shock of the conquest, the herding of the Indians into the backlands or their utilization as forced labor, the introduction of epidemics, the destruction or hispanization of aboriginal frameworks, and perhaps also the dominant internal traits of the Indian societies themselves, such as a certain vigorous pessimism or an excess of totalitarianism—all these factors provoked the downfall of the cultures and societies existing in America before the arrival of Columbus.

As to the first missionaries, their concern for evangelization during the period of "spiritual conquest" led them to seek a cultural integration of the aboriginal populations. But most often this was attempted through a total and rapid transculturation. Both in North and South America even the most primitive peoples, who lived by hunting, fishing or from the natural products of the land, believed in a "Supreme Being" who was master of the earth. But this vague belief occupied a poor second place in their lives compared to magic, which was so important that it actually helped determine the degree of development of the tribal cultures.

Among the peoples of a more highly developed culture, like the Aztecs, religion had a funereal aspect; there were human sacrifices and ritual practices resembling certain Christian sacraments, like baptism and confession. The Mayas believed in the existence of an all-powerful God and in numerous secondary divinities. Their cities were great religious centers, and their priests were the trustees of Mayan wisdom, the most highly developed of all American civilizations. The Incas had divinized their kings and gave worship to the sun, the moon and the stars, as well as to material objects, like the *hindeas*. Their priestly class was hierarchical; and they had numerous monasteries for men and women.

It is interesting to observe that most of the Indian beliefs included prophecies, and notably one concerning the conquest by foreigners. The penetration of Christianity was perhaps facilitated by this idea.

How did the missionaries act toward these peoples? It should be remembered, first of all, that the Church's freedom of action was very limited at this time. As a result of the secular struggle of the Iberian Peninsula against the Moslems, the Spanish Crown had been invested with many powers in the religious sphere. Thus it was that as early as 1493, one year after Columbus' voyage, Pope Alexander VI established the line of demarcation between Spain and Portugal, and conferred on the Spanish kings the exclusive right to take possession of and evangelize the newly conquered territories, and to exercise the right of patronage over the churches to be established. In 1501 the Pope accorded the tithes collected in America to the Spanish Crown in perpetuity; in return, the Crown was charged with the responsibility of founding and endowing the churches. Such were the stipulations underlying the *Real Patronato*. In the New World, the Spanish kings were by pontifical mandate the founders, protectors and administrators of the Church. The Crown could present for the various ecclesiastical offices those persons it judged suitable; it was the Crown that gave authorization to erect religious establishments; and later on, the kings were to obtain the power to change diocesan boundaries. Thus it is evident that evangelization was far from falling under the exclusive initiative of the Church.

Scarcely off the boat, the missionaries were confronted with all kinds of problems in the new continent, not the least of which was language. For a start they had recourse to sign language, but soon they developed native interpreters to pass on the instruction they gave. The Indian and Spanish children contributed measurably to the assimilation and spreading of the language. The work of conversion was further aided by Spanish families living in contact with the aborigines. However, if evangelization was accomplished by diffusion of the spoken and written word, by the martyrs and by the good example of Christians, the fact must not be passed over that coercive means were also used, means approved by most of the theologians of the time, when military submission and forced baptism went hand in hand, in a confusion of values and aims quite characteristic of the Catholic *Hispanidad*. Fortunately, it seems that this recourse to force took place only in a few sectors and was used only during the first stages of evangelization.

Supplementing its mission to spread the gospel, the Church soon displayed great activity in the social and cultural domains. It very often took up the defense of the Indians in the various problems created by the conquest: the distribution of profits, the collection of taxes, the repression of rebellions which resulted from these, the maltreatment and subjugation of the riffraff in the *encomiendas*,[5] slave traffic and political corruption. It was through the activities of the missionaries, particularly of Bartolomé de las Casas, O.P., that the Indians obtained, as early as the beginning of the sixteenth century, a declaration of liberty and the repatriation of all those who had been deported to the Iberian Peninsula. The efforts of the Church finally resulted, in spite of the frantic opposition of the colonies, in the promulgation of the "Laws of Burgos," which delegated three religious to study a governmental reform of the Indies, and which provided for a Protector of the Indians and the removal of corrupt public officials.

The Church gave equal concern to the organization of social

life. It concentrated its action in the ordered planning of towns and in the creation of centers destined principally to diffuse the teaching of Christianity. If these centers did not always effect the rapid assimilation of the natives, at least they made possible their progressive adaptation to the new civilization. The first towns were developed in the Antilles, then throughout the rest of the continent, where traces of them are still discernible today.

The preaching of the gospel was generally coupled with cultural activity. Instruction in the new culture was imparted either by Spanish families or by monastery schools. The first dictionaries and grammars of the Indian languages date from this period.

THE COLONIAL PERIOD, 1520–1810
The Social Categories

Once the conquest was completed, who held the power? As a matter of fact, it was divided among four principal groups, each having their own particular interests: the *conquistadores,* the capitalists (tradesmen and industrialists), government officials, and the clergy. Several years were necessary before a true political and administrative organization was set up, so that the beginning years were characterized by improvisation and adventure. It was during this period that a social stratification was formed, certain characteristics of which are visible even today.

Once their weapons had partitioned the territory, the *conquistadores* began to exploit their immense fiefs, first by reducing their populations to slavery. They moved in, got organized, constructed their residences. From conquerors they became lords; and soon Charles V officially recognized the reality of the situation by instituting the *encomienda.*

The *encomendero* was entrusted by the king with a group of Indians. He imposed on them a heavy tribute, which they had to pay with materials, money and work. He thus realized a substantial profit. In return, the *encomendero* had to assure the defense of the territory, its civil administration, and the evangelization of the Indians confided to his care. The structure of the *encomienda,* therefore, was basically territorial. There were other origins of property, however: the distribution of lands for services rendered, the sale of public domain, and out-and-out confiscation.[6]

Soon the *encomienda* gave way to the *hacienda,* a large rural estate where the Indian labor was theoretically free but, because of its debts, was maintained in circumstances bordering on slavery. Many classes of individuals were able to acquire large estates: the newly-arrived from Spain, the financiers, the successful tradesmen, the mining industrialists. The multiplication of estates—one could even say their "vogue"—was encouraged in the seventeenth century by the policies of the State. It sold domains, legalized the possession of usurped lands, and instituted a system of laws by which the family patrimony remained undivided. The owner of a large estate was more concerned about the social prestige and the power which the property provided than he was about really making his land valuable. He lived in town, entrusted the management of his land to major-domo, and rented or leased parcels of it to expropriated Indians who, now as simple farm hands, would contract to work a certain number of days without pay in exchange for the patch of ground at their disposal. Finally, whole sections of large estates often remained completely idle. In Brazil, however, the *fazendas,* and particularly the sugar plantations, created a somewhat different social structure, the *fazendero* usually living on his own property. Otherwise the same traits are discernible.

The existence of this agrarian structure, the unproductive character of the large estates, the lack of an enterprising spirit, the antipathy toward change—all these factors held back economic development. They are still today the principal characteristics of the rural areas in a great number of Latin American countries.

Along with these feudal-like elements, the colonial period also had its capitalistic side: the accumulation of riches (chiefly through exploitation of the Negro), the importance of capital investments (by the generalization of credit), the orientation of production toward trade and toward the needs of the mother country.

The most important capitalistic enterprises were the mines, the tropical plantations, and the flour mills. Although the extractive industries were at the base of the whole Latin American economy, and although they made possible the blossoming of Western capitalism and, in the last analysis, the industrialization of Europe, they did not give birth to an industrial bourgeoisie in Latin America. The revenues of the mines did make possible the importation of servile labor and manufactured products, the embellishing of towns, and certain cultural strides; but they did not contribute to the development of native industries (with the exception of silk and leather). This coincided nicely with the interests of the Crown, which was anxious to prevent the colonies from endangering home industries.

Thus did colonial capitalism assume a commercial pattern, which was to remain long after Latin America's independence. In addition to the property owners, the merchants constituted a very strong economic force. Since the expansion of credit was highly irregular, they joined their capital with that of the bankers, controlled the shipping trade, and, by holding mortgages, got their hands on a goodly number of rural plantations.

The third influential group in the spectrum of power was the colonial administration. It became strongly centralized during the second half of the sixteenth century. Public offices, which at first were considered merely as favors or remunerations, became the prerogative of a salaried bureaucracy. Colonial affairs were directed by the mother country herself through the Council of the Indies, the highest legislative and administrative body. In America, royal power was executed through the office of the Viceroy, through the captain-general in the *capitanias,* and through the *Audiencia* which enjoyed both administrative and judiciary powers and constituted the Council of the Viceroy. The administrative control of the Spanish Indies was accomplished on all levels by the *Residencia* and the *Visita.* This political organization, composed of officials selected by the Crown and provided with temporary duties, was very rigorous, but slow and costly. According to Pierre Chaunu, it absorbed 50 per cent of the revenues from the Indies in the sixteenth century, and 80 per cent in the eighteenth.[7] For reasons of economy, therefore, the Crown was to get rid of a certain number of public offices by sale. Little by little the administration became more corrupt, so that by the eighteenth century the public official "became a businessman who would dip into the money under his care and utilize quite profitably a good portion of state revenues."[8]

Along with this development, the multiplication of public offices effected a profound political decentralization. At the end of the eighteenth century the Bourbons undertook an administrative reorganization by setting up intendancies, but it came too late to have any lasting results and it included too many measures which were unpopular with the creoles, who were excluded from all posts.

Economic policy was based on mercantilism and the tightening of monopolies. Controlled by the *Casa de Contratación,* trade between the Indies and the homeland had its only port of entry at Seville. It was only in 1717 that this commercial privilege passed on to Cadiz, which in turn held the monopoly until 1765. This centralization permitted a more rigid control over the imports of gold and other precious metals, and over the *Quinto,* a tax which the Crown levied on the products of the mines. The traders of Seville, however, could not meet the increasing demand of the Indies for European products and manufactured goods. Prices mounted higher and higher, along with increased costs in transportation and taxes.

Soon Spain could no longer control the shipping between the colonies and the homeland. The ships found it necessary to travel in convoys. Still many profits were undercut by pirates. By the end of the seventeenth century, the chief beneficiaries of the trade between America and Seville were foreigners; it has been estimated that 90 per cent of the capital exports passed through the hands of Frenchmen, Genoese, Hollanders, Englishmen and Germans. Smuggling struck the final blow to trade monopoly. It was encouraged, on the one hand, by the strict supervision or suppression of regional trading and, on the other hand, by Spain's incapacity to meet the competitive prices of other countries.

There was another consequence of this policy of regional trade restriction, namely the emergence, at the end of the colonial period, of autonomous economic blocs, a phenomenon which in turn was to prove favorable to the political breakup of the Indies. Thus, by her policy of trade monopoly, Spain got nowhere; and by the progressive corruption of her administration, she eventually lost economic and political control of her colonies.

We have thus far described very briefly the first three social groups that exercised power, by authority or by fact, during the colonial period: the *conquistadores,* the capitalists, and the civil officials. There remains the clergy. During this period, the regular clergy like the secular clergy will see their wealth increase, and they will constitute at the end of the colonial period an important economic power. They will gain possession of huge estates as a result of gifts, inheritances, grants, and mortgages. The fixed capital of the Church will often represent little productive value, except in the case of the Jesuits who were great producers, achieving high standards of administration and capitalistic technique.

The Social Situation

What was the social structure of Latin America during the colonial period? Two observations give the general picture: first, there existed a clear-cut hierarchy of social and racial groups; second, between the ethnic groups there was a geographic as well as cultural gulf.

The basis of this social hierarchy was both feudal and economic. It was feudal in the sense that, although the government officials and the rich tradesmen were becoming more important, it was really the *conquistadores,* the Crown's privileged ones, who seized the power, who became lords, *encomenderos* and property owners. It does seem, however, that feudal ideas did less to stabilize the social stratification than did the desire to maintain the economic privileges once they had been acquired. The crystallization of colonial society into castes took place in the seventeenth century, in spite of the sharp increases in population and interracial marriages which were factors of social mobility capable of doing violence to the dichotomy on which the colonial system rested.

The classical metaphor of the pyramid might be best suited to bring out the general outlines of this hierarchy. At the top were the Spaniards. At the base, the blacks and the Indians. Between the two extremes, proceeding from bottom to top: the mulattos, the Indian mestizos, or half-breeds, and finally, the mestizos of Spanish culture.

The summit of the pyramid, then, was occupied by the whites, but with certain distinctions. The higher positions both in the administration and in the Church were awarded by preference to the Spaniards born in the homeland rather than to the creoles, that is, whites born in America. Outside of the high governmental bureaucracy and the high clergy, social rank was a matter of birth or family position based on the ownership of land or mines. Since birth and landed property were accorded so much prestige, and since lucrative operations were looked upon with such disfavor, the traders, merchants and industrialists, in spite of their economic power, did not enjoy the highest social status.

At the base of the pyramid, the lowest group was the Negro. They supplied much of the labor force, both slave and salaried, and had no participation in the political and cultural life of the country. Also blocked in the lower stratum were the Indians who were attached to the *encomiendas,* then to the *mitas,*[9] and later to the *haciendas.* The passage from one system to another (*encomienda, hacienda, mita,* etc.) did very little to alter the social condition of the Indian. As a matter of fact, all these systems tended to push him toward the bottom.

It must be mentioned, however, that at least at the beginning of colonization some of the more noble Indians were able to maintain a certain rank and prestige, but only in proportion to the amount of Spanish civilization they were able to absorb. Also, the administration did make some attempts at assistance indirectly through the Indian chiefs. But the latter were under the authority of the *encomenderos* and had as their main duty the recruitment of the labor force and the collection of taxes. Whenever they would show too much concern for the interests of their people, they would be dismissed and replaced by more hardened individuals.

It can be said that, in general, the Indian population was cut off from the elite (which, as is the case with most populations of higher culture, was urban) and that the Indian could not aspire to a new cultural and social order.

Between the upper and lower strata one would expect to find a "middle class." But, properly speaking, one did not exist. Some groups of mestizos who, by their geographic location (towns) and their professional occupations (small artisans and tradesmen), were able to dissociate themselves from the lower stratum, were nevertheless still attached to it by their way of life and their illiteracy. Little by little certain mestizos did enter into competition with the whites; they were the artisans, tradesmen, small impoverished landowners, adventurers without any precise qualification who formed the category, "little whites." But this whole intermediate group was not able to evolve into a middle class until the end of the colonial period, for its development was retarded by the caste system and a series of economic restraints. To mention but a few: the impossibility of acquiring small property, the restrictions in manufacturing, the absence of a free international market, and the barriers on domestic trade. Many segments of this intermediate mass even underwent a profound cultural regression and were eventually absorbed by the lower groups.

Coinciding with this rigid hierarchy of social structures during the colonial period was the geographic and cultural distance between the ethnic groups. Indeed, parts of the aboriginal populations, like the Indians of the woodlands, lived literally "outside" the colonial society. This segregation was not always natural, but often the result of a retreat before the conquest; such was the case of several groups of Guarinis after the destruction of their villages. Moreover, some populations, like the Indians in the reductions, maintained—and still maintain today—a relative cultural and social independence, even though undergoing a certain amount of culturalization, at least in the religious domain. But this autonomy was rather shaky. The reductions had been "institutions of refuge" for a poor population exposed to land speculations and subjugated to the forced labor of the *mita*. The "Christian-communist" republic of the Jesuits of Paraguay constituted an interesting attempt at integration on the social, economic, cultural and religious levels, but it had a tragic epilogue due to the too "paternalistic" character of the experiment.

Finally, it must be pointed out, as did Sergio Bagu in his study on the social structures of the colonies,[10] that there existed another whole group, a population of unproductive outcasts, more or less permanently unemployed, who lived by occasional favors or by expediency. This group was comprised of mestizos, Negroes, and fugitive Indians who had been expelled from their communities or who fled to avoid forced labor. They usually lived on the outskirts of the towns.

Such was, in its broad outline, the social panorama of the Latin American countries on the eve of their independence. All will not seem unfamiliar, for certain characteristics have persisted even to our day without undergoing any really profound changes.

The Church during the Colonial Period

Two documents underlie the missionary structure of the Church in Latin America: the brief, *Expani notis peristi,* and the bull, *Omnimoda,* both promulgated in 1522 by Pope Adrian VI at the request of Charles V. There are two major sections. The first recognized the canonical and pontifical mission of religious in the evangelization of the Indians (conditioned by the approval of their religious superiors and of the Crown) and accorded them the right to organize expeditions. The second part spelled out the powers given to superiors in the exercise of their ministry and government, powers delegated either by the general superiors or by the pope himself. Among these powers, the most important was the authority, *Omnimoda*: privileges in the internal and external forums which included prerogatives ordinarily reserved to the episcopate; these could be used whenever distance made recourse to the bishop or to official quarter impossible. Particularly active in sending expeditions were the Franciscans, the religious of Our Lady of Mercy, the Dominicans, the Augustinians, the Jesuits, the Discalced Carmelites and the Capuchins. The structure of the organizations developed by these orders in America was modeled after those in Europe, and eventually they became independent provinces.

It was also under the reign of Charles V that the hierarchy was definitively established. During the course of the colonial period the number of dioceses steadily increased: by 1520, seven dioceses; by 1540, nine more had been added; five more by 1550; two by 1560; and yet another four by 1570.

Just how were bishops nominated in Spanish America? After a preliminary investigation, the Council of the Indies would present their candidates to the king; he then sent his proposals to the pope. The Council notified the interested party, who would, in cases of emergency, serve notice directly to the government of the diocese. Ordinarily, however, before being consecrated, they had to wait for a bull of nomination and a new notice from the Council. This lapse of time enabled the nominee to refuse the office, which, in fact, many did. Some declined out of humility, others out of ambition, feeling that the income they would derive from the diocese in question would be insufficient!

Generally, the candidates were chosen from the secular clergy. At Rome, seculars were preferred to religious, and Charles V shared this preference. On the other hand, the Council of the Indies was of the opposite opinion; it felt that religious managed the tithes and incomes much better because of their vow of poverty!

The first cathedral chapters were constituted in 1512, the capitular officers being appointed by the king. Until a diocese was formed in a particular area, parishes did not exist. The administration of the sacraments, preaching, and teaching were taken care of by the missionaries and the chaplains of the expeditions. When a diocese was finally erected, a diocesan clergy would be organized to take charge of the Spanish and Portuguese parishes while the missionaries continued to work among the Indians.

The first parish was always the cathedral. It would be erected in an area thickly populated by whites which was automatically recognized by the pope as a city. Division into parishes moved very slowly. The priests who left for the Indies with a papal mandate were, for all practical purposes, the king's chaplains; they were paid by him and had as one of their principal duties the collection of the tithes.

It should be remembered that it was during this period that the *encomiendas* were created. The heads of these organizations were also responsible for providing centers of religious activity for the Indians. There were, at first, simple lay chaplaincies outside of canonical supervision; but eventually they became regular parishes administered by religious.

The year 1530 marked the departure of the first women religious for the Indies. They were, for the most part, Franciscan tertiaries sent by the Empress to engage in social work and to found boarding schools for children between the ages of six and twelve. The Council of the Indies was not in favor of cloistered nuns in America; as a result, the first convent was not established in Mexico until the sixteenth century had passed the midway mark. After that, however, new foundations multiplied, and by the end of the seventeenth century there numbered more than 80 convents.

The Inquisition was inaugurated in Spain by the Catholic kings shortly after the discovery of the New World. Its main purpose was to combat any lingering Judaism or Islamism in new converts. So great was the fear of possible "contagion" that even the descendants of converts were banned from America. But since this prohibition did not prove very effective, the American bishops petitioned the king to set up courts of Inquisition on the continent. The first courts were established in Mexico and Lima in 1569 and had jurisdiction over all Europeans, mulattos and mestizos. Only the Indians came directly under the jurisdiction of the bishops, who, it must be mentioned, judged with more clemency.

It was the responsibility of the Inquisition to protect both faith and morals. Its courts intervened in crimes against religion (heresy, apostasy, sorcery, sacrifice), against discipline (bigamy, forbidden books), against the priesthood and religious vows. During the sixteenth and seventeenth centuries they were principally engaged in combatting Protestantism; in the eighteenth century they intervened only in cases of church discipline; finally, they disappeared completely.

Relations between Church
and State

It was mentioned at the beginning of this introduction that Church-State relations had been determined by the system of patronage. Before analyzing its evolution during the colonial period, it would be well to enumerate the principles which governed these relations.

Luther had defended the thesis that the secular prince was the religious pontiff of his subjects. Calvin had likewise proclaimed the divine origin of royal authority, and considered that the ultimate purpose of the State was to assure the external worship of God and the unity of the Church. A century later, the Treaty of Westphalia (1648) was to add an international character to these principles by confirming the right of temporal authorities to intervene in religious matters. These principles were adopted not only by many Protestant churches, but even by Catholic monarchs, who sought more direct control over national churches so as to be able to override or even contradict papal policies.

The *Patronato* was a double-edged sword. Charles V's interpretation of it was essentially the same as Ferdinand's had been, namely, that by virtue of the privileges accorded to the Spanish Crown by the Holy See, the government of the Church of the Indies was under the dependence of the king. The Emperor was the first to commit an abuse of his powers by sending bishops to America who had not received bulls of nomination. On the other hand, he did not assert all his rights; and it must be admitted that during the last years of Charles V's reign the Church enjoyed a much greater autonomy than during his predecessor's.

Philip II, in the first decade of his reign, strengthened the organization of his temporal and religious power. In 1568 he created an assembly to study American problems. It eventually prepared the famous *Cedula Major* of 1574 by which the whole organization of the Church and its missions was centralized in the hands of the king and his Council, or *Junta*. The resolutions of the *Junta* extended to three areas:

1. *The nomination of pastors.* No ecclesiastical benefice could be conferred without the approbation of the king and his council. It was the same for bishops and, all the more, for heads of territories.

2. *Tithes.* The *Junta* decreed that it was urgent that tithes be collected from everyone, without exception. This meant a levy of 10 per cent on all agricultural and industrial products as well as on personal incomes. The total revenue collected was to be divided into nine parts and allotted to the parish councils, to the king (2 parts), to the bishops and chapters (3 parts), to the hospitals, and to the parishes for the administration of the sacra-

ments (2 parts). But Pope Gregory XIII was not to approve his proposal.

3. *The organization of chapters and ecclesiastical benefices.* In the large metropolitan areas (Mexico, Lima, Bogotá, where the majority of the population was Spanish) the cathedrals and churches were to be ministered by bishops and religious priests who lived a community life and owned the church income in common. This measure was aimed at avoiding friction between the secular and religious clergy, cutting down expenses, and reinforcing the centralization of church government (the religious orders being much more dependent on the Crown than were the secular clergy).

The hierarchy was faced with other problems of a more general nature. The contacts between the Church of the New World and Europe were being made directly with Madrid, and not with Rome. This situation seemed to call for the establishment, in the large metropolitan areas of America or Spain, of ecclesiastical authorities to whom the Holy See could confer extraordinary powers. Rome decided, therefore, to create papal nuncios. But the *Junta* did not approve of this plan, since tradition excluded from the Indies any kind of foreign delegation, and since it always had looked upon the king as the responsible head of the evangelical mission, on an equal footing with the Holy See. The *Junta* favored a compromise solution, a patriarchate of the Indies. The patriarch would be presented by the king and named by the pope. He would reside at the royal court and be the focal point of all jurisdiction. The *Junta*'s plan was never realized. During the pontificate of Pius V Spain expressed no desire to negotiate a solution; and later on, Gregory XIII turned down the proposal.

Failing to obtain the patriarchate, Madrid came up with another proposal: give the king the title, "Vicar of the Indies and Delegate of the Pope." Theologians and canonists went to work using historical arguments to forge a theory that would legitimize the title and progressively amplify the powers of the Crown. According to them, the king, the "Vicar of the Indies," would assume the right to expel priests and religious, to authorize the construction of churches and convents, to intervene in the nomination of commissary-provincials and vicars of religious orders, to set boundaries of new mission territories and to entrust them to whichever congregations he wished, to prohibit publications dealing with religious matters, including pastoral letters and decisions of provincial councils or diocesan synods, and finally, to bar entry into America of papal nuncios.

While Spain was becoming more adamant in her demands, Rome was organizing the Congregation for the Propagation of the Faith, whose jurisdiction was to extend to the whole missionary world. The Council of the Indies reacted immediately by opposing the entry into Spanish possessions and missions of any delegate of the new Congregation. Rome counter-replied by banning the works of Solorzano, who justified the actions of the Crown. This spirit of high tension characterized the relations between Spain and the Holy See throughout the entire seventeenth century. As it turned out, the theory of the king's "Vicariate" received *de facto* application in all the American territories; and the Council of the Indies continued to regulate the life of the Church in the New World.

In 1701 the Bourbon, Philip V, came to the Spanish throne; and a new dynasty, directed from Versailles by Louis XIV, took control. The absolutist ideas of the new king squared well with the anti-Roman feelings quite widespread in the Peninsula. The patriarchate now tended to be thought of as a royal right rather than a privilege to be granted by the Papacy.

Philip's son, Charles III, was to state the Bourbon thesis in his decree, *Real Cedula* (1765), by publicly and officially proclaiming himself the "Vicar and Delegate of the Sovereign Pontiff." Once more in history, practice gave birth to theory, at the expense of a grave doctrinal error. During this period, however, when Europe was in the throes of schism (Gallicanism and Josephism), this proclamation was paradoxically equivalent to a declaration of allegiance to the Holy See. The Monarch would invoke the Roman Pontiff every time he could derive certain advantages by doing so, but he would repudiate him whenever his royalist interests would dictate. In 1776, a new code of laws was devised for the Indies. It limited communications between the bishops and the Holy See, reduced still more the freedom of diocesan curias regarding tithes and construction, and increased royal authority in the juridical domain.

The Jesuits came with the liberals and were suppressed with the Conservatists.

This chapter could not close without mention of an event that had very serious repercussions in the history of the Church in Latin America: the suppressions of the Jesuits.

In the ideological conflicts of the seventeenth century, the Society of Jesus had been the butt of attacks from all sides, from Protestants, Gallicans, Jansenists, "philosophers" of the Enlightenment, all of whom viewed with particular disfavor Jesuit sympathy with the Papacy. There is no doubt that during this period the Jesuits were very powerful within the Church; also, because of the various secular functions they assumed, some of them were involved in matters quite foreign to religion. Even in ecclesiastical circles, notably, in the Roman Curia, they made many enemies, particularly because of their missionary methods.

The anti-Jesuit campaign began in Portugal under the ministry of Pombal who claimed that the Order was amassing riches in the reductions of Paraguay and was inciting the Indians against Portuguese authority. From there the attack spread to countries dominated by the Bourbons: France, Spain, Naples, and Parma.

In Spain, it was under Charles III that the Jesuits were finally expelled. To obtain from the Holy See the definitive suppression of the Order, the king exerted pressure on the American bishops, then meeting at the Council of Mexico, to petition the pope. A good many bishops were not favorable to this course of action, but fear of reprisals finally obtained a unanimous vote. In 1767 the Jesuits had to give up their American missions, and in 1773 the Society was suppressed by Clement XIV.

This expulsion had dire consequences. It can be said that the institutional crisis of the Church in Latin America dates from that day. If in 1750 there were only 779 inhabitants per priest on the continent, after the departure of the Jesuits there remained only 2,267 religious, who had to operate 4 universities, 22 seminaries, 100 high schools, 70 missionary centers, and 300 reductions containing 500,000 converts. The departure of the Jesuits, moreover, marked the beginning of a socio-cultural regression among the Indians.

NOTES

[1] The term "Indies" in the context of this work refers, of course, to the American continent.

[2] As a good example, see the excellent account of the conquest of Darien in Kathleen Romoli's *Balboa, Conquistador du Pacifique* (Paris: Plon, 1961).

[3] Pierre Chaunu, *Histoire de l'Amérique Latine* from the series, *Que sais-je?* (Paris: Presses Universitaires de France, 1949).

[4] The Anglo-Saxons, however, were equally, and even more radically, destroyers of culture. They all but decimated the Indian populations by putting into actual practice the popular saying, "The only good Indian is a dead Indian."

[5] Groups of Indians entrusted to the *conquistadores*.

[6] In Brazil the establishment of large territorial properties was quite similar.

[7] Pierre Chaunu, *op. cit.*

[8] J. Vicens Vives, *La sociedad americana en los siglos XVI y XVII.* Vol. 3.

[9] The *mita* was a legal institution by virtue of which the free Indians of a region were obliged to furnish a certain number of work days per year either for the Crown or for private citizens. (They received a salary for this work.)

[10] Sergio Bagu, *Estructura social de la Colonia. Ensayo de Historia comparada de América Latina* (Buenos Aires: Libreria "El Ateneo," 1952).

2

Independence,
1810 to the Present

The authoritarianism of the Spanish Crown had not been conducive to education in self-government, for the administration had
remained in the hands of native-born Spaniards. Moreover, even
though the later Bourbons terminated the trade pact with the
colonies, the monopoly system had stifled the exercise of economic
freedom and the spirit of enterprise. One thing trade restrictions
did encourage, however, was regional self-sufficiency. Finally, the
social structure remained undemocratically based on privileges and
castes, while culture was controlled by censorship and inquisition.

As the Mexican philosopher, Leopold Zea, says: "The democratic or republican spirit and technical know-how appeared to
the Spanish Americans as values yet to be acquired, for they
were not part of the Western world's heritage." In another place
he says: "The assimilation of the new ideals from the 'Western'
world was one of the most difficult tasks imaginable for the
peoples of Latin America, for it represented the abandonment of
their way of life for one that was radically different."[1]

The Spanish patrimony had not, of course, been completely
impermeable to certain ideologies capable of opening Latin
America to new currents which would enable it to shed the ethics
of an absolutist regime. The democratic theories of Suarez and

24

Vittoria had reached the New World. The Bourbons, and especially Charles III, under the influence of the Enlightenment, had tempered their despotism with certain admixtures of liberalism. Freemasonry had gotten its foot in the door, and its provenance was, of all places, Spain, where under Charles III it was enjoying a certain amount of non-interference. The Jesuits, who often worked closely with the rising local bourgeoisie, were representatives of the advanced element of colonial culture, and had, in their teaching, contributed to the introduction of the pre-revolutionary ideas of the late eighteenth century. The Mexican Jesuits, for example, spread the theories of the social pact, of progress, and of equality.

The expulsion of the Jesuits in 1767 had effected a cultural void that proved most harmful to Latin America. We can posit the hypothesis that the colonies' apprenticeship in self-government would have greatly benefited by the spirit of enterprise, of realism and progressivism that was evident in many of the members of the Society of Jesus.

The creole revolutionaries had been in unbroken contact with the movements of revolutionary ideas in France and England. The Declaration of the Rights of Man had been translated into Spanish and printed clandestinely in Bogotá in 1794. The writings of the French Encyclopedists and of John Locke as well as the Declaration of Independence of the North American colonies were known and discussed by the creoles.

In the eighteenth century, therefore, Latin America was open to modern ideas. But her revolutions were unleashed without her being blessed with the social stability of the western European countries or the United States. Whereas in these countries there was an already rich and organized bourgeois class prepared to take advantage of the revolutions by means of economic expansion, in Latin America the revolutions did not raise up a class firmly oriented toward an important economic revival. Latin America armed itself with liberal constitutions, but without a social structure capable of guaranteeing them and without the technical means to secure its economic independence in the jungle of the economic and political expansions of the great powers.

Internally, the countries of the new continent were at grips with a social structure that represented no national unity. Geographic isolation, the decadence of the colonial administration, and the rising power of the *hacendados* fostered the feudal tendencies which favored the take-over by special-interest groups or by *caudillos,* local despots. In the actual struggle for independence, the popular masses took very little part; in fact, they were more of a dead weight. Except for the first uprisings in Mexico, they were often in opposition to the rich creole councilors of the municipalities; and in Venezuela they passively followed the royalist *caudillos.*

The revolutions of Latin America, therefore, were political, not social; their goal was not power for a new social class. On the contrary, they resulted in the birth of militarism, of armed bands which, as Bolivar observed, were a necessary evil for independence, but in time of peace, a danger for order and tranquillity.

THE NEW POLITICAL AND
SOCIAL STRUCTURES

The state of the existing social structures and a series of centrifugal forces (the feudal *caudillismo* of rich property owners and military men) brought to power new independent regimes, which were either oligarchies or dictatorships. As Leopold Zea indicates:

The conservative forces were so powerful that they had no trouble in utilizing the opportunities afforded by a democratic regime for the destruction of freedom; and the liberal forces burned themselves out in never-ending political battles with their enemies and among themselves. Thus was destroyed another indispensable condition for the solidification of a nation: progress and prosperity. Faced with the peril of conservative action in a democratic regime whose very institutions were used to overthrow it, and faced with a lamentable material stagnation, these countries fell quite easily into the opposite extreme, into dictator-ships. They called these, "dictatorships for liberty." In the history of our countries this was a necessary stage in the formation of a nucleus of a national spirit. But these dictatorships, soon forgetting their *raison d'être*, became purely and simply dictatorships for the protection of the interests of a given social group.[2]

Without the social and cultural basis for the establishment of a true democracy, the Latin American countries underwent a succession of enlightened dictatorships, oligarchies, and minority governments. These theoretically represented the people, and at times were interested in the progress of the nation, but they governed "more for the future than for the present" and found their justification "in the realization of future projects more than in the will of the governed." These governments of "democratic Caesarism," restraining liberties as they did, were hardly conducive to training in democracy, nor did they even provide the means that could put democracy within the people's reach. They were interspersed with military dictatorships which represented private interests and which, from the second half of the nineteenth century on, were to serve foreign economic powers.

Rev. Raul Cereceda, S.J., in his study on the civil and political institutions of Latin America,[3] gives a description of a *caudillo* at three stages of his career. The first step is the allurement of the people. He builds up local support, assures his predominance over the other local leaders, acquires regional power by posing as a *libertador,* justifier and renovator, defies the central authority, and finally overthrows it by a revolution. In the second stage he imposes his style of government, but attempts to legalize his power by holding an election and making the people adopt a new constitution. In the third stage, he uses his Machiavelianism to eliminate all opposition, and sets himself up as the dispenser of public favors, i.e., government posts, establishing a veritable nepotism.

These political practices were to taint every facet of life in the Latin American republics. They quite naturally permeated the political parties. The parties that were defeated at elections, or the parties that could not present their candidates in a favorable light, had recourse to force. Afterwards, of course, they would establish legal recognition of their rights. These parties were not organizations with an ideological platform, but groups of political aspirants who exercised, as Frank Bonilla states, "a charismatic influence over mass movements, with little continuity from one electoral campaign to the next."[4]

Such policies were quite normal consequences of the conditions in Latin America after independence; but by enduring, they created a permanent cultural phenomenon. Politics and the exercise of power were based on values quite unrelated to social and political goals, and were not thought of as a method of administering the common good. On the contrary, they were merely an institutionalized expression of the privileges accorded to the family clan or to individuals. Making its debut at a time when national unity was non-existent and when large segments of the social strata were not integrated with society, political activity could not perform the function of "defining or integrating the global objectives of society."[4] It became completely entangled in private interests.

The army was in much the same category. For the most part, it did not fulfill its normal function of national defense; its main occupation was intervening as a private force in the internal political struggles. The army's function did undergo, however, a gradual evolution. At first it was an agent of the *caudillos* and private interest groups. Later, with the birth of the new social classes, it attempted to represent the national conscience as the champion of social justice. Finally, as the best organized element of the new middle classes, it sought to play the role of arbitrator.

To understand the political evolution of Latin America, consideration must be given to the political isolation and economic subjection that most of these countries experienced shortly after their independence. Latin America was the victim of the expansionist policies of the very countries that, on the ideological level, had so generously contributed to her independence. As Leopold Zea writes:

The revolutionaries who emancipated Latin America always considered England, France and the United States as natural allies. . . . But events proved how wrong their judgment was. The great nations of the Western world, though they acted in the name of liberalism, did not wish to extend the application of liberal principles to the Spanish-American countries. The peoples of Latin America were denied the fruits of these ideas and were looked upon as completely foreign and backward as the peoples of Asia, Africa and Oceania.[5]

Latin America served as the target for the annexationalist aims of several countries. Mexico lost half of her territory to the United States in 1848, and was the victim of Napoleon III's dream of establishing a vassal empire. Between 1845 and 1847 England tried to claim her rights on Venezuela. Between 1862 and 1867 France and England set up a blockade of Rio de la Plata. At the end of the nineteenth century Puerto Rico was annexed to the United States, which acquired, at the beginning of this century, the *de facto* protectorates of Cuba, Haiti and Santo Domingo, not to mention the sovereignty of the Panama Canal. Concurrent with this military and political expansionism, the Latin American countries became the depository of foreign investments and served as veritable financial and commercial colonies of European and North American capitalism. The underdevelopment of the Latin American countries and their social and political imbalance are the result of "a contact of societies of unequal power," as Georges Balandier indicates when speaking of underdeveloped countries in general.[6]

The development of Latin America was curtailed not only by her international economic situation, but as far back as the colonial period there prevailed destructive economic practices which exhausted rather than developed her resources. The get-rich-quick desire, to which was coupled neither a spirit of enter-

prise (in the capitalistic sense) nor an appreciation of the value
of hard work, engendered in the countries of Latin America a
spirit of economic speculation. This attitude, devoid of national
interest, defensive and narrow in character, prompted the rich
classes to invest their capital abroad rather than bolster the
national economy. On the lower social levels this spirit of speculation emerged in the form of lotteries and games of chance. Last,
but not least, economic speculation found a made-to-order base
of operation in the political institutions.

ENTER A TECHNOLOGICAL CIVILIZATION

By way of conclusion, we can briefly summarize the history
of Latin America as follows. The colonial period saw only incomplete socio-cultural integrations. There was no fusion of the
different cultural groups, and the feudal spirit of the social and
political institutions held back the realization of economic objectives. It must be added, however, that if colonization brought
about only incomplete integrations (and they are still not complete at the present time), it did give birth to a process of miscege-
nation which, as Angel Rosenblat says, "was in some countries
the formation of the national soul."[7] This cultural cross-breeding
expressed itself, for example, in some remarkable artistic works;
to mention only one aspect: the exuberance and extraordinary
vitality of baroque architecture.

The period of independence witnessed a rupture with the anti-
modernism, political unity and commercial control of the Crown;
but this rupture did not succeed in transforming social and economic realities. It had its greatest effect on the ideological and
political levels, and in the development of a secularization whose
manifestations were anti-clericalism, positivism and the success
of freemasonry. The new political ideology, instead of influenc-
ing political practices, was usually relegated to formal phrases in
constitutions. And a certain legalism did not discourage contro-
versies between political factions. The current of new ideas co-

existed with archaic structures, which it lacked the means to eradicate. The economic structures that had been inherited from the colonies made the countries of Latin America most vulnerable and facilitated the machinations of economic imperialism. Finally, Latin America, even after independence, conserved, as a vestige of its archaic structures, a good number of outmoded behavior patterns and mentalities. These consisted especially in a disdain for manual occupations, and in a "personality cult" which found expression in politics and in the spirit of speculation.

From a positive point of view, however, the struggle for economic independence developed in the young nations of Latin America the will to assert themselves and to prove their originality. "The epic of the liberation and of its heroes, Hidalgo, Bolivar or San Martin, is characterized by vigorous ideas and is pervaded with the atmosphere of a bustling, perpetually renewed myth."[8] The search for a spiritual autonomy and for liberation from economic exploitation would engrain in the people of Latin America, as positive, dominant traits, the ideals of grandeur and intellectual independence.

We have described a certain number of manners and structures anterior to the process of contemporary social change. Contemporary change received a very definite impetus from the large-scale inter-continental immigrations which developed in the last quarter of the nineteenth century.

In Latin America's past we find a series of traditions and positive values capable of guiding her to original solutions of her social problems. There are also cultural creations whose value can be an inspiration to the whole world. To quote Jean Cassou's penetrating observation:

Civilization is in continuous change there. It can no longer rely on those ancient principles which, in our old world, have so often assumed worn-out, hardened, scholastic forms, drained of all their vitality. But this budding American humanism, with all its anxieties, exigencies, irrepressible nationalism and indigeneity, possesses the power to renew the vitality of those principles and apply them to specific conditions. . . .

This humanism is a vital power in which inheres the possibility of an extraordinary future. Its hope is as large as the planet.[9]

THE CHURCH AFTER INDEPENDENCE

During the crises of the independence movements, the Church also experienced difficulties inherent both in the political circumstances and in her own organization. The reactions were indeed varied. A part of the hierarchy, which was European in birth or training, was unsympathetic to the revolutionary currents and openly displayed its solidarity with the colonial authority—it was, after all, one of the elements of that authority, at least indirectly through the system of patronage and the double perspective of the colonial enterprise. The situation naturally differed according to the country and region.

On the other hand, in all the countries some members of the clergy played an active and sometimes preponderant role in the liberation movements. This was especially the case in Mexico, Colombia, and Argentina. All this resulted in an extremely confused situation, the final chapter of which has hardly begun.

The history of the Church since the independence unfolds in three phases: a period of confusion between the Church and the State, whose duration varied in each country, but which generally lasted to the end of the nineteenth century; a phase during which there was a regrouping of Catholics (running to the 1930's); finally, the present period characterized by the discovery of a new mode of existence for the Church in the world, due to its encounter with the social change and the extraordinary renewal of thought and action among the clergy and laity.

As an introduction to the analysis of the present situation, however, we shall concentrate on a few basic considerations which illustrate the gradual calming of relations between the temporal and spiritual powers, and the reorganization of Church structures, such as the realignment of dioceses, the multiplication of religious orders for men and women, and the creation of seminaries.

The Evolution in Church-State Relations

The relationships between the Church and the Latin American governments of today are quite diversified, in spite of a common colonial inheritance. In certain countries Catholicism is the official religion, and relations with the public powers are cordial. In other countries, even though the Catholic religion is officially recognized, its activities have been reduced by the civil code. In still other countries, the system of complete separation prevails.

In each country since 1810, there has been a partial but continuous liquidation of the political past, to which is very strongly linked the whole problem of Church-State relations. The first initiatives were the abolition of the Inquisition, the limitation of clerical participation in censorship, and a partial curtailment of the Church's influence in education.

But one of the first problems which the new States had to resolve was the relations with the Holy See. It was the opinion of the new leaders (who were still strongly tainted with the absolutist theories of the Spanish dynasty) that the rights of the *Patronato* should be automatically inherited by the new heads of state. Other questions, moreover, were connected to the problem: the civil status of the Church, and the attitude to be taken toward the Protestant religions in the new territories. In these matters, fidelity to the idea of religious unity impelled the constitutional recognition of the Catholic religion as the state religion. The government, however, could not impose public worship on members of other faiths who had the right to practice their religion in private. The decisions of the governments were influenced by the idea of tolerance, but even more so by the desire to encourage immigration and strengthen commercial relations with the United States and Great Britain.

The right of presenting candidates for the episcopacy was one of the essential powers of the *Patronato*. Even during the colonization period it was the source of many conflicts. It was once again to cause an eruption when independence was achieved, for most of the new states laid claim to it immediately. They soon discovered, however, that the Holy See in granting simple political recognition was not at all disposed to accord the right of patronage.

The Congress of Gran Colombia and its famous law of 1824 validated the *Patronato* as if it had been inherited by the State. In Argentina, in 1819, the *Patronato* was claimed by the State, but was not used for several decades. Other States preferred to deal with each Church-State problem as it arose by direct negotiations with the Holy See. In spite of continued efforts, no concordats were concluded during the first half of the century. The first was signed with Guatemala in 1852. It recognized the right of patronage, but when new agreements were established in 1884 this right was revoked. The concordat with Colombia in 1887 did not recognize the *Patronato,* but stipulated that preference would be given to the candidates recommended by the government. In other countries, although the Church did not recognize the right of patronage as being inherent in the sovereignty of the State, it did several times tolerate the exercise of this right.

If most of the first constitutions made no formal declarations concerning the Church, the new States did, in fact, give it official recognition. On the other hand, certain intellectuals favored a separation of Church and State. They were influenced by their European education, their acquaintance with eighteenth century literature, and the French Revolution. In general, however, they accepted the fact of an official Church as an historical tradition, because of the permanent influence she exercised over the conscience of the faithful.

As the nineteenth century ran its course, anti-clerical ideas found concrete form in a series of legal measures decreeing the abolition of ecclesiastical privileges, the prohibition of tithes, and the secularization of numerous activities, such as education and cultural services. There were stipulations concerning civil registration, the obligation of civil marriage, the suppression or restriction of certain activities of religious orders. In some countries, moreover, were included measures expropriating or nationalizing church property, and curbing or forbidding the participation of the clergy in political affairs. While these measures varied from one country to another, they did indicate the State's will to assume rights and activities that formerly constituted a monopoly of the Church.

The growth of anti-clericalism was due to a variety of causes. In some countries it was the influence of anti-clerical personalities for whom politico-spiritual problems assumed a major importance, even if they were not appreciated by the majority of the population. In other countries it flowed from the situation created during the colonial period. By the end of that period, the Church, because of the extensiveness of her intellectual, economic and social activities, was exercising a real power over civil society. It was almost inevitable that she should take a position against the revolutionary changes that would affect her vast interests. As time passed, the Church's opposition (whether alleged or real) to an economic and social evolution provided the opportunity to attack the social activities and economic possessions of the clergy. This is why certain intellectuals, like F. Bilbao in Chile, Gonzales Prada in Peru, and I. Ramirez in Mexico, attacked the Church not only as an agent of colonial heritage, but also as a spiritual and social force opposing the realization of democracy. When the temporal functions of the Church were secularized, the anti-clericals invariably claimed that they were not attacking religion; quite to the contrary, they argued, secularization meant giving back to the Church her true mission, and no longer handicapped with temporal preoccupations, she would be free to turn all her attention to spiritual labors. Such affirmations were not completely devoid of truth, but, as one would expect, they were rejected by the conservative elements.

Furthermore, the Church, as an economic institution, was accused of allying herself with the land barons and the conservative classes. Thus she was considered an obstacle to social progress. This is why she was relieved of the major portion of her rural properties in Mexico, Guatemala, Honduras, Haiti, Colombia, Venezuela, Ecuador, and Paraguay.

Anti-clericalism, however, was not always involved in the opinions for or against the separation of Church and State. During the first half of the nineteenth century, in fact, the prevailing opinion favored union, considering it the best system for both parties. Furthermore, no law of separation was promulgated before 1853. The defenders of separation were branded as avowed enemies of the Church, and some of them really were. But separation did not necessarily imply unhappy consequences for the Church, any more than union necessarily implied advantages. For example, union of Church and State such as it was applied in Venezuela produced more disastrous effects than any separation. On the other hand, while separation following the civil wars in Colombia (1853–87) and Mexico (1873) was a victory for sectarianism; in Brazil (1890), Cuba (1902), Panama (1904), Uruguay (1909) and Chile (1925), separation came about peacefully and the Church was the major beneficiary.

All these events exerted a definite limitation on the Church's capacity to develop. The expulsion of the Jesuits had already been a heavy blow to the organization of the Church, and especially to the missions. Then the crisis of independence accentuated the burdens, for the re-establishment of the hierarchy was slow and this had profound repercussions on vocations and the education of the clergy; all this at a time when the flow of missionaries from Europe was cut off.

Now new problems were arising in regard to the organization of dioceses. In the Spanish and Portuguese colonies there were 6 archdioceses and 38 dioceses. If this number was adequate during the colonial period, it was hardly the case later on when the territory was cut up into numerous independent states.

But that was not all. Disharmony between the Church and the State was further evidenced by the measures against the religious orders: they were either secularized or severely curtailed in their activities. This inflicted many hardships especially in the rural areas where the suppression of the small monasteries and the scarcity of missionaries in no time deprived the populations of all religious assistance. In certain countries it took many years to revoke the secularization of religious orders.

The confiscation of the property of the diocese and of the religious orders eliminated the sources of revenue which would have been sufficient to assure the independent activity of the Church; but these revenues were part of a feudal system.

How did religious matters evolve in Brazil? The situation there was rather particular since the Empire lasted so long. The religious history of Brazil can only be understood when seen in the context of Portugal's religious history. Many factors, not the least of which was the University of Coimbra, put the Church in Portugal within the encircling hands of the State; and during the eighteenth century, the Church felt the grip tightening. One by one a great number of privileges had been accorded to the civil authority by the Church in recognition for services rendered in the spreading of the faith; but this power was quickly abused, until finally the Church was all but smothered by the Marquis Pombal, who incarnated the doctrine of state domination. The turn of the century witnessed a fully absolutist regime.

In Brazil the situation was even more acute. Under the pretext that Rome was too far away, the Crown assumed here a "universal power" in the religious sphere. The civil authority had the right to name bishops to vacant posts; Roman documents had to have the visa of the king's secretary before being published; there was an administrative office which did nothing but survey public worship; all books were censored by civil authority. These actions received their vindication in the doctrine of royal absolutism that was being disseminated by the University of Coimbra. There resulted a clergy imbued with a mentality of political servitude, which they proceeded to justify theologically.

The Nuncio Caleppi, who fought against the royalist influence, was among the many first-hand witnesses of these developments who left us a detailed description of the state of religion. Popular faith was superstitious, morals were depraved, and worship was purely ceremonial, as society was basically irreligious.

As significant a factor as any in this state of affairs was the clergy. They were either poorly educated or simply neglectful of their pastoral duties. The faith of the people was deteriorating, for it was usually transmitted from father to son without any systematic explanation. When religious instruction was given by the clergy, it was pure rhetoric. Thus religious feasts became mere occasions for expensive celebrations and debauchery. Seminary training was wholly inadequate. The clergy in Brazil, for the most part, lived in a most lamentable moral state. They were ignorant and partially influenced by the ideas of the Encyclopedists. As can be expected, there were a great number who abandoned the priesthood completely. If such was the condition of the secular clergy, the regulars were not much better. Pombal's royalist policy of centralization had little by little subjugated all the religious orders.

Such was the state of affairs until the end of the Empire (1889), and it was not before Don Pedro II was deposed that the Church finally sprang back to life. The end of the imperial regime was marked by a truly profound religious decadence. Freemasonry and other anti-religious forces had utilized the union between Church and State to cut down the Church by every legal means. For example, it was against the law for a Brazilian subject to join a religious order.

Into a New Century

If the Church in Latin America somehow weathered all the storms and rough seas of the nineteenth century, the present century has not exactly provided smooth sailing. We need only refer to the persecution in Mexico, the difficulties that arose at the end of Perón's regime in Argentina, and the present situation in Cuba. In general, however, relations between the Church and State have been less rocky. Slightly different conditions prevail, of course, in each country. Church structures and organizations, such as diocese, parishes, congregations and sisterhoods, have been able to develop; and the Church has resumed some activity in the educational field.

In spite of all this, during a rather long period, until about the 1950's, those responsible for the various sectors of apostolic action found it difficult to admit that the Church was now in an entirely new situation. Many still imagined that, in spite of the many persecutions and oppositions that the Church had suffered, she remained fundamentally the expression of the culture and values of a people whose Catholicity had never changed. Such an attitude was evidenced in many ways. The Church's past was extolled. A great importance was attached to juridical questions, or to declarations affirming the rights of the Church. Prestige became a goal, especially in external signs of a feudal nature: episcopal palaces, imposing cathedrals, exterior respect for the hierarchy. In brief, they were fashioning an image of the Church which corresponded less and less to the real situation on the continent.

Certain groups of laymen and priests, however, understood the situation. They thought and worked in a new direction. Some of them had been formed by the Catholic Action movement which had assumed a vigorous activity about 1935 in countries such as Argentina, Chile and Mexico, thus laying the foundations for a new generation.

Little by little there dawned an awakening over the land. It was quickened by the ever-increasing contacts with Europe and North America, especially Canada. Like a spot of oil it spread and permeated every level of the Church: the laity, the clergy and the hierarchies of the various nations. The creation of a large number of dioceses gave birth to a new generation of bishops who assumed a greater importance, if only numerical. Nuncios in countries like Brazil and Chile began to take positive action. Certain institutions of a continental scope made invaluable contributions. In particular, the creation of CELAM (The Latin American Bishops Council) in 1955 indicated the episcopate's awakening to its continental dimensions; and the resultant inter-communications not only permitted a more realistic picture of the problems of Latin America, but at the same time restored to the episcopate the self-confidence it seemed to lack.

This, then, was the climate in which the Church of Latin America encountered the great social and cultural change that was to plunge her suddenly into a new world. Would she understand it? That will be the subject of the following chapters.

NOTES

[1] Leopold Zea, "L'Amérique hispanique et le monde occidental," *Esprit,* No. 10 (Oct. 1958), pp. 482–83.

[2] *Ibid.,* p. 484.

[3] Raul Cereceda, S.J., *Las Instituciones políticas en América Latina* (Fribourg: FERES, 1961).

[4] Frank Bonilla, "Sobre la estructura de clase en América Latina," *Ciencias Sociales,* Vol. III, No. 40, pp. 263–276.

[5] Leopold Zea, *op. cit.,* p. 486.

[6] Georges Balandier, "La mise en rapport des sociétés 'différentes' et le problème de sous-développement," *Le Tiers-Monde* (Paris: Presses Universitaires de France, 1956), pp. 119–32.

[7] Angel Rosenblat, *La Población indigena y el Mestizaje en América* (Buenos Aires: Ed. Nova, 1954).

[8] Jean Cassou, "Vers un humanisme?" *Esprit,* No. 10 (Oct. 1958), pp. 458–59.

[9] *Ibid.,* p. 459.

II

Social Change
in Latin America

3

The People and Their Groups

It is impossible to understand the social change in which the individuals of a region, of a country, or especially of a whole continent are involved, without placing it in a broader evolutionary and historical context. Probably no one today would think of explaining an existing circumstance except by reference to its past evolution. The present moment cannot be separated from history. *How I wish it could!!!*

On the other hand, since we have so many methods at our disposal for better understanding the economic and social processes, and for making certain prognostic calculations, it is equally indispensable to peer into the future. Gaston Berger has termed this *"la science prospective."* We cannot look upon history as ending today. The peoples of Latin America are now engaged in an irreversible movement; we shall try to capture not only its present moment, as in a photograph, but also the dynamism which propels it toward the future.

Such a broad view is also necessary to avoid approaching the problems of social change with a purely negative outlook. Wilbert E. Moore declares: "Among contemporary theorists, Sorokin and MacIver stand out as scholars who show a major and insistent concern for change as a part of the very nature of social existence, rather than as a regrettable disturbance in the normally placid interdependence of self-equilibrating systems."[1] This moti-

vates us to present the Latin American problem in its true
perspective.[2]

One can manage, of course, to consider the situation on the
continent as catastrophic. The population explosion is much discussed. Many are uneasy about the socio-cultural transformations
in the family, in the rural areas, or in religious values. Some are
shocked by the upheaval of traditional society, or by the pitifully
low standard of living of the lower classes. Others are terribly
alarmed by the many revolutions, such as in Bolivia, Mexico or
Cuba. We shall attempt to rectify this one-sided pessimism by
realistically viewing present conditions in their evolutionary
context.

But before treating all these questions, let us first take a closer
look at the people who live on this continent. Four main socio-
cultural groups are distinguishable: 1) the whites, who up until
the nineteenth century were almost exclusively of Spanish or
Portuguese origin, but who now are more heterogeneous; they gravi-
tate toward the centers of modernism; 2) the traditional rural
population composed, for the most part, of mestizos; 3) the
Indians, who are generally marginal in relation to the global society; 4) the Negroes, who are either the dominant element of
a country, as in Haiti, or the coastal population, as in the Caribbean islands, Colombia or Peru, or a constituent element of the
population and culture, as in Brazil. The make-up of these socio-
cultural groups is quite diversified. The racial factor is still today
a predominant basis for distinction; not because there are dis-
criminations in the law, as in the United States, but because the
social levels of the races have been very different, if not in complete opposition, ever since colonization. The whites represented
the transplantation of European culture, and for others to marry
into the white race implied a closer communication with the dominant culture. The Negroes bore all the marks of an inferior social
condition, even after the abolition of slavery in Brazil at the end
of the last century. As for the Indians, even though they some-

times enjoyed equal legal rights, their social status was, in fact, quite distinct.

Although race is a basic consideration, other factors have combined with it down through the centuries to shape Latin American culture. From the very beginning of colonization, for example, some elements of the white population were assimilated by the lower groups. And today in Brazil there are segments of the white population, like the caboclos, whose standard of living and cultural level are relatively similar to those of the mestizos, or sometimes even those of the Indians in neighboring countries.

Moreover, the white immigration of the nineteenth and early twentieth centuries deeply transformed social structures. It laid the basis for an urban middle class which found its economic integration in industry and commerce, and which was quite different from the traditional elite class that had evolved from the colonies. It is no coincidence that the countries that received most of this immigration are today among the most highly developed: Argentina, Uruguay, and Brazil, particularly in its southern and central regions.

Small cells of modernism, with a predominantly white population, have cropped up, especially in the large cities. One of the obvious traits of urban development has been the concentration of a large segment of the population into a small number of cities —and in the case of some countries, into a single city. This is both a heritage of colonial times, when a city became the seat of power quickly monopolizing all roles and activities, and the result of the endemic underdevelopment of the rural areas during the population explosion.

The large metropolitan areas of Latin America serve as magnetic poles, particularly of modernism. This does not mean that they are always centers of progress for the surrounding region. They are more like small oases in an economic and cultural desert. The white population, taking over the political, social and economic roles, has become predominant in the large cities. For a very long time it had the monopoly of all these activities. During colonization the white population was made up of an elite from Europe; gradually, however, a local elite formed, and it was this group that brought about the political revolutions of the nineteenth and twentieth centuries.

When European migrations started, new cultural types were merged with those already existing in Latin America. Indeed, the immigrants did not come solely from the Iberian Peninsula, but from other European countries as well: Italy, first of all, then Germany, Poland and central Europe. The influx took place especially in the southern countries of the continent and had a decisive influence on industrialization.

The large cities thus became the melting pot of a new elite. In those cities that have conserved a traditional character, such as Lima, Bogotá, Quito and others, one finds both a traditional society of Iberian culture and a new society influenced essentially by the technological values of northern Europe and North America. The universities have been most influential in the development of this new society. The present urban elite classes, therefore, are hybrid in make-up; they are torn between two contradictory systems of values.

In most of the countries where the Indian component of the population is considerable, their mere presence in the towns makes them significant as a proletariat or as a marginal group. In Mexico the mestizo element is of major importance. They played a predominant role in the revolution, and today they are integrating socially with the urban class.

The traditional rural population is a mixture of races: white, mestizo, or Indian, depending on the country. It has generally lived on the fringe of all political, economic and cultural life, but forms the most sizable segment of the Latin American population. Only in Uruguay and Argentina does the urban population account for more than 60 per cent of the total. Living in areas where towns are few and far between, often scattered in the mountains or across the plains where communication is difficult,

TABLE 1

Distribution of the Population in Latin America and Neighboring Areas according to Sociological and Geographical Divisions (c.1950)

Type of Population	Latin America	Mexico and South America	Central America	Antilles
Urban (towns of 5,000+)	49,911,425—32.9%	43,722,476—33.6%	1,702,203—19.6%	4,486,746—33.8%
Small towns (under 5,000)	12,105,127— 8.0	10,541,076— 8.2	945,797—10.9	618,254— 4.6
Rural	89,852,967—59.1	75,639,901—58.2	6,030,573—69.5	8,182,493—61.6
Total	151,869,519	129,903,453	8,678,573	13,287,493

the rural population has remained marginal in relation to the total development of Latin America. In the chapter concerning agrarian problems, it will be seen how this class was affected by a social structure that had been stagnant for generations. The result was a rather particular kind of cultural universe, generally geared to a pre-technological existence. They lived in complete isolation, having no influence on the national life.

TABLE 2

Percentages of the Urban Populations in the Various
Latin American Countries (c.1960)*

Mexico and South America		*Central America*	
Argentina	67.6	Panama	41.0
Chile	62.9	Costa Rica	37.8
Venezuela	61.7	El Salvador	32.6
Mexico	53.6	Nicaragua	33.9
Colombia	46.1	Guatemala	31.0
Brazil	39.4	Honduras	22.5
Ecuador	34.7		
Peru	35.8		
Paraguay	33.8		
Bolivia	29.9		

Antilles	
Cuba	54.6
Dominican Republic	30.5
Haiti	12.6

* UN's Economic Commission for Latin America (ECLA). Urban population refers to localities with 2,000 or more inhabitants.

The rural population today is in full transformation. On the one hand, there is the ever-mounting population increase due to a lower mortality rate, especially among infants. On the other hand, the rural masses are becoming more and more aware of their situation, hence desirous of a fuller participation in the culture of the nation. They still represent one of the principal elements of the Latin American social system. The present social reformers understood this when they included in their programs agrarian reforms and facilities for more accelerated training. It is hoped that these will help the masses emerge from their sub-cultural state.

The Indian population has reached high proportions in certain countries. Various estimates place their number anywhere between 14 and 40 million (1950 figures). The figures vary according as the criteria used are linguistic, racial or cultural. Included by some in the indigenous populations are the mestizos, whose culture is predominantly Indian, and whose numbers are steadily increasing. At the present time, 80 per cent of the Indian populations of Latin America are concentrated in five countries: Bolivia, Ecuador, Guatemala, Mexico, and Peru. In the other countries the Indian population is relatively small: Colombia, 400,000; Chile, 250,000; Argentina, 130,000; Paraguay, 30,000; Venezuela, 100,000.

It is important to realize that the greater part of the Indian masses live completely outside the rest of society. This marginal existence is evidenced by the social system they have conserved and by the continued use of their native languages. Some countries are making serious efforts toward integration. This is especially the case in Mexico, and the effects can already be seen in the penetration of Indian values into revolutionary Mexican art.

In some regions the Indian, still using primitive techniques, lives by hunting, fishing, and the natural products of the land. In other regions, he lives in reservations or communities, he is Catholic, and his techniques and social organization have been influenced by Spanish culture. In still other regions, he is completely without roots, social sense, specific language or culture; he lives from day to day as a hired hand on the farms of the whites or mestizos, or else he gravitates to the outskirts of a large city.

The growing nationalism of several of the Latin American countries, however, is being nurtured by a return to their indige-

nous sources of culture, and this should enable the Indian populations to become one of the important socio-cultural components
of society. This is actually happening in Bolivia and Peru.

TABLE 3

Evolution of the Ethnic Composition of the Population between
1650 and 1950 (population figures in millions)*

Groups	1650 Population	%	1825 Population	%	1950 Population	%
Indians	9.13	80.4	8.2	35.6	14.3	8.8
Negroes	0.83	7.3	4.07	17.8	13.7	8.0
Whites	0.72	6.4	4.3	18.8	72.0	44.5
Mestizos	0.67	5.9	6.2	27.1	61.6	38.1

* W. S., and E. S. Woytinsky, *World Population and Production: Trends
and Outlook* (New York: Twentieth Century Fund, 1953).

The Negro population is localized in certain well determined
regions of Latin America. Their most predominant influence,
with the obvious exception of Haiti, is in Brazil. The books of
Freyre and Bastides have effectively brought to light the Negro's
contribution to Brazilian culture. Certain phenomena, such as
spiritism—which we interpret as an attempt to adapt to a changing
culture—can be traced back to the African peoples.

The sub-cultural influences, the living conditions, and the types
of social stratification are naturally all interdependent. One must,
therefore, take into account the interaction of these three elements
in order to assemble any kind of global picture of the social
change in Latin America.

In closing this introductory chapter, it bears repeating that we
consider the social change in Latin America as the preparation
for a new type of society—a rather laborious preparation, but one
full of hope for the future. All change is difficult. Every birth
is painful. But a realistic picture of the problems of Latin America
can be obtained only by placing them in the context of the past

and future, rather than concentrating solely on present difficulties. The crisis of Latin America is growth. This is the perspective in which her problems must be viewed.

NOTES

¹ Wilbert E. Moore, "A Reconsideration of the Theories of Social Change," *American Sociological Review,* Vol. 25, No. 6 (Dec. 1960), p. 811.

² In this attempted new vision of the real Latin America, sociological and economic research plays a major part. Fortunately, the social sciences are making rapid strides in Latin America; and this is a rather new development, for these sciences were very often bogged down with philosophical and literary considerations. Various universities, such as the University of Bogotá, the Catholic University of Santiago, the University of Mexico, of Buenos Aires and of São Paulo, have contributed largely to the movement. Mention must be made of UNESCO's Centro Latino-Americano de Pesquisas em Ciencias Sociais at Rio de Janeiro (see especially: L. A. Costa Pinto, "Pesquisas sobre mutanças socialis en América-Latina, tendencias e problemas," *Boletim del Centro Latino-Americano de Pesquisas em Ciencias Sociais,* Vol. IV, No. 1 (Feb. 1961), pp. 5–17). The following publications also deal with the problem: *Revista Mexicana de Sociologia, Quadernos de Economia Humana,* the studies of FERES (The International Federation of Institutions for Socio-Religious and Social Research), the important studies of the United Nations (CEPAL) and of the Organization of American States. FERES has made available the results of three years of research in a series of over forty books, many of which are referred to in the present work. For a background study of this series, the reader might consult Eugene K. Culhane's "The FERES Study of Latin America," *America* (Sept. 26, 1964). In addition to this and other series, FERES also publishes a journal, *Social Compass* (116, rue des Flamands, Louvain, Belgium).

4

The Origin
of the Social Changes

A change is endogenous when its origin is within the very society which undergoes it. Such is the case, for example, with the new scientific and technological discoveries: they are fruits of the culture in which they occur, but their application gradually, and sometimes suddenly, transforms the whole social system. A most striking illustration is the industrial revolution in England. An exogenous change is one whose origin is exterior to the society in which it occurs. The perfect example of this is colonization. People come from the exterior to take root in a new territory, bringing with them a totally different social and cultural system which either disintegrates and supplants the pre-existing civilization, or synthesizes with it.

In Latin America, social change has been both endogenous and exogenous. It is important to understand this, otherwise the effects of these transformations will be judged quite differently. There are, of course, a good number of traits traceable to non-Latin-American societies; but most of the elements of change were already present within the continent, above all, in those cells of modernism previously mentioned. This factor alone makes the social change of this continent quite unlike that of Africa, for example. The cells of modernism are, in large measure, made up of a population that has been indigenous for a good many generations. In Africa, by way of contrast, the modernistic circles, even today, are composed mostly of European elements.

THE ENDOGENOUS CHANGES

Part of Latin American society has for decades now been undergoing changes similar to those in Europe and North America. This is particularly true of the more industrialized nations. Although the remote origin of these transformations must ultimately be traced to non-indigenous economic causes, they have nevertheless taken place in a society basically Latin American.

We are referring here specifically to the urban areas, for the rural masses lived apart for several centuries. Rural change is very recent, and we shall later treat of it at length. In the cities, the large cities especially, one social group, which enjoyed the monopoly of the economic, political, social and educational institutions, constituted the only integrated society of the continent. Before the revolutions for independence, most of the leadership was exercised by the whites who had been born on the Iberian Peninsula. After independence, the creoles took over these roles, becoming in turn the elite class, without, however, transforming the social structures. During the entire nineteenth century, and in some countries even until recently, this same group of individuals and families, though relatively fewer in number, continued to monopolize culture and the socio-economic functions.

As the economy of the countries evolved, some changes came about in the controlling social group. In some cases it adapted to the new conditions by assuming administrative and commercial roles, in other cases it simply did not concern itself with new developments. The social structure of the colonial period was thus carried over in spite of the many changes that the nineteenth century brought.

The birth of social groups situated between the upper classes and the masses was likewise a product of developments. In general, the intermediate categories descended from the upper class and, for a long time, entirely depended on it for their development. Only in areas where industry grew up did a middle class—if we can use that term at all—emerge from the lower social strata. This latter type of evolution became common only recently. It was more accelerated in regions where the newly–arrived European immigrants settled, for they formed the principal components of this new class.

In the cities there has always existed a lower class destined for menial labor. Moreover, there was always a floating population of unstable elements, parasites of the colonial and post-colonial urban societies.

Beginning in the 1940's, a veritable urban revolution took place in Latin America. (See Appendix Table I.) Huge masses of the rural populations moved into the cities. This occurred because the population explosion was not accompanied by an adequate expansion of rural activities, and because the industries which attracted the influx were not sufficiently dispersed.

This transplantation from the country to the cities gave birth to a new marginal urban population. Yet these new city-dwellers, abruptly encountering a new civilization, did not become conscious of themselves as a group. Except in cities like Buenos Aires or São Paulo, they have not as yet formed a true "social class." Instead, they have remained a frustrated mass, living in the midst of a society in whose activities they take very little part.

The changes we have been describing can probably be classified as endogenous, that is, produced by the Latin American society itself. It is difficult, however, to isolate the endogenous from the exogenous, since developments within the continent are so clearly dependent on the outside world.

THE EXOGENOUS CHANGES

The very fact that the economy of Latin America is essentially non-autonomous implies there will be exogenous influences. Economic troubles in Europe and North America automatically have repercussions in Latin America. The fluctuations in the price of raw materials, fundamental for the Latin American economy, depend not on the latter, but on the sensitive markets of Europe and North America. It should be immediately evident, therefore, that a large part of the transformations in Latin American society depend ultimately on outside influences, hence should be considered exogenous.

Even the recent industrial developments in Latin America are predominantly exogenous. In countries like Argentina, Brazil, Venezuela, or Chile, the initiators of important industrial and commercial enterprises are very often foreigners. It is rare to find regions like Medellin in Colombia, Monterey in Mexico, or Cordoba in Argentina where the majority of the industrialists are native to the country. It was mostly, then, foreigners who introduced technological values, whether industrial or commercial. This partially explains the conflict of values experienced by the traditional elite class.

When the different Latin American countries will have worked out a truly original synthesis of the values they have received from the outside and those which they draw from their own vigorous cultures, they will then be ready to make a creative contribution. There is no doubt that the social, economic and political structures themselves have significantly limited the absorption of the technological values which are indispensable for the development of Latin America. A transformation of her social system, a certain independence in her economy, and a more real participation of the masses in her political life will profoundly influence her cultural evolution.

Orlando Fals Borda expresses this very vividly in his report to the sixth Latin American Congress on Sociology:

Latin America has not experienced such changes [the industrial development] except through cultural contacts with the Old World. It is interesting to notice that the "industrial revolution" had scarcely reached its peak in Latin America by the third decade of the twentieth century. We might ask why the delay was so pronounced. Since the knowledge of technical inventions was so widespread, was there no way of bringing about a transformation in Latin America simultaneously with that of Europe during the nineteenth century? It is easy to understand, however, that such a transformation was not previously possible, because the necessary transformation in beliefs, attitudes and motivations, i.e., the "ethos" of the population, had not yet come about in Latin America. It took over a hundred years for our continent to lay the foundations and prepare the ground for the operation of the "*Kürwille*."[1]

Such a process perhaps began with the first contacts of the Latin American elite with the French Encyclopedists at the end of the eighteenth century, and received impetus from the anti-Spanish reactions after independence when, for the first time, public schools were established. The construction of one of the exotic, but inefficient railroads, the establishment of small factories and banks helped create the necessary atmosphere; to such an extent that even the natural conformism of the masses was weakened and they began to question the merits of the existing order. It was only when the peasants freed themselves of their confinement, of their fatalism, of their conservatism, of their state of dependence, it was only when they first experienced, by migrating or through education, the existence of social injustices, only when they began to desire their emancipation and when new needs and ambitions gave them new motivations—only then did rapid progress become reasonably possible.

This is what had fed not only the industrial and urban revolutions of today, but also the tensions and conflicts that our society is undergoing.[2]

Foreign influences have also directly marked Latin American social transformations. A major part of social legislation has been inspired by the evolution of laws in Europe and North America. But the result has often been a perfectly elaborated legal text which is inapplicable or unapplied to daily realities.

The labor organizations have likewise suffered considerably from foreign influences. The first unions were heavily dependent on the union organization in Europe. The history of the Latin American labor movement during the last fifty years shows to what extent political influences, be they socialist, anarchic or communist, have perverted labor activity.[3] The labor organization on the continental level, and more so the national groups, have been guided more by events abroad than by the continent's own needs. The Communists' involvement in the situation is only too clear: unions are made or broken in Latin America, depending on how the party line evolves in the East.

Of equal importance is the influence of North American unions. They have become especially interested in the Latin American labor movement since the war. It was not long before it became evident that policies were being dictated by exogenous interests. Characteristics of North American unionism, such as anti-Communism and neutralism, governed the attitudes of labor organizations of the south, notably concerning the granting of subsidies.

It should be evident by now that the social change in Latin America is very complex. It is both endogenous and exogenous. It shall be the task of the future to strengthen the native elements which influence social change. This must be done in all areas, the economic and the cultural as well as the social.

NOTES

[1] Term used by German sociologists to indicate the creative will.

[2] Orlando Fals Borda, "La Transformación de la América Latina y sus Implicaciones Sociales y Económicas," an address to the 6th Latin American Congress of Sociology, Caracas, April 1961, and published in the review, *La Nueva Economia*, No. 2 (1961), pp. 17–18.

[3] J. A. Arcos, *El Sindicalismo en América Latina* (Fribourg: FERES, 1964).

5

The Masses on the Move

A significant development in present-day Latin America is the entry of the masses into the deep and moving stream of social change. Until recent years, only a relatively small part of the population was involved; the social transformations were operating almost exclusively within the upper echelons. Today, the whole of society is in movement. The changes in society formerly had little effect on the basic social structures of most of the Latin American countries, for it was being absorbed by the elite. Now it is passing to the masses.

The majority of the population had not been integrated into the economic system. They continued a day-to-day existence while the more dynamic sectors of society were already participating in a market economy. The masses lacked the same integration in other areas: in politics because of their non-participation in normal elections; in education because of their high degree of illiteracy; in social relations because of their physical isolation and lack of communication. They lived literally outside of society. These conditions, originating in colonial times, carried on through independence to the political and economic regimes of the nineteenth century. There was really nothing novel about this type of social structure; it was basically the same as existed in Europe during feudal times. The ignorance in which the common people

58

lived led them to accept their lot, for they had nothing to measure it against. Harry M. Johnson writes:

Once a system is more or less stabilized, people tend to be immersed in it and do not seriously consider whether some other system might be possible. In such a system, people are like fish who, swimming around in water all their life, presumably are unaware that there is or could be any other milieu in which to live.[1]

The same author also points out that in every feudal society the marginal population forms a social category even more heterogeneous than the upper classes:

Since all members of the upper class are educated in the same sacred classics, that class is more homogeneous than the mass of the population, whose members, tied to their villages, may develop local sub-cultures that prevent effective communication between one small group and another.[2]

Two types of society can coexist, therefore, in the same territory with very little contact between them and function as almost independent entities.

Two basic factors operated to change this situation in Latin America. The first is the numerical expansion, i.e., the population explosion; the second is the communication which began to operate between the marginal masses and the rest of society.

Let us first examine the phenomenon commonly called the population explosion. In ten years, from 1950 to 1960, the population of Latin America increased by about 50 million. A large part of this increase did take place in the cities, particularly the large cities, but it was the rural areas that most drastically felt the pressure. Within a few short years the average rural family found the number of its children increased by a third or a half. Advances in hygienic methods had very rapidly decreased the infant mortality rate.[3] Unfortunately, the sources of family income did not keep pace with the growth of the family's size; very often the income actually decreased. The very structure of rural property was the cause.

It was practically impossible for the small peasant farmers, and even more so for those who held no title to property, to increase the size of the arable land at their disposal; the large plantations and estates formed an insurmountable blockade. In an effort to get more out of their land they often impoverished it. The ignorance of elementary measures against erosion, the almost total absence of fertilizer (either because it was too expensive or its use was unknown), the unfortunate overworking of the land, all these factors combined to drain the productivity of the soil.[4]

TABLE 4

The Relative Number of Large and Small Farms, and the
Percentage of the Total National Area They Encompass
(national agricultural statistics, c. 1955)

	Small Farms		Large Farms	
	% of total number of farms	% of land owned	% of total number of farms	% of land owned
Argentina	34.4	0.87	1.2	41.43
Bolivia	59.3	0.20	8.1	41.43
Brazil	34.43	1.30	14.58	64
Chile	23	1.70	2.1	40.50
Colombia	60.5	6.88	0.87	40.22
Cuba	39.07	?	1.46	46
Ecuador	73.13	7.20	10.7	56.62
El Salvador	80.61	2.0	0.55	?
Mexico	79.16	1.42	1.42	89.43
Uruguay	25.89	0.62	1.34	34
Venezuela	80.62	?	1.70	?

The situation of these peasant farmers was, then, quite paradoxical: more mouths to feed, less crops from their land; yet nearby, large estates lay uncultivated, or exploited well below their potentialities. Moreover, the modifications that were possible in the global structure of the rural world were insignificant and incapable of resolving the problem.

Since the farmers could not move socially, they moved geographically. This, and not the need for an industrial labor force, is the key to the excessive rural exodus to the cities. These very large groups of rural immigrants were put in contact with the centers of modernism. They increased the marginal population of the cities without significantly modifying their former social status. Yet their very contact with a new civilization revealed to them the unnecessary character of their social state. Raymond Frost considers this one of the most important results of the contact between advanced and retarded social groups.[5] The social and economic structures of the rural world cannot remain stationary much longer. The pressure is too great. In some regions the peasant masses are starving.

The second factor of contemporary social change is the broadening of communications. We have already pointed out that the rural migrations toward the cities put more people in contact with modernism. This affected not only those persons who actually came into the city, but also the families who stayed in the country and with whom they were now able to maintain communication.

There was an expansion of both the physical and ideological means of communication. We shall not go into the subject of air travel, which greatly facilitated interchange between the various centers of modernism and linked them more closely with the North American and European continents. Instead, we would like to turn special attention to communications on the local level.

Today there is no village, be it the most isolated hamlet of Cordillera, that is not linked to a nearby city by bus, at least once or twice a week. The "bus" is rather primitive (in fact the people there call it a "truck"), but it is of prime importance. Gradually the network of bus lines made possible a greater mobility for the marginal populations. It put them in contact with new ways of life, at first in the small cities, then in the large.

Today even in the most progressive neighborhoods of the large cities you see individuals whose dress and manners betray their country origin and pre-technological civilization. Networks of communication have also made possible a gradual integration, though still very slight, into the market economy. Even the Indian communities have adopted the use of money. Small country towns have become centers of commerce, and only an extremely weak purchasing power has kept them from developing more rapidly.

If buses bring the rural populations into the city, they also take city folk to the country. The contact has been reciprocal and is not limited to economic influences, but includes social and cultural exchanges as well.

The means of physical communication are, of course, important in the contact between civilizations, but more important yet is the extension of ideological communication. A considerable effort has been made in the Latin American countries to combat illiteracy. It is still very high (nearly 50% of the total population, with fluctuations in some areas from 20% to 80%), but it seems to be gradually giving way. Through printed media the literate populations are now discovering how other people live. Newspapers, magazines and pamphlets have begun to be a major force in the shaping of mentalities. Little by little the rural masses of Latin America are coming to realize that theirs is not the only way of life.

The power of radio in recent years simply cannot be overemphasized. And now, with the advent of transistors, the boom in radio broadcasting is bound to become even more pronounced. The radio has not merely enabled the marginal populations to shed their ideological limitations in national affairs, it has put them in contact with life around the world. The immediate effects of this can be exaggerated, but the long-range influences are extremely important. The Colombian peasant can listen not only to his national programs, but those of Cuba, Moscow and Peking as well.

The consciousness of living in abnormal conditions is day by day seeping into the mentality of these people. Already their minds have begun a process of transformation. The fact that social structures are so rigid and economic development so inaccessible makes this awareness that much more explosive:

A traditional society that is isolated and out of communication is not underdeveloped as far as its own members are concerned, but they begin to consider it as such when they are able to compare their condition of political, economic and cultural dependence with a more "developed" society. Moreover, even if their traditional "pattern" does not change one bit, it is still not the same as it was before the awareness of its underdevelopment.[6]

In Colombia, the *Acción Cultural Popular,* especially through educational broadcasting, has had great success in combating illiteracy and in progressively transforming the values of the rural world.[7] It has been very effective in raising the basic standards of living in relation to hygiene, housing and farming techniques. It should be obvious, however, that these cultural programs which increase the awareness of the peasant masses must be accompanied by very basic structural reforms, if a social explosion is to be avoided.

The pressure of a growing population and the new means of world-wide communication have been favorable to a very rapid diffusion of modernistic values. The most noteworthy of these are democracy, the secularization of certain social and personal activities, the raising of the standard of living, and better education. All segments of the population are not uniformly affected by these ideas. Most receptive are the younger elements (40% of Latin America's population is under 15 years old) and the new leaders in the urban and rural societies. As can be expected, there are conservative elements that play restraining roles: the property owners, the "ancients" of the rural society, and certain priests who are still the organizers and leaders of local communities.

The transmission of new values is essential for future change.

Indeed, an important social change must receive its impulsion from the masses; and since the desire to change is essentially an acquired capacity, contact with new values is necessary to encourage it.

The awareness of which we spoke is reinforced by revolutionary ideologies. This is where the West shows its great weakness. In contrast, Marxism, symbolized today by the Cuban experiment, not only gives an ideological objective to the uneasy masses, but even spells out the specific methods of attaining it. A striking example is the book by Ernesto "Che" Guevara entitled, *Guerrilla Warfare*. The author, who is Minister of Economic Affairs in Cuba, paraphrases, for the most part, the works of Mao Tse-tung. He not only explains the philosophy of social revolution and guerrilla warfare, but goes into the concrete details of how to accomplish it: the type of equipment to be used for ambushes, for fighting in the mountains or on the plains, how to transform a hunting rifle into a "Molotov cocktail," etc.

For the masses, the Cuban experiment meant the rapid attainment of a real social status. It can even be said that the purely economic aspect of the problem is secondary. The day Fidel Castro permitted the common people of Havana to use the beaches, which up till that time had been reserved for Cuban capitalists, or North Americans, or tourists, he did more to fulfill their expectations than if he had raised all salaries. The desire for status in society, for real participation in cultural and political activities, and for raising the standard of living, is an undercurrent which in the years to come will sweep the Latin American masses into movement. The rapidity of this movement will perhaps depend upon the degree of awareness of their relatively low condition, consequently, upon the development of the means of communication. We shall see later that this awareness is not by itself sufficient to stimulate popular uprisings; nevertheless, it is at the base of the present transformations.

The Marxist ideologies have done much to accelerate change,

but their influence has been favored by the international situation and the East-West conflict. The campaign against the United States has been facilitated by the masses' awareness of the economic influence which certain American companies exerted in that country and in many other Latin American nations. This reality has been used to feed an embittered nationalism and serves as the launching pad for a whole ideological program. Communist propaganda has thereby become most effective.

Such an ideology can only be counteracted by one equally coherent and equally capable of mobilizing the forceful energies of a nation for boldly accomplishing the necessary basic reforms. Unfortunately, at the very moment when the Latin American masses are becoming increasingly conscious of their plight, the economic evolution in most of the countries is actually widening the gap between the income brackets of the different social classes. During the last ten years almost all the southern countries, especially Argentina, Brazil, Chile, Bolivia, Uruguay and Paraguay, have been weakened by continual inflation. In Chile, for example, the 1960 cost of living index was ten times its 1953 level. During the same period in Bolivia, the index tripled. In these countries the salary increase has not kept pace with the depreciation of the currency. (See Appendix Table III.)

NOTES

[1] Harry M. Johnson, *Sociology—A Systematic Introduction* (London: Routledge and Kegan, 1961), p. 637. Cf. also the American edition published by Harcourt, Brace and World, Inc., in 1960.

[2] *Ibid.*

[3] The infant mortality rate still maintains a relatively high level in the majority of Latin American countries. For the period 1950–55, the United Nations supplied the figures of 12.5% to 17.5% (in western Europe and North America they fluctuated between 2% and 5%). A downward tendency is noticeable, however, in Argentina, Jamaica and Puerto Rico, where the rate is about 7.5%; in Chile and Costa Rica it is between 10% and

12.5%. In some regions of Latin America, for example, the northeastern part of Brazil, the rate is still as high as 50% to 60%.

⁴ B. Corredor and I. Torres, *Transformación en el mundo rural Latino-Americano* (Fribourg: FERES, 1961).

⁵ Raymond Frost, *The Backward Society* (New York: St. Martin's Press, 1961).

⁶ Gino Germani, "Démocratie représentative et classes populaires en Amérique latine," in *Ouvriers et Syndicats d'Amérique latine*, No. 4 of the series, *Sociologie du Travail*, under the direction of Alain Touraine (Paris: Editions du Seuil, 1961).

⁷ C. Torres and B. Corredor, *Las Escuelas Radiofónicas de Sutatenza (Colombia)* (Fribourg: FERES, 1961).

6

The Disintegration
of Traditional Society

Disintegration of a structure implies that a change has taken place in its most important functional elements. Some social changes can be a simple replacement of one element by a similar one fulfilling the same functions. Thus, when one political clan is overthrown by another of the same type, it cannot be called a fundamental change. As Johnson states: "Of structural changes the most important are those that have consequences for the functioning of the system."[1] We can cite as fundamental changes in Latin America the progressive transformation of a feudal type of social stratification, and the rapid urbanization of a predominantly rural society.

Among the basic social structures that we shall treat, emphasis will be given to the marginal rural masses and the former elite class. It is around these two groups that revolves a social system that is presently undergoing a violent upheaval. No doubt this is somewhat simplifying reality, since numerous sub-groups could be mentioned; but the fact remains that these two groups form the axis of the whole social system.

It is difficult in a sociological analysis to distinguish precisely between the changes in social structure and the changes in culture, for these two elements are intimately bound together. A society cannot exist without a culture any more than a culture can exist

67

without a society. The distinction, therefore, is purely rational. The evolution through which Latin America has been passing for the past several decades is a classic process that has been described by all the eminent sociologists from Max Weber to Howard Becker. Each has utilized a personalized nomenclature in explaining the passage from one system of values, which we call "pretechnological," to a system of technological values. Harry Johnson writes: "According to Weber, the process of rationalization is one of the most important trends in human history."[2]

Depending on the localities where social change takes place, however, the cultural aspect can either precede or follow. In European society at the end of the eighteenth century, the transformation of values preceded the application of the new scientific discoveries. Technology was born of a culture. Once off the ground, technology became, in a sense, independent of the cultural system and, in turn, initiated very important structural changes; the latter finally necessitated a transformation in the system of values. From new methods of production, for example, were born new relationships between men, based on an entirely unprecedented social hierarchy and stratification.

On the Latin American continent, however, cultural change has been a necessary consequence of social change and the introduction of technology. It is therefore more of an effect than a cause. On the other hand, the economic, technological and social developments must suppose that the cultural system will adapt. Progress, therefore, is not merely an economic question. Without a change of values in the Latin American peasant one will never change the agricultural system, and thereby profoundly influence his productivity. That is why the educational system is so important in a growing society, and why institutions, like the Catholic Church, which traditionally have influenced values, can play a preponderant role. In Latin America, Catholicism represents a system of values that has always exerted a great influence. Rather than oppose the Church on the grounds that it is too integrated in an ancient social system and too hesitant in becoming a part of the new structures, every initiative should be taken to make of it an element of cultural and social dynamism.[3]

A certain equivalence can be ascertained between what Max Weber terms "the process of rationalization" and what Redfield calls "the passage from a folk society to an urban society." Other sociologists have their own terminology: Howard Becker labels it "the process of secularization," and Gino Germani refers to it as "the passage from prescriptive action to elective action." They are all speaking of the transformation of values which is effected by the introduction of new technological elements into traditional society. This society is affected to such a degree that its very bases are modified, i.e., its roles, norms, social hierarchy and institutions.[4]

It is important to understand well the terminology of these authors. Becker categorized a society as sacred or secularized, based on its openness to change. That which is "sacred," according to current usage, is that which cannot change. Thus any social system whose coherence is assured by an ensemble of norms, hierarchies and values, and which is considered as unchangeable, is qualified "sacred."[5]

The utilization of such a framework of terminology could help us in the discussion at hand. Indeed, in Latin America we are dealing with the passage from one type of society, which considered certain things as "taboo," to a social system that is not only open to change, but quite prepared to provoke change when necessary. As should be evident, the terms which Becker uses have nothing to do with the religious character of values, nor do they imply a moral judgment on change. In fact, he deliberately excludes this aspect. Note, however, that while religious values have a "sacred" character *par excellence,* they can also undergo a process of change. In fact, the religious values of Latin America can emerge from this evolution purified of many superfluous elements which formerly had encouraged a confusion between the temporal and the spiritual, between transitory religious manifestations and spiritual reality, between religious structures and religion itself.

When change occurs, especially when it is abrupt as in Latin America, the passage from one system of values to another is not made without some reaction. The result is often a very painful period of transition. Today the continent is experiencing a genuine disintegration of traditional values. The ancient norms, based on a well-defined scale of social values, are incapable of coping with new situations. A determining functional element, therefore, is lacking to the present social system.

Before new values make their appearance, are circulated among and accepted by the various social groups, a space of time elapses during which is created a condition of *"anomie,"* to use Max Weber's expression, that is, an absence of norms capable of producing integration. It is naturally the younger elements of the population and the rising classes of society that are more susceptible to transformations, hence, new values. They consequently have a better chance of integrating into new-fledged systems. These are the social groups, therefore, that must be counted on in any attempt at renewal.

THE MARGINAL RURAL MASSES

Before social change affected the traditional rural masses, they were living in a very particular kind of social system. Numerous sub-cultures existed and still exist in the different regions of Latin America. In some regions the family structure was patriarchal, in others, matriarchal. The effect of the varied cultures on the small local communities was not always the same. The social groups living in the mountains of Cordillera are very different from those living on the coast. But, in a sense, all these societies can be described as "closed," and based on pre-technological values.

They were characterized, first of all, by a patriarchal type of family. This means that the family group formed the basic economic unit, that the role of parents and relatives was highly important, notably in the education of the children, and that the "ancients" had the monopoly on authority, for all human knowledge was acquired by experience. Rural society was characterized by the importance of minute rural communities. These small groups still exist today in most of the Latin American countries and are called *aldeas, veredas, fundos, caserios,* etc. Although they did not form the actual basis of formal society, as the towns, they did constitute the most solid unit of rural society above the level of the patriarchal family.

These two basic elements, the family and the small social group, form the essence of the economic, political and social systems of the pre-technological rural world. The social hierarchies were built around them. They naturally resulted in very different structures, ranging from the Indian communities isolated in the mountains or forests, as far as possible out of contact with Western civilization, to the mestizo communities, or even whites, like the caboclos of Brazil.

Religion, it should be mentioned, was very often closely integrated with the social system. The role of the "ancients" likewise had a religious value.

Today, as a result of the factors already described, a profound transformation is operating in the social structures of the rural world. We have already spoken of urbanization as a reaction to the immobility of the social structures. We can also mention the change in the type of jobs; and in this area the place of agriculture is diminishing—as everywhere else in the world. All this is bringing on basic transformations in the type of social relations, in the organization of communities, in the forms of social control and leadership. Since, in such an evolution, the role of the ancients is gradually being taken over by "technicians," the social relationships in the very interior of the family are changing. And

since an economy of subsistence is being replaced by a market
economy, the patriarchal structure of the family will not be able
to hold up much longer.

New roles are coming into being. Local political administration is developing. Model economic organizations, such as cooperatives, are making their appearance. Unionism is spreading
to the rural areas. To meet the challenge of these new roles, the
pace of leadership in this traditional world is gradually quicken-
ing. The changes in structures, roles and leadership are producing
an evolution in the type of social control. The over-all control
which certain individuals or offices had exerted is diminishing.
Typical in this category is the priest. He was formerly the leader
of the community in Latin America, and still is in some localities.
His role generally had beneficial effects, for he defended the community against the central political powers or against the abuses
of the landed gentry. It was normal, however, that the appearance
of new roles should gradually reduce his traditional social leadership.

More important yet is the fact that these structural changes
are deeply altering the traditional channels through which culture
has been transmitted. For indeed, the patriarchal family, the small
rural groups and, in general, the whole rural structure acted as
funnels of cultural values. And among these we include religious
values, which, in spite of the absence of priests and the fierce
anti-religious struggles, have been passed down to the Latin
American masses of today. There are some old values which must
be replaced by new ones if there is to be a reintegration of the
whole social system. There are, however, some basic values of
another order which also threaten to disappear. Regarding these,
and we have especially in mind religious values, the solution
seems to consist in withdrawing support from the transitory traditional forms and searching for new channels of transmission and
new forms for integrating with a society on the move.

Lastly let us point out that the transformation of the social
structures of the marginal and rural masses of Latin America is

accompanied by a whole cortege of very serious difficulties. In some regions the result has been poverty and hunger, in others, like the northeast of Brazil, social disturbances. These consequences are not unavoidable. They come from the uneven development of the different factors of the social system. Some of these remain unchanged, like political power or the ownership of lands, while others change profoundly, like the population increase and the reduction in illiteracy.

The Latin American masses have lived on the outer limits not only of the economic and political systems, but also of the culture of the rest of society. It could not be otherwise, so closely are these systems bound together. That does not mean that the "culture" of this population had no scale of values. As a matter of fact, they formed an infinity of "sub-cultures" which have provided anthropologists with almost unlimited material. In this sense, it is entirely incorrect to speak of *the* culture of the Latin American rural masses.

Yet all authors agree in labeling this cultural diversity "pre-technological." This is a rather broad generalization, but it is justified in that the present upheaval has in a few short years accomplished a technological revolution similar to the one which Europe spread over some 150 years before bringing it to complete maturity, at least in its concrete applications.

The values of traditional rural society made possible the continued existence of patriarchal families, small rural groups, a backward economy, and certain social traditions, like the *fiesta,* which served as a sort of safety value to an excessively closed and normative society.

But today, owing especially to the developments in communications, the rural masses are entering into contact with other social forms and other values. Even though old structures have held together, it will not be for long, for mentalities are already changing. The most dynamic elements, the most "desacralized," are turning toward new values, and this is a prophetic sign of structural transformations. The new contacts are giving rise to the need and desire for better education, better farming methods, and a greater buying power.

These are the new values being introduced into traditional society, and not without a violent reaction. Moreover, other values are being assailed: the authority of the older generations, the quasi-magical ways of treating the soil and the livestock, the rites accompanying daily activities. And the more "sacred" these things are, the greater is the resistance of the traditional elements. Thus the very painful conflict between generations.

Disintegration does not stop here. New roles are making their appearance: merchants and administrators who are beginning to take an interest in the marginal populations; teachers who are instilling an appreciation of knowledge, so indispensable to change; all kinds of political leaders, some concerned only with their own career, but others with the emancipation of the masses at heart; social organizers of cooperatives, of unions, or of programs for communal development. These roles are in themselves transmitters of values.

The normal reaction of the present social system has been one of resistance to change. Very often the chief "guardians" of traditional values go overboard in stressing the veneration in which these principles should be held. Thus there is always present the risk of fierce oppositions and tragic conflicts. For the one camp, everything new is evil, the work of the devil. For the other, everything even remotely connected to the traditional social system must disappear to make way for a new utopia. Adding to the confusion is the fact that this opposition is taking place in a political and ideological context, and, as so often happens, is influenced by national and international events. The old guard puts the tag of "Communist" on all those who stand for new values, while their opposition labels "clerical reactionaries" those who would attempt to distinguish between those things which are not essentially "sacred" and the immutable values which have their origin in divine reality, such as the value of the human person, of the family, and of worship.

In a great number of villages in the northern mountainous

regions of South America, action was recently undertaken, with the support of civil authorities, to aid the development of the communities. It is interesting to observe the reactions of the pastors of these villages, who up till then had exercised the social leadership. The older pastors, especially, adopted an aggressive attitude from the very beginning. They figured that such an initiative had to be inspired by the Communists since it created new social roles in competition to their own, and by that very fact reduced the place of religion in society. They forgot that their social function was only secondary, that they were only filling in until such time as society could produce its own leaders, thus permitting the clergy to concentrate more fully on their spiritual mission.

Other pastors assumed a polite neutralism, a sort of wait-and-see attitude. One pastor, having understood the importance of the changes that were about to take place, lost no time in designating the persons who would fill the new posts. He chose, however, not his most competent parishioners, but his most docile; as he himself explained, he wished to maintain control of any new initiatives. He completely confused his social and spiritual functions. The former was used solely as a means to reinforce the latter. But according to Catholic theology the social role has a value in itself, as do all secular functions. It cannot be diverted from its proper end, as in the case in question, even if the short-range effect is a more efficient accomplishment of religious responsibilities.

Finally, a certain number of priests, realizing the significance of the new developments in their community, offered their complete cooperation from the outset, in spite of the fact that their leadership, in certain respects, was bound to be affected. They set themselves to the task of giving a deeper religious training to the new leaders so that their social and cultural development would not take place in an atmosphere of religious stagnation. The attitude of these priests was the one that the bishop of the diocese in question held up as an example to all his clergy.

It is not by chance that the incident we selected to describe concerns a religious question. From earliest times, the society and culture of Latin America have been impregnated with religious values, and to ignore this fact deliberately would be to throw away a most valuable key to the understanding of the continent.

Since social control is so closely connected to social leadership, it is likewise changing hands. As the newly created social roles become more important and more appreciated, there is a proportionate decrease in the power and prestige of the landowners. Many of them, instead of adapting to the new situation by heading and collaborating with movements of reform, have decided to oppose energetically anything that might spread the new ideas, anything that might affect the servile submission of the rural populations.

Even in the country areas an intermediate class is coming into its own. It is comprised of farmers to whom technical advances in mechanization and fertilizer have been made available, and of the new leaders in cooperatives, unions, administration and education.

The pattern of the new revolutionary movements in Latin America has been to make the masses aware of their sub-human condition by putting them in greater contact with the outside world, then to call them to revolt internally and externally. The apparatus has been set in motion and no one will be able to stop it. The rural exodus and communications with the city have destroyed the traditional isolation which had made possible the coexistence of two independent societies, without any relationship between them except one of master and slave. Now the new technical media transmit ideas almost as soon as they are born, without any frontiers or obstacles whatsoever. One simple incident can illustrate this. One Sunday, in the Church square of a small Indian and mestizo village of Cordillera, a blind Indian, a few short months after Caryl Chessman's execution in the United States, recited poetry extolling him as a victim of a capitalistic regime.

This cultural permeability, a result of the new social developments, is by its very nature provoking a disintegration of traditional values in the masses. They are rapidly moving toward a participation in society, even if this participation has up till now consisted merely in a gradual awareness of their marginality.

THE TRADITIONAL SOCIAL ELITE

Although the traditional society of Latin America has been based on the ownership of land or mines (a carry-over from the *encomienda,* and later from the *hacienda* or *fazenda*), the social elite has generally been urban. Except for certain parts of Brazil, where the rural lords lived on their own property, most of the landed gentry resided in town. Social prestige was based not on the productivity of the lands, but on their size; which explains the paradoxical anti-economic attitude of the property owners. As they formed closer contacts with the capitalistic society of Europe and North America, they began to invest more of their revenue abroad. Monopolizing social prestige and cultural, political and economic power, they constituted the only segment of the population capable of living in step with the rest of the world.

However, under the influence of contacts with the exterior world and the large immigrations from Europe, this elite class was to see its power and prestige become less solid. Orlando Fals Borda writes:

It seems evident that power, in the Weberian sense of the word, is no longer the privilege of a privileged class whose superiority is based on land, education, race and family. The emergence of a middle class and a new upper class challenged the status and survival of the established interests on which the power structure was based. Special note should be taken of the following symptoms which are particularly indicative of the profound mutations our continent has experienced: the decline of *caudillismo,* whose origin was in the setting up of large estates, and which had military and agrarian after-effects; the decline of the traditional elite class; the decline of the traditional political parties, and the emergence of young parties of different mettle; the importance of women in political life; and the growth of bureaucracy and state power.[6]

Their monopoly is breaking up not only in the economic and political domains, but also in education. For a long time a secondary education and more so a university education were reserved to the social elite. Today, an ever-increasing number are finding these within reach. The universities have become an important avenue of social ascension for the new middle classes. There can be no doubt that this will result in a more pronounced transformation of the upper class.

While on the subject of education, we should note that the Catholic Church has played a very important role, especially on the secondary level where it operates 60 per cent of the schools. Since these schools are usually not subsidized, the payment of tuition is a factor; thus Catholic education today is considered too exclusively reserved to a privileged class of the population. And after an analysis of the facts, it is probably true that it has been the "social elite" who have most profited by this service that the Church renders to culture. Hence the Church appears to be trying to prolong the traditional structures of society and to be blocking the social rise of the new elite. Although most of the teaching clergy would not agree with that observation, the Church in its desire to help elevate the standards of culture has become too attached to traditional forms. Little by little secondary education, as conducted by the religious orders, has had the final effect of maintaining the cultural monopoly of one social class without contributing to a social evolution and without truly integrating religious values into the changing social order.

But to make a valid sociological judgment, the situation must be analyzed in all its details. Some interpret it as the Church's desire to maintain outmoded social structures. Others see in it one more example of the Church's attachment to reactionary values. In reality, the Church, in its desire to contribute to the development of civilization, has made an error in the interpretation of this development through lack of a positive analysis of the social systems. The *Acción Cultural Popular* movement in Colombia and the Institutes for training rural leaders in Chile are sufficient examples of how the clergy can reorientate cultural activity once they have grasped the meaning of the present evolution.

Another type of force which is diminishing if not totally disappearing from the Latin American scene is the army, at least as an agent of *caudillos.* The military dictatorships of today are quite different, except in some countries like Paraguay and, until recently, the Dominican Republic, where they drag on as outmoded symbols of the past. The army still performs an important function, but more like the French army it has become the arm of the government in times of crisis, or the support of the political parties of the right, sometimes the extreme right. The Brazilian and Argentine escapades demonstrate this, not to mention Peru and Ecuador.

The political influence of the urban masses is gaining momentum. On the whole, the masses have not reached the point of playing a significant part in the national life, but in countries where an industrial tradition is already well established or where they have already been utilized for popular movements (for example, by Perón in Argentina), their political influence is growing. Gradually they are becoming a political force with which governments must reckon, rather than mere clientele for a political clan. But because of their disorganization, their unstable economic condition, their lack of social integration, these masses are easy prey for extreme leftist or fascist movements. In the more developed countries, moreover, political heads are turning toward the urban masses to establish their power.

The labor unions, though still in an embryonic stage and still plagued with major organizational problems of their own, are becoming a telling force in organizing the popular masses. They will probably become even more influential than the unions in Europe or North America. The situation in Bolivia since the 1952 revolution is a living example. A solid labor organization is the only hope of providing a structure for the emancipation of the Latin American masses.

And yet, the mass of newly-arrived city-dwellers does not form a true social class. It still constitutes a marginal population in the process of disintegration, a simple product of the big cities' role of demographic safety-valve. It is surprising to observe just where attempts at socially integrating these marginal populations have led. Unlike the workers they have not achieved class consciousness. The living conditions of the inhabitants of the *callampas*[7] in Santiago, for example, act as a mere common denominator and have produced *ad hoc* organizations which include social types of all sorts, from the well established merchant to the poorest, most unstable hireling who changes jobs almost every day.

In spite of its variety, this mass represents a new social structure, and hence, a break-up of the old. Even though an oligarchy rules in many cities, like Lima, the violent contrast between the old and new elements in society can only result in an acceleration of the changes already in progress.

These changes were further facilitated by a steadily increasing social mobility. As a matter of fact, one of the chief characteristics of the traditional society was the almost total absence of any kind of mobility. During the colonial period it was blocked by both juridical and economic measures. During the nineteenth century, when the urban elite were surcharged with a liberal and egalitarian ideology, they would talk about it, or fashion magnificent constitutions around it, but they made sure not to give it any real application in social relationships. As to the situation today, Orlando Fals Borda declares:

In general, the traditional elite are in the process of losing their intellectual vigor, their ideological monopoly, and their economic pre-eminence. They are being reduced to a few bureaucratic positions, and sometimes to a simple oligarchy. A new intellectual elite is forming. They come both from the new group of the upper class and from the upper middle class, whose members possess a totally different mentality, and who are changing or have already changed the face of old Mount Parnassus and Mount Olympus.[8]

Thus it is that the new classes are entering into competition with the "ancient" elite.

This competition is most obvious in those sectors that are expanding, namely, industry, commerce and administration. A new leadership is issuing forth, and the former elite are practically absent from it. Certain members of the younger generations have understood the necessity of getting into those areas that control the present society. But for many of the traditional elite, who in their turn are becoming more and more marginal, engaging in industrial, commercial or administrative activity is still considered degrading. It will not be many years before this mentality is completely foreign to the real leadership in all the Latin American countries. The traditional elite will then be reduced to the second or third level of the social hierarchy, or will have to shut themselves up in complete isolation where they can cultivate outmoded values and an artificial hierarchy—if the coming revolutions permit them such leisure.[9]

We shall not go deeply into the subject of the disintegration of the traditional elite's values. That they considered these values as "sacred" is for the most part due to the fact that they considered their own superiority as "providential." During the nineteenth century they did accept new respectable ideas, but these were usually imported from European circles and had not the slightest relevancy to local conditions.

This fact alone throws much light on why in less than 150 years the Latin American countries adopted some 200 constitutions.[10] They were mostly simple transcriptions of European constitutions superimposed on feudal social structures in countries whose illiterate masses comprised 90 per cent of the population. It also explains the origin of liberal economies in monocultural countries, as well as the introduction of an Iberian Catholicism among Indians and Negroes whose cultural norms would reinterpret the rites without always understanding their meaning.[11]

As long as the double stratification lasted, the values of the traditional elite were functional. But as soon as industrialization was introduced (and this dates in some countries from the end of the nineteenth century) and as soon as the marginal masses began to develop (a very recent phenomenon), the ineffectualness of the scale of existing social values became boldly conspicuous. There followed a process of rapid disintegration due to transformations within the upper class and the birth of an intermediate class.

This intermediate class, however, still offers a curious spectacle of an incoherent mosaic. Fruit of a social change whose origin was essentially technological, this group still aspires to certain elements which constituted the prestige of the traditional elite. Except in the cities where a genuinely new class formed around the industrial, financial, commercial, and administrative functions, this intermediate category vacillated between two sets of values. The result is its cultural disequilibrium. This often degenerates into a feeling of frustration, complicated by the many obstacles to social ascension. Such circumstances do not make of this group an element of social and political stability, as is the case in other Western nations, but rather easy game for all the subversive ideologies of the right and left.

Orlando Fals Borda describes the characteristics of this new class in the following manner:

Some claim that elements of the middle class can become the true pillars of democracy. But in reality, they still seem to feed on the ideologies of the traditional upper class, whose intolerance, defense of established interests, and conservatism in dress they attempt to emulate. It is obvious, however, that mere growth in number is making of this group a real entity. It has been estimated that 50 per cent of the populations of Argentina and Uruguay and 40 per cent of Chile belong to the middle social categories.

The emerging middle class is predominantly urban and is formed of three elements: 1) the civil servants, tradesmen and artisans, who for centuries have filled in the gap between the elite in power and the masses, without changing their own social level to any appreciable degree; 2) the descendants of the great families who have adopted liberal professions because their properties were abandoned or did not yield steady incomes; 3) the elements of the lower classes, the immigrants and their descendants who took advantage of the possibilities for social ascension offered by industry, technology, education, and the very growth of the cities with their insatiable markets and anonymity.[12]

The same author notes that the result of this variety is a mélange of values, which include a very strong feeling of family solidarity, a certain intellectualism coupled with disdain for manual labor, and a sense of personal dignity which sometimes borders on the ridiculous, as in their *hidalgo* ancestors.[13]

Apart from a few countries in Central America (or Peru, where the monopoly of the traditional classes is still powerful) it can be said that social change has already penetrated the traditional elite. In what we have referred to as the cells of modernism, this change has created a kind of dichotomy, where a certain amount of political and economic power is wielded by minorities of both the traditional and new elite, where the middle class is undergoing the growing pains of contradictory values, and where a popular mass represents both the continuation of the backward rural class and the spearhead of a broader participation in society.

THE CONSEQUENCES OF DISINTEGRATION

When the values which integrate a social structure undergo change, there inevitably results a derangement of social norms. We are speaking here of the rules of conduct which orient the individual in his social life. These range from the *mores* of a people to simple customs, but do not refer to norms of morality based on religious beliefs.

When this change of norms reaches a significant intensity, anthropologists and sociologists describe it as a state of *"anomie"* or "normlessness."[14] It is the result of a too rapid process of "desacralization" or "rationalization" which is unable to create a new system of values that would be functional in the new society. Scholars like Malinowski, Redfield, and Radcliffe-Brown have studied these phenomena, especially in primitive cultures. Radcliffe-Brown concludes:

A society insufficiently integrated will generally, if not always, suffer from moral insecurity, and this is expressed in various ways. A growing rate of suicides, an increased number of neurotics . . . political revolutionary movements, the formation of new religious sects, particularly when they are accompanied by forms of hysteria and emotional excess, any of these can be looked upon as symptoms of a lack of social integration.[15]

We find such a state of normlessness in certain cultural zones of Latin America where the social impacts have been the most violent. This state occurred formerly when Spanish civilization met head on with the Indian cultures. But even today the same situation arises in all the sectors undergoing change. Suffice it to recall the situation in some regions of Mexico at the time of the revolution and the establishment of the first *ejidos,* collective farms which somewhat resemble *kolkhozes* or *kibbutzim;* or else the reaction of the rural Indian masses in Bolivia after the agrarian reform. Or simply consider the masses of rural immigrants in the cities, the *callampas, favellas, villas de miseria* and other slum areas, all dramatic expressions of the state of normlessness.

Total normlessness, of course, does not exist, for it would be a negation of social life. Certain norms always exist, and if they almost disappear in a given sector, they become stronger in another. The family solidarity of the outlying urban districts is a typical example.

There can be little doubt that political and social anarchy, popular spiritism, and the diversity of religious sects are all manifestations of a state of normlessness.[16] In Brazil, for example, such a state proved particularly favorable to the development of the *umbanda* and the *kibanda,* institutionalized forms of African emotionalism.[17]

But not all the results of social change are negative. The introduction of technological values is prerequisite to any progress in the modern world. The elimination of the traditional two-class system, and the upheaval of the values which permitted it to exist is in itself a positive good, for it will facilitate the gradual abatement of the marginality of Latin America's masses, and make possible their integration into society on the national and international levels. And although change has produced some disequilibrium in religious values, positive results have followed: an awareness of the fundamental values of Catholicism, the birth of a more mature laity, and a spiritual life less contaminated with the traditional myths of the rural world.

NOTES

[1] Harry M. Johnson, *op. cit.*, p. 626.

[2] *Ibid.*, p. 644.

[3] Of course, this must not be understood as a recommendation to return to the outmoded relationships between Church and State, which still exist in certain Latin American countries. Rather, we mean concrete collaboration for progress, especially cultural and social.

[4] See, among others, Hans Gerth and C. Wright Mills, *From Max Weber: Essays in Sociology* (New York: Oxford University Press, 1946); R. Redfield and M. B. Singer, "The Cultural Role of Cities," *Economic Development and Cultural Change*, Vol. III, No. 1 (Oct. 1954), pp. 53–73; Howard Becker, "Current Sacred-Secular Theory and Its Development," in Howard Becker and Alvin Boskoff (ed.), *Modern Sociological Theory in Continuity and Change* (New York: Dryden, 1957), pp. 133–85; Gino Germani, "Secularización y desarollo económico," in *Resistencias a mudança* (Rio de Janeiro: Centro Latino-Americano de Pesquisas, 1960), pp. 261–66.

[5] "Reluctance and readiness to accept or initiate social change provide the construction lines of what may be called a sacred-secular scale or continuum. Any society or part thereof that imparts to or elicits from its members evaluations that can be altered, if at all, only in the face of definite emotionalized reluctance is a sacred society. . . . Conversely, any society or part thereof that imparts to or elicits from its members evaluations leading to well-marked readiness to change is a secular society. . . ." Howard Becker, *op. cit.*, p. 142.

[6] Orlando Fals Borda, *op. cit.*, p. 8.

[7] *Callampas* (literally, "mushrooms") are the slum areas which crop up on the outskirts of the big cities.

[8] Orlando Fals Borda, *op. cit.*, p. 10.

[9] F. Debuyst, *Las Clases sociales en América Latina* (Fribourg: FERES, 1962).

[10] R. Cereceda, *Las Instituciones políticas en América Latina* (Fribourg: FERES, 1961).

[11] Centro de Investigaciones y Acción Social, *La Variable política*. Preparatory Document for the Opening Session of the OAS, Mexico, Dec. 1960 (Santiago de Chile, 1960).

[12] Orlando Fals Borda, *op. cit.*, p. 6.

[13] *Ibid.*, p. 7.

[14] Howard Becker, "Normative Reactions to Normlessness," *American Sociological Review*, Vol. 25, No. 6 (Dec. 1960), pp. 803–810.

[15] A. R. Radcliffe-Brown, *Social Change* (London: Ibatts, 1958), p. 27.

[16] J. Ycaza Tigerino, *Hacia una Sociologia Hispano-americana* (Madrid: Ed. Cultura Hispanica, 1958), p. 63.

[17] C. Procopio de Camargo, *Aspectos Sociológicos del Espiritismo en São Paulo* (Fribourg: FERES, 1961).

7

The Necessary Conditions
for Reintegration

In a period of social and cultural upheaval, such as Latin America is now passing through, the various segments of society react by searching for a new equilibrium. The reaction will vary according to the social values of the groups. It might be a search for new forms, or a violent break with the past in the hope of a better future, or even a dogged attachment to crumbling structures.

The social change runs so swift and deep that the choices are rather limited. To cling to the social structures and values of traditional society in an effort to keep them alive is necessarily doomed to failure—and this is not an ideological evaluation, but a simple sociological observation. When a continent grows by nearly 50 million inhabitants in ten years, and when according to modest estimates (which are already proving too conservative) the population 40 years hence will have tripled the 1960 figure of 200 million, which it took four centuries to attain, how is it any longer possible to believe in the virtues of social immobility? Moreover, when this quantitative change is manifestly accompanied by a qualitative transformation of every aspect of society and culture, even compromise is out of the question.

There are, in fact, only three alternatives: a radical transformation, but consciously directed; a revolution, obliterating the social structure to construct an entirely new one; or a prolonged anarchy, bestrewn with *pronunciamentos* and social conflicts. The concept of reintegration is applicable only to the first alternative. Revolution is the simple replacement of one system by another, as in Cuba; and anarchy, or chaos, implies the negation of reintegration.

A constant state of change is, of course, a characteristic of any social system, so that its very existence implies a need for continuous reintegration. But in Latin America, we are not dealing with simple recurring changes; the situation is much more complex. There are at least three major aspects. First, the passage of the masses from marginal existence to social participation; then, the solidifying of an industrial type of society based on the national economy and influenced by modernism; and finally, the intermingling of two types of society which previously had merely coexisted.

In all three cases the consequence is the spontaneous but organized progression toward a technological civilization. The first case is the result of the pressure of the population increase, and hence is bound up with the technological advances in hygiene, medicine, and the means of communication. The second is directly the fruit of industrialization; and the third is dependent on social mobility, hence on progress in transportation and communication.

This means that Latin American society, in varying degrees according to the country and region, is passing from a narrow and simple system of social integration to a broad and complex one. We have already mentioned the resulting rapid changes in social control, leadership and values. Effective reintegration, therefore, must go beyond purely structural measures and penetrate the social values themselves. The principal task will be to integrate technological values and to re-evaluate social functions and institutions. That cannot be accomplished overnight.

Examples are legion, but let us pursue one case in point. The continent's population explosion is essentially due to the sharp reduction in the infant mortality rate. Only a few years ago the peasant, for whom every additional child meant increased earning power, could only expect that one out of every two or three of his children would live past birth. Today, two out of three, and in some areas eight out of ten, babies survive.

Whether he stays in the country where, for various reasons explained above, the land cannot provide a decent living for his family, or whether he migrates to the city, swelling the already overcrowded slums, his children have now become a burden. The lower his standard of living drops, the heavier this burden becomes. The problem is further intensified by obligatory schooling since children are prevented from rendering immediate service to their family.

That these children live at all, to be sure, represents a remarkable progress. It indicates that mankind is steadily gaining mastery over the unknown forces which, until recently, had prevented half of these children from reaching adulthood. But it also indicates a total change in the structure of the peasant family. The child no longer has the same value. The meaning of birth is no longer the same: whereas ten births were necessary to have five children, now only six are needed.

It will take a long time, however, before the peasant families of Latin America become fully aware of the true significance of this change and adapt their behavior patterns accordingly. It will perhaps take several generations, for a cultural change in a matter as "sacred" as life itself does not come about without passing through stages. Something has to give, however; this biological fecundity will not be compatible with present conditions for very long. A change must eventually come about; in fact, there is already indication of it in the urban societies.

The main point we are trying to get across with this one example is that the process of change is complex and includes both structural and cultural aspects. No action which would deliberately ignore one of these aspects could be faithful to social realities. As another example, a structural modification, like an agrarian reform, without an attempt to educate the peasant masses, would be doomed to failure. Conversely, education without changes in agrarian structures would only aggravate frustrations. The two are so inseparable, that reintegration must work with one only in relationship to the other.

We are obviously reasoning from a well determined hypothesis, namely: *only by integrating into a technological civilization will Latin America be able to solve its problem of development.* While the objective is clear, there remains a wide choice of means for attaining it, and these are not exclusively technological. When Castro chose Marxism, he did more than adopt a technique, he introduced new values.

It is in this sense that one can speak today of the existence of two basic systems: that of the West and that of Marxism. If Marxism does not always faithfully put its own principles into practice, at least its choices are clear and unequivocal; the West, on the other hand, seems full of contradictions. We have already spoken of the ambivalence of the *Hispanidad,* but so-called "Western civilization" can be qualified in much the same way. The fruits of its system of values are, at first view, contradictory: everything from a highly developed intellectual and spiritual life to the most brutal manifestations of capitalism and deplorable social injustices, such as still exist in Latin America today. The ambiguity of its values are often deliberately maintained; and a fierce anti-Communism changes nothing.

The development of Latin America, more than a mere problem of economic and social techniques, hinges primarily on a choice of values. If the representatives of Western civilization can successfully make the distinction between what pertains to a just evaluation of man and his place in this world, and what pertains to the enrichment of private-interest groups or the conservation of those social and cultural privileges unjustifiable in the present evolution of society, they can still give a direction to social change in Latin America. Otherwise, a latent anarchy will threaten the continent for many years to come, until finally some popular leader crystallizes the aspirations of the masses, who tend more and more to put their hope of emancipation in another Castro.

We shall now examine, in their broad outlines, the attempts at reintegration which have been made within the basic institutions on the economic, social, political, family, educational, and religious levels. We shall try to determine how the functions of these various elements are changing, what measures are being attempted, and what hindrances are impeding their progress.

8

Economic Development

We treat the economic aspect of development first, not because we are doctrinally persuaded that this aspect is the root of all others, nor because it is logically first—we would then begin with the family—but because it plays such a major role in the total evolution of Latin America. A social and cultural reintegration supposes an economic base. On the other hand, it would be incorrect to think that the economy develops independently, as if it existed in a vacuum. All the aspects of society are interdependent. As a matter of fact, both the motivations and the effects of economic changes are to be sought outside the economic sphere, properly speaking.

We shall give special attention to two problems: national consumption and savings, and the diversification of products. They seem to be at the very root of Latin America's economic difficulties, for their solution would put these countries in a position to make their own decisions on economic matters, an indispensable condition for national development. Without this power, their economies would indefinitely retain their "colonial" aspect.

NATIONAL CONSUMPTION AND SAVINGS

The national revenue of a country is utilized either for consumption or for savings. Economic growth depends on that part

92

of the savings effectively invested in economic activities. In most Latin American countries the over-all level of savings is very low, which means that the national revenue is directly consumed. Such a situation is the result of many factors. First of all, the rate of increase of the national revenue scarcely surpasses the rate of population growth. There are, of course, differences from one country to another, but on the whole, the situation prevails. Secondly, there are causes of a social nature. The majority of the Latin American population, which we have described as marginal, lives in a state of under-consumption.[1] This condition exists to such an extent that the per capita calculations of the national revenue have little or no meaning. In Mexico, for example, 51 per cent of the national revenue is absorbed by 1 per cent of the population, in a country more advanced than many others in economic development and social reform.

Another factor is the substantial foreign investments of the rich class. Capital is leaving the country for North America and Europe; some estimates put the amount between 10 and 14 billion dollars.

Finally, the national revenues are being bled by plethoric and often meddlesome administrations, as well as by military programs which, for prestige purposes, are expanded far out of proportion.

The basic problem of a functional readjustment of the economy is, then, achieving a sufficiently high level of domestic investments. Two elementary measures are indispensable. First, since investments depend directly upon the level of savings, the saving power of the masses must be increased, beginning with the lower levels of society. Second, battle must be waged—and several countries have already begun—against the outflow of capital and the massive repatriation of the interest on foreign capital. At times in the past it has happened that in several Latin American countries the interest on foreign capital has actually equaled or surpassed the total amount of new investments. This naturally poses the inherent problems of an economy based unilaterally on profit. It has become evident that the capitalistic system, as such, is incapable of resolving the question.

Foreign investments are also necessary. But except for rare cases, they would only partially or temporarily provide the necessary capital. The economic problems of Latin America will never be solved without bilateral or multilateral foreign aid, and this means a very well-defined policy on the part of Europe and the United States. Moreover, to assure the effectiveness of this economic aid, there must be attached certain conditions, not political or military, but social and cultural. It is in this direction that the programs of Bogotá and Punta del Este (1960 and 1961) have been orientated.

Since the problem of Latin America's economic development is so vast, the methods to be adopted must be well chosen. Among those which seem particularly indicated is the vitalization of centers of development. Such a concentration of forces is necessary to produce effects that will reverberate and whisk away certain structural bottlenecks. It is imperative, however, that these centers do not become small oases in the middle of a vast economic desert, as they are now in most of the countries. They must be evenly distributed and joined by relay posts.

THE DIVERSIFICATION OF THE NATIONAL PRODUCT

There should be no need to describe at length the excessive sensitivity of most of the Latin American economies to the price fluctuations of raw materials (tin, copper, oil) or certain agricultural products (wheat, coffee, sugar, bananas). So important are these to the national economy that any one of them can produce a chain reaction. This undiversified production also creates a favorable climate for monopolies, and control of several sectors of economic life by a single group.

In recent years the market price of raw materials and agricultural products has gone down, whereas that of the manufactured products of developed countries has shown a continuous upward trend. It has been estimated that between 1870 and 1930, the world price of raw materials dropped 40 per cent. Since then it has plunged even lower. This is a rather paradoxical development in a system described by the puritanical euphemism "the international division of labor."

The result has been a monetary instability which creates vicious cycles in the economic processes. Since the national revenue fluctuates according to the economic imperatives of the developed countries, any economic planning has been impossible. The only factor that has provoked a rapid and substantial rise in the price of raw materials has been the periods of crisis outside the continent, such as the Second World War and the Korean War. But since these situations were only temporary, and because of the nature of the existing social structures, any additional profits went to the established rich and not to the nation as a whole or to the State.

Various efforts have been initiated to "reintegrate" the economic system. The first was a request for the stabilization of raw material prices on the world market, at least over relatively short periods. Up to the present time, this request has not had much hearing in the economically developed countries, since they would have to transform the very bases of their economy to accept it.[2] Yet, in recent years, the loss suffered by the falling off of world prices has, on several occasions, surpassed the entire economic and military aid granted by the United States, Europe and Russia. This prompted the representative of Chile at the 1958 session of the Economic and Social Council of the United Nations to say: "In studying the aid given by the developed countries it is difficult not to think of the popular Spanish saying with reference to a hospital founded by the very rich Don Juan de Porres:

> The lord Don Juan de Porres,
> Whose charity will never fade,
> Constructed this wonderful hospital
> For the poor—whom he had so made.

The most concrete effort toward reintegration has been the creation of national industries, which are gradually progressing beyond the field of ordinary consumable goods. Countries like Argentina, Uruguay, Chile, Brazil, Colombia, and Mexico have already made advances in this direction. Slowly their economy is becoming more diversified. Although production is often backed by foreign capital or controlled by foreign permits, the label *Industria Nacional* must be stamped on the products to show the domestic character of the enterprise. It goes without saying, however, that the development of such industries supposes the existence of a market; in other words, the buying power of the masses, who so far have led a marginal existence, must be increased or, in some cases, created from nothing. It also supposes that the national capital, whether derived from landed property, or raw materials, or international commerce, will be invested in new sectors of the economy. And needless to say, any economic development has a series of social and cultural prerequisites.

Finally, mention must be made of the zone of free exchange, a sort of common market, established as of June, 1961, among seven Latin American countries: Argentina, Brazil, Chile, Mexico, Paraguay, Peru, and Uruguay. This had been preceded by a similar initiative of the Central American countries. But the difficulties of the enterprise must not be under-stressed. The most concrete advantage will be to create a broader market for certain new industries, but often the products of these industries are competitive rather than complementary.

NOTES

[1] See on this point: F. Debuyst, *Las Clases Sociales en América Latina* (Fribourg: FERES, 1962); and S. Torres and B. Corredor, *Transformación en el Mundo rural Latino-americano* (Fribourg: FERES, 1961).

[2] In a particularly courageous effort, President Kennedy proposed in 1962 a stabilization in the price of sugar and coffee.

9

The Indispensable Social
Revolution

THE TRANSFORMATION OF
SOCIAL STRUCTURES

In order to satisfy in a functional way the necessities of development, according to the basic hypothesis we have adopted, in other words, in order to answer the vital material and cultural needs of a population which is growing at a vertiginous rate and which is headed toward social and economic participation, a profound alteration of the social structures is necessary. Certain obstacles must be cleared away. But time is running out, for life, health and social status are basic human rights, and the urban and rural masses are bound to become more restless and more demanding.

Change would have as its starting point a feudal-type society coexisting with a few centers of modernism, but without any real interchange between the two. What must be effected is a national integration. There must be a passage from the colonial economic system and the feudal social structure to others more adapted to the development of the rural masses. Let us examine once more the various levels of this society.

The rural social world, as we have already described, is based on a restricted class of property owners who derive their social prestige from the size of their land. But it also includes the enormous mass of landless peasants and small-farm owners. The only way of transforming this social structure is by changing the distribution of property through agrarian reforms.

The complexity of the agrarian reforms should not be minimized. Some conceived them—and this is quite typical of the speculative tendencies of the Latin American mind—merely as a series of legal documents logically spelling out the details of land distribution. Often such documents got nowhere because they were unrealistic and impractical. Such was the case of the Colombian law of 1936 concerning the expropriation of uncultivated lands. No one was ever able to define the term "uncultivated."

Several agrarian reforms, however, have already been initiated in countries like Mexico, Bolivia, Cuba, and Venezuela. In Mexico, the *ejidos* were organized as early as 1911. Although their economic success cannot be considered brilliant, they did have beneficial social consequences. In Mexico today, however, numerous large estates have been re-established, partially because the peasants, having received the land, did not have the financial or technical means to cultivate it. In Bolivia, the revolution of 1952 finally abolished the most feudal regime of the whole continent.[1] While this revolutionary action is quite understandable, it must be noted that the Indian masses were plunged into a state of normlessness and social and economic disintegration that the government-oriented farm syndicates have not been able to rectify.

In Cuba, the agrarian reform has been accomplished in the most radical and extensive way. But it has been steadily approaching pure collectivism. In Venezuela, the experiment seems to be following a well thought-out plan which takes into account economic and cultural necessities—but will it go far enough?

Agrarian reform is one of the prerequisites to the economic development we spoke of in the last chapter, but it is, above all, a reform in social structures. Though it is basically social in character, it does rely on political activity (legislation), economic activity (financing, expropriations, cooperatives, the organization of markets, transportation, etc.) and cultural activity (basic education, training in techniques).

It is clear that the efforts to reconstruct rural society on entirely new bases is encountering and will continue to encounter enormous difficulties. Some are of a technical nature: the perplexity of finding suitable economic solutions or of educating the people to technical values. Other difficulties come from the severe opposition of the social groups that are benefiting the most from the status quo.

This process is common to the history of all social change. It is unfortunately rare that the privileged classes have the foresight and the courage to execute the necessary reforms themselves. Every institutionalized social system has in its very make-up mechanisms which resist social change. But when a relatively simple system like a feudal-type society feels threatened, not only will it fall back on the ordinary means of resistance, such as political power, ideology or the army, but it will not hesitate to have recourse to intimidation, corruption, calumnies, violence, new ideologies, or a very special use of the existing ideology.

Thus, even the anti-Communist campaigns often have this ulterior motive. They carefully create and maintain a confusion between Communism, collectivism, Marxism, and every initiative of social reform. Another method in Latin America is recourse to religious principles: reforms are opposed in the name of Catholicism and of the Church. Of course, the individuals who use this tactic do not present direct arguments. They claim to defend respect for the human person, liberty, the right of private property, and the superiority of spiritual values. In reality, these are only apparent objectives, though in some cases sincere. The underlying objective is to strengthen their defense of the existing social order and their opposition to any social reintegration based on new structures.

Here is a typical example of how the Catholic Church was utilized in this defensive tactic. In September of 1960, the Colombian bishops collectively published a letter on agrarian reform which caused a great stir not only in Colombia but throughout the Latin American continent. In analyzing the lowly condition of

the Colombian peasant, the pastoral letter concluded that an
agrarian reform was necessary. It then indicated certain principles
and norms which should guide the reform: family property, the
organization of the economy, the education of the peasants, etc.

The reaction in conservative circles, and especially among the
landowners, was antagonistic but restrained. Indeed, the hope of
using religious motives to support opposition to the proposed laws
of agrarian reform seemed to be vanishing. They decided it best
to let a little time pass, then to take up the religious argument
from another angle.

On May 6, 1961, a rightist newspaper in Bogotá published a
special letter to the farmers from Monsignor X, titular Archbishop
of Y, on the subject of agrarian reform. Now the venerable prelate
was almost 90 and had been retired for several years because of
age. The paper naturally made no mention of this fact, but instead
ran a first-page-article whose headline read: "The proposed
agrarian reform is worthy of condemnation, irreligious and inadmissible."

After recalling the hardships of the peasants in the atmosphere
of violence which had existed for several years in the region in
question, the prelate broached the problem of the agrarian reform.
Here is his first sentence: "There is much talk today about the
Agrarian Reform, with which I am personally not well acquainted;
nor do I understand exactly what they are going to reform. . . ."
After this declaration he proceeds to enumerate a certain number
of postulates which should govern any agrarian reform. It would
be painful to give the details. Here is the conclusion, which the
newspaper printed in italics:

In recent days, a well known and respected member of the clergy
proved, with lucid arguments, that the Agrarian Reform in its present
draft contains venemous sectarian threats against the Catholic Social
Action Movement,[2] which is like the pupil of the eye of the Roman
Pontiffs and a sacred legacy of the holy hierarchy. This priest demon-
strates unequivocally how the present draft of the Agrarian Reform is

an impious and genuinely apostate attack against the Catholic social organizations, which exist in the Capital and elsewhere under the vigilance and direction of the Episcopacy, and which up to now have been exquisite, zealous, flourishing, and most beneficent. This means that an Agrarian Reform of this kind is irreligious, and worthy of condemnation. Eternally inadmissible!!!

No further comment is needed.

Similar instances can be cited in other countries, in spite of the vrey clear declarations of the bishops of Chile, Peru, Bolivia, Brazil, and Ecuador, as well as the general statements of the bishops of Latin America through the intermediary of CELAM (The Latin American Bishops Council).

The urban structures are likewise undergoing transformations. Since cities present a more favorable climate for innovations, change had advanced more rapidly than in the rural regions. Three major developments are taking place: a transformation of the elite class, the establishment of a middle class, and the emergence of a working class.

The breakup of the old elite class is being brought about by new roles in a more industrialized society, a development that is functionally necessary for a social reintegration. As can be expected, this is not happening without the resistance of the traditional elite. But the change is being stimulated both from within and from without. Within the old elite class, new leaders are emerging. But more of them come from the intermediate classes and from the second generation of immigrants. Their scale of social values is approaching that of the social elite of the technologically developed countries.

The middle class is experiencing difficulty in solidifying. As far as we can see, this results from the fact that society in most of the countries is insufficiently fluid, and there is an absence of a well developed secondary sector. Since Latin American society is, on the whole, modeling itself on industrial-type structures, partly in imitation of Europe and North America, the tertiary sector, which constitutes the essential of this intermediary class, called "middle," is developing healthily.[3] A very harsh struggle is now underway to close the gap in social differentiation and there is a fierce competition for social status. From this flows the proliferation of administrative posts, the utilization of political influence and the institutionalization of bribes. The more rigid the social structures are in denying social ascension, the more susceptible will this class be to the political movements of the extreme right or the extreme left. A broadly developed social mobility and a healthy middle class are important factors of political stability. In Europe, the middle class has often been defined by a criterion of socioeconomic independence, whereas the American middle class is based on income. Both criteria seem to be valid for Latin America, with emphasis on the former.

The oppressiveness of their condition and their embittered awareness of it are strongly shaping the social values of the middle classes. The possession of a material sufficiency assuring a social status certainly forms the key value, toward which the others are oriented. It is striking to see, for example, that vocations to the priesthood are not as numerous as should be expected from a fairly developed middle class. No doubt there are other factors involved, but the hierarchy of values seems to be the determining one.

Finally, as a logical consequence to industrialization, a working class is forming. Its history differs sharply from one country to another. It is significant, however, that it has played an increasingly important role in the social upheavals in Latin America, sometimes as the dynamic element, but more often as the object of the preoccupations or demagogy of certain regimes. Such was the case in Brazil with Vargas, in Argentina with Perón, in Bolivia, Chile, Mexico, and recently in Cuba.

It is understandable that the working class has not found its true integration in the social system. Class consciousness has not developed in many countries because of the hybrid nature of the social and economic structures. Nothing works against the class consciousness of this marginal urban population more than their country origins. They put up with the inhuman living conditions of the cities and factories because in spite of everything they are better off than they were in the country. They are essentially preoccupied with a day-to-day existence, working at a hundred small, interchangeable jobs. Mostly illiterate, they form an unskilled-labor reserve, ready to accept any kind of a wage.

To these factors must be added: geographic dispersion, especially in the mine and plantation countries; an indigenous European, or North American capitalism which is operating in many areas today without restraint, creating social conditions comparable to those in Europe and the United States during the nineteenth century; finally, the ever-changing political regimes, utilized by the economic powers, or themselves utilizing the embryonic labor organizations as political support. In such circumstances, it is no wonder that the labor organizations are weak and ineffective. Few countries have labor organizations of any firm structure; one could hardly mention more than Argentina, Chile, and Colombia.[4]

The organizations are also characterized by internal disunity. In some countries the turnover in national and even international labor organizations is equalled only by the number of constitutions or *pronunciamentos*. Apart from political repercussions or violent repressions, most of the disharmony stems from clearly exogenous factors. Large factions form around anarchist, Socialist or Communist ideologies. These factions rise or fall with their parent organizations, generally in Europe, or according to international politics, as in the case of Communism. Furthermore, between the two World Wars, but especially since the Second World War, the American unions have taken an interest in the labor movement in Latin America. Finally, the International Confederation of Christian Unions is beginning to operate with a truly remarkable dynamism, especially in view of the means at its disposal. This organization offers the double advantage of independence from national and international political powers, and a spiritual framework well in harmony with the basic culture of the Latin American continent.

It will take much time and effort to strengthen the labor organizations of Latin America. In the process of social integration they will play a role that it would be difficult to overestimate. Their failure would represent a major setback to progress.

THE TRANSFORMATION OF SOCIAL VALUES

We have not been able to speak of structural changes without constant allusion to cultural factors. They are inextricably woven together. The type of social organization depends upon the scale of values, which in turn is often obliged to evolve because the structures change.

Social values are most essential in the reintegration of a society. Some values are clearly disfunctional. Two examples come to mind: at a time when productivity is the prime factor of development, landowners still base social prestige on the size of their property; secondly, many peasants still consider vegetables as fit nourishment for animals, but not for humans.

The essential action to be undertaken for continued progress would consist in introducing, at all levels of society, the values of the technological world without, however, destroying those values which are not obstacles. The structural changes, which have already been transforming behavior and mentalities, must be accompanied by an educational program which should extend from the basic education in the rural regions all the way to the university level, without neglecting any of the technical and administrative areas. In this sense, it can be said that education is a factor of development.

It is remarkable how much opinions have evolved concerning the interpretation of underdevelopment. Whereas a few years ago it was spoken of essentially in economic terms, today, without denying this aspect of the problem, more importance is given to the cultural factor. The development of the Western countries was not the effect of pure chance, nor was it the automatic consequence of their abundant natural resources. Recent discoveries have shown that most of the underdeveloped countries, including those of Latin America, possess natural resources at least equally abundant. The basic problem, then, is one of culture, i.e., of values.

A civilization which attaches a value to positive facts, to their scientific discovery, and finally to their technological application necessarily develops a certain number of activities. It organizes itself around these activities and produces results on the technological level. Consequently, the passage from a pre-technological civilization to a technological one is essentially a cultural fact. This is the factor which must command attention if the problem of underdevelopment is to be solved at its roots. It is not sufficient to break the chains of Latin America's economic dependence. Nor is it enough to build dams, roads or railroads. A more basic need at all levels of society, from the small farmer to the industrial entrepreneur, is men who can assimilate the technological values which would enable them to resolve their own problems. As Jean Fourastié explains:

The scientific and technological advances which would quickly improve the condition of the underdeveloped countries have no chance of being rapidly applied on a large scale, for one cannot put new techniques of production into use without "technicians." Production cannot be improved without improving the work of the masses, and this cannot be improved without first educating men capable of understanding and applying the modern techniques.[5]

Fully appreciating this need, the *Acción Cultural Popular* movement in Colombia has undertaken an educational program chiefly through radio broadcasting. The initiative is based on the idea that the underdevelopment and undernourishment of the Colombian peasants are due in great measure to their ignorance of technical methods. Since this problem is inseparable from that of cultural attitude, their social values must be transformed. Thus the program is striving to change their attitudes toward the different problems of life, toward the new techniques in fertilizers, the prevention of soil erosion, the necessity of hygiene, decent housing literacy, basic mathematics, etc.

NOTES

[1] See S. Torres and B. Corredor, *Transformación en el Mundo Rural Latino-americano, op. cit.*

[2] It is important to note that the Church was officially represented on the commission for drafting the proposals of the agrarian reform by Monsignor Calderón, the auxiliary Bishop of Bogotá, in the name of Cardinal Concha, the Archbishop of Bogotá, who personally was present for some sessions.

[3] See F. Debuyst, *op. cit.*

[4] See Juan Arcos, *op. cit.*

[5] Jean Fourastié, *Histoire de demain* (Paris: Presses Universitaires de France, 1959).

10

Political Life

The instability of Latin American political regimes has become a legend. It is the outgrowth of the social and cultural imbalances which encourage despotism, and of governments structured on French or American constitutions which are unsuited to the real conditions of the country.

Important changes have occurred over the last few decades. *Caudillismo* is no longer a fact, except in a few countries untouched by the mainstream of political and economic developments.[1] Fewer military men are heads of state, and the role of the army has evolved. A new reality is making its appearance: a Latin American Communist regime. A slow evolution toward a national reintegration is taking place, but so great are the obstacles that political life remains today one of the most serious weaknesses of the continent. For any progress to be made, however, a minimum of political structure is indispensable.

It is, of course, impossible in a few pages even to survey all the political problems of Latin America. The purpose of this chapter is simply to provide a background for the interpretation of social change.

THE POLITICAL PROBLEMS INVOLVED IN THE EVOLUTION OF SOCIAL STRUCTURES AND PRESSURE GROUPS

The social "orders" which previously held the prominent position in society were the components of the traditional elite class: the owners of land or mines, the rich tradesmen, and later, military men. As this group underwent a gradual transformation, political power came to be shared by the new groups making their appearance: the industrialists, the middle class, and lately, in some countries, even members of the working class and peasants.

Political power and the elements which enter into its make-up have further been affected by greater efforts in the educational field: the fight against illiteracy, the multiplication of news media, and the enormous vitality of the universities. The political parties, which previously consisted in a mob supporting *caudillos* or family clans, are now becoming organized around social objectives. Orlando Fals Borda, after describing the evolution of countries like Brazil, Bolivia, and Colombia, declares:

all this can be a symptom of the formation of new parties or ideological groups which will attempt to confront the grave social and economic problems of today in a more realistic and effective way, basing their action on the inevitable awakening of the masses and their increased political participation, on the improvements in education and communications, on the disappearance of rural isolation, on the existence of a much broader community, and on the growing consciousness of nationality.[2]

Among the serious problems to be solved, priority must be given to the political integration of the marginal masses. Their awakening to a political consciousness can be an explosive factor, if certain structures are not prepared to absorb them. Probably the most concrete project to be realized is the preparation of local leaders by the establishment of new economic and social structures, on a small scale to begin with, then on the regional and national levels. This is why the cooperative movements, the labor organizations of workers and farmers, community development, and the educational efforts of the Catholic Action organizations assume such great importance.

Naturally, there are the restraining forces of the old social "orders," although a few of their members have had the courage to play a progressive role. In some countries the army has resumed its normal functions while continuing to serve as a counterweight in periods of crisis. Unfortunately, such is not the case in the majority of crises, especially in the larger countries. This can be more easily understood if attention is drawn to the excessive number of superior officers maintained by some armies. Argentina alone has 30,000, including more generals than the United States.[3]

In the struggle against political change, just as in the struggle against social change, various means are employed. Anti-Communism is an effective weapon, and it has the advantage of promoting a clean conscience. When not utilized directly to battle political adversaries, anti-Communism takes on, for some, the aspect of a modern-day holy war, which quickly banishes other motivations. And sometimes, democratic labels are used to conceal reactionary ideas. This is not a case of new wine in old skins, but of old wine in new skins.

While political restraints have been keeping the power structures from adequately meeting the needs of development, there has been an increased number of revolutionary movements. But even these have taken on a new meaning. A sociological study of the Latin American revolutions would show how much they are the reflection of the state of normlessness which has prevailed since the crises of independence. But indeed, there is a world of difference between the take-over by a Trujillo in Santo Domingo and a Fidel Castro in Cuba, between the *coup d'état* of a Perón and of a Somoza, between the palace or barracks revolutions of the last century, and the revolutions in Mexico, Bolivia, and, to a certain extent, in Guatemala, Venezuela, or even the 1948 uprisings in Bogotá.

At least by intent, the popular masses are participating more prominently in the revolutions. Gone are the days when revolutions were merely conflicts between political clans or *caudillos,* provoked by *pronunciamentos,* although this myth still persists in Europe and in North America. The revolutionary attempts of recent years in Mexico, Argentina, Bolivia or Cuba, had as their purpose the transformation of social structures, which had not been effected by independence, nor by the political regimes which followed. Yet only the Cuban revolution seems to be truly complete. It has overthrown all the social structures, the economy, the organization of the army, and cultural life, and has introduced a completely new scale of social values. These developments could only be brought about by a revolution. It was not possible to effect a "reintegration" of the social system, it was necessary to demolish it and replace it with another. This supposed a complete upheaval which would change not only the political power but the economy, which would accord a social status to the rural and urban masses, and which would initiate campaigns against illiteracy and for the rapid training of technicians.

It is evident that the Cuban situation merited a "revolutionary" change. Many were those who hailed the birth of the Castro movement and the objectives it pursued. A Catholic elite, small in number but of true merit, participated in the revolution. The majority of democratic countries approved the movement. Gradually it evolved toward Communism, for both internal and international reasons. These reasons are still difficult to determine precisely, but no matter how one assesses the events, one fundamental fact still remains: what can be called the first total revolution in Latin America has been absorbed by Communism. It stands as a particularly clear sign of the times, if not a signal for those who are contemplating the social emancipation of the marginal masses. The new situation in Chile, therefore, may possibly offer a new model for social change.

It should not be concluded, however, that similar revolutions are about to take place in all the Latin American countries. No doubt in most of the countries the social, economic and political conditions have deteriorated to a point where some are thinking more of a revolution than of a reintegration. But several factors must be conjointly present for a popular revolution to succeed.

The sociologist Harry M. Johnson gives the following conditions for a social revolution.[4] First, there must be a pronounced rupture within the social order, in other words, a broad marginal population confronted by a small group monopolizing the principal elements of political, economic, social and cultural power. This first condition is found in many of the Latin American countries.

The second condition is an alerted public opinion. As a matter of fact, as long as the masses are not aware of their marginal situation, the probabilities of a popular revolution are not very high. A minimum collective consciousness of the problem is necessary. This is being created today in Latin America by the communication media, whose effectiveness is enhanced by the increasing rate of literacy, and also by the considerable activity of revolutionary forces.

An explosive situation and the consciousness of its existence are still not enough to create the movement. A leader is necessary who can gather together the diverse aspirations of the masses and thus incarnate a revolutionary drive.

A single individual, however, is not enough. A leader never rises without a revolutionary group around him, be it a political party, a pressure group, a secret society, or a guerilla band. The existence of the group is very important, for it provides the masses with a concrete reality with which they can identify themselves. Mao Tse-tung, and Guevara who paraphrased him, understood this when they underlined the role of guerilla bands in national or social revolutions. That is why many Latin American governments have declared the Communist Party illegal.

Another condition is a revolutionary ideology. To gather together all the motives for action, its arguments must be simple but resounding. Nationalism has constituted the most common basis for the recent popular revolutions on every continent. It can offer a common objective, mobilize energies, appeal to traditions, and easily find a scapegoat abroad. Communism has added philosophical and social dimensions to nationalism, in addition to placing it in a universal perspective. This global aspect of Communism explains the spell it casts over young intellectuals even before penetrating the masses.

The sixth condition is a weak government, weak not only materially, economically and militarily, but especially in the moral sense. An indication of this moral weakness might be a prolonged period of social troubles, the inability to effect the structural reforms demanded by public opinion, or the procrastination or corruption of the officials in power.

Johnson cites, as a final condition, the idealization of the future. To stimulate the masses to decisive revolutionary action, their imagination must be fed with a certain number of dreams which contrast with their present frustrations.

If in most of the Latin American countries the first conditions are already realized, what is most often lacking is a leader. Prerevolutionary groups exist almost everywhere. Nationalist and Marxist ideologies have merged to provide a dynamic revolutionary doctrine. For many revolutionary aspirants, Fidel Castro represents the leader they are lacking. His image threatens to be much more significant than any former revolutionary leader in America, except for the great names in the struggles for independence.

THE TECHNICAL PROBLEMS OF POLITICAL ORGANIZATION

A modern State, confronted with problems as complex as those of the Latin American countries, must exercise a number of functions which were unknown in the nineteenth century. This supposes *ad hoc* organizations, financial means, and capable men. We would like to give brief consideration to four problems: public administration, financing, economic planning, and social security.

As we have already pointed out, public administration in most of the countries we are considering is excessively overstaffed. Argentina, with 20 million inhabitants, recently had 1.3 million government workers. The State of Guanabara in Brazil, a territory with a slightly larger population than the metropolitan area of Rio de Janeiro, according to the latest figures has more on the government payroll than the State of New York.[5] An administration which knows that it is oversized will inevitably try to make itself as indispensable as possible, inventing, if necessary, all sorts of ways to do so. There results a paralysis in the administrative machine. To make matters worse, hiring is based on favoritism, and this lowers professional standards.

In the culture of Latin countries, in Europe as well as in America, public administration constitutes a value. The persons who are attached to it enjoy a certain social prestige. In conditions of economic underdevelopment, such a value appears as functional, i.e., it substitutes a social status for an economic one. In view of the fact that a similar standard prevails on other continents, one wonders if this is not a universal characteristic. One reflection of this prestige value is the delight occasioned by a finely elaborated legal text, even when it is of no practical consequence. This mania is nothing new for Latin America; the laws of the Indies already suffered from it. The prestige of official papers, impeccably drawn up, with innumerable seals and hidalguesque signatures, is still very much alive not only in the civil administrations, but in those of the Church as well. Perhaps that is what inspired the Brazilian proverb: "Our country makes progress during the night, when the politicians sleep."

None of this, of course, is functional in a period of social change, when rapid, effective and sometimes radical measures must be taken. In fact, the administrations are often a restraint to development, resulting in a kind of vicious circle. This is why good schools of public administration should be organized in the social science departments of the universities. To be unaware of the importance of administrative deficiencies would be dangerous to the efforts at social reintegration, for it could do considerable damage to such initiatives as foreign aid and internal industrial expansion.

To operate, the State must have the financial means, and one of the principal sources of revenue is, of course, taxes. The fiscal system today, however, assumes prime importance, for in the modern State it has become not just a means of collecting public finances, but equally a method of orienting economic life and redistributing the revenues. But the fiscal system is considerably disoriented in those countries where the transformation of political power has not yet taken place. It is still based on privilege. In some countries, direct taxation is almost nonexistent. To accomplish a true reintegration, fiscal policies must evolve in such a way as not to paralyze development but to make it possible for the State to play a dynamic role.

Another technical problem which presents itself to all governments without exception is economic planning. For reasons indicated above, this obviously poses very great difficulties. Yet economic planning is essential if the standard of living is to be raised through a greater number of investments and the utilization of international aid, to which more and more technical conditions are being attached. Once again, this supposes technical means and men capable of accomplishing the projects.

Finally, the organization of a modern State must include a system of social security. It should be needless to explain why such a system is particularly difficult to inaugurate in countries where the population is rapidly evolving, where industrialization is in its first stages, where the majority of the population is economically marginal, where a certain under-consumption is necessary for development, and where the State is not in a financial position to support such a social policy.

The popular masses, however, enlightened by the more developed means of communication, are beginning to have the same expectations as those in Europe and the United States. Social legislation of this kind has been enacted in some countries, but—

a simple detail—it has not been put into practice. And yet, a system of social security is necessary. It is bound up with the other aspects of social change, especially with the economic aspect and with social structures. Perhaps foreign aid could have as an indirect purpose the stabilization of social security in countries where a working class and a middle class are already developed.

THE ROLE OF EXTERIOR FACTORS

We think it useful at this point to broach two subjects of prime importance for the Latin American continent: the role of the United States, and the role of Communism. Of course, volumes have already been written on these subjects, and it is very difficult to classify them for they treat simultaneously of economic, social and political matters. But the point of view which interests us in this synthesis on social change is not economic techniques, or investment figures, or military aid, as such. We are more concerned with their significance in the process of socio-cultural transformation, hence, as elements of reintegration on the structural and cultural levels.

Role of the United States

As is common knowledge, the interest of the United States in her neighbors to the south is not recent. In 1823, Monroe proclaimed his famous Doctrine, which can be paraphrased, "America for Americans." This must be viewed as one of the remote sources of "Pan-Americanism," which became institutionalized toward the end of the century and which has since experienced high and low peaks. New life for the Monroe Doctrine was occasioned by recent events in Cuba. And the more the grip of the Communists tightened, the more did the United States try to persuade the other American nations to take a stand against extra-continental interventions. In this situation the United States played two roles: leader of the Americas, and leader of the non-Communist world.

But the United States does not merely have a political function. It has a considerable economic leadership. If the Latin American economy continues to be subsidiary, it is because it has furnished the economically strong countries with an important part of their raw materials. Among these countries, the United States occupies first place. It is also Latin America's banker, furnishing the major part of foreign investments. Political and economic considerations clearly influence each other, as was shown in the Cuban affair, where the American investors were the first victims of the revolution.

It must be avowed that the political and economic role of the United States has been quite disfunctional in relation to a balanced development of the Latin American nations. The question of the price of raw materials is not specifically an American problem since it arises between all countries that are basically producers or consumers. But it is one of the principal aspects in the economic relations between North and South America. It has not yet been resolved, and one wonders if it ever will be, in spite of the attempts of the late President Kennedy.

The countries where American economic interests were powerful almost inevitably maintained conservative regimes, controlled by the traditional elite or by military dictators. Although this was in complete contradiction with the democratic political traditions of the United States, maintenance of the status quo in the Latin American countries was generally beneficial to the business groups, who with goods or money could easily assure the good will of the political regime. The regime might be overthrown, but the tendencies stayed the same, even if the personnel changed.

The direct aid extended by the United States to Latin America has not been proportionally as great as the aid accorded to Europe and Asia. Moreover, it has partially been military aid, and we have already commented on the role of the army in these countries. Since 1963, however, the situation has evolved considerably.

Even before John F. Kennedy assumed the presidency, voices were raised in the United States for a change in its Latin American policy. The real turning point, however, was the Kennedy Administration's new view of the problem. It attempted—to use the terminology of our previous discussion—to make the mutual political and economic relations functional for development. This attitude is quite new.

Alliance for Progress

The principal means was an economic aid conditioned by social reforms, essentially agrarian and fiscal. Such measures, however, met with fierce opposition both on the part of the Latin American governments and parliaments, who globally still represent established interests, and on the part of the groups in the United States that were affected by these reforms. At the present time, certain points have yet to be sufficiently clarified: the question of raw material prices has consistently been dodged; and the limits of social reforms have not been precisely defined: for example, the reforms would certainly not include measures such as Castro has taken, but just how far can they go, which measures should receive the Castro label and which should not? As a last point, the sums proposed are quite insufficient to resolve the problem. The 500 million dollar total for the ten-year social program, which was proposed in Buenos Aires in 1959, decided in Bogotá in 1960, and contracted in Punta del Este in 1961, is equivalent to about 1 per cent of the United States' military expenditures for the year 1962.

The anti-Yankee attitude is more complex than might be imagined. It is not merely the natural consequence of the relations between two neighbors unequal in strength, producing, on the one side, jealousy, and on the other, an abuse of power. It is today a very functional element for the revolutionary doctrine of the nationalists, like Perón in Argentina, and the Marxists. It would be naïve to think that it was created by these ideologies. It is simply utilized and amplified.

A survey conducted by an American sociologist in 1961 to sound out the opinions of 162 leaders in various fields in nine Latin American countries lists the following causes of anti-American sentiment.[6] In first place came the problem of raw materials;

secondly, the habitual alliances with conservatives. The Americans
were also reproached for their lack of disinterestedness. They
offer 500 million dollars to the Bogotá conference, but merely to
stem the spreading influence of Castro. Next comes the memory
of a series of historical events: the conquest of New Mexico and
California, the interventions in Panama, Central America, and the
Caribbean. The rich-neighbor aspect was also mentioned in the
report, as well as the fact that the Americans could never conduct
business at home as they do in Latin America. Finally were cited
the Americans' superiority complex and their "savior" mentality.
It should be noted that this inquiry was conducted after President
Kennedy took office.

No doubt a more penetrating study of this important question
is needed to uncover all the aspects, but it is easy to see how
such a psychological factor can serve as a basis of nationalist or
Communist ideology.

Role of Communism

In such circumstances, Communism appears perhaps less under
its class-struggle aspect than as a technique for development, to
which it provides both an ideology and a system. This is why
Chinese Communism attracts more attention than Russian.

Communism is a radical solution of the problems of social
change, for it proposes the replacement of the old system by a
totally new organization. There is no need for a long commentary
on this view, because Communism in Latin America is the same
as elsewhere. Three aspects, however, merit mention.

First of all, Communism exploits the *flagrant structural deficiencies* of Latin America, and this is indeed a very solid starting
point. It is not obliged to wage a thunderous propaganda. It simply
has to awaken the social consciousness of the masses and bring
to their mind the simple facts of reality. At the present time they
are capitalizing on the inability of the governments to realize
projected social reforms, like the agrarian reforms, because of

the organized resistance against them. The Communist slogan is simple: the projected reforms are excellent. Since experience has proven that the present political regimes cannot possibly effect them, a social revolution is the only solution. Every delay in carrying out reforms is like money in the bank for the Communists, who really have to expend very little effort. Such a situation exists in several countries, especially in Brazil and Peru.

The second aspect flows from the first and from the very exigencies of revolutionary tactics. It is the fact that the organized action of the Communists, apart from Cuba and a few exceptions due to accidental circumstances, is always directed toward a few *key points,* and relatively little toward the marginal masses. The key points are those categories of persons who have developed or are susceptible of developing a social consciousness. The first two pressure points, therefore, have been the labor organizations and the university students. In those places where the working class is more developed, Communist activity is more extensive. The concentration of efforts has also shifted from one country to another according to historical circumstances: Mexico, Argentina, Venezuela, Chile. . . .

Until very recently, Communist influence was little felt in the rural regions. It is now gaining momentum; which shows that the Communist leaders feel that the moment has come to stir up the rural masses. It probably will not be long before concentrated efforts will be initiated in one region or another, or before groups are organized similar to those in northeastern Brazil. This is the stage that Gino Germani called the "mobilization of the masses," during which Communism serves as a catalyst.[7]

The middle classes, although it might not be expected, also offer a fertile ground for Communism because of the many frustrations they are experiencing. In fact, a considerable number of Communist leaders come from this group. *strange!*

The third aspect worthy of mention is the powerful *ideology* that Marxism presents to a Latin America undergoing a sociocultural transformation. It awakens social consciousness, and it offers not only a solution which appears ideal, but an ideological framework which both explains phenomena and inspires devotion. Ideological arguments have a much more powerful effect than the distribution of material goods. The Communists do not distribute powdered milk, but they do offer a social status. It should not be believed that the Communists' strength lies in the astronomical sums they are said to be spending on Latin America. It is rather in the faith of their members, who are willing to undergo great sacrifices for a cause they hold sacred.

Most of the anti-Communist campaigns are ineffective. A Catholic leader of Cuba, who since has been imprisoned, said in 1960: "The anti-Communist campaigns conducted in Cuba before the Castro regime were such that now that Communism is here, the people do not recognize it." How many of these campaigns were based on the Communist atrocities; yet, to the people, the Communists appeared in no way violent. How many campaigns affirmed that Communism destroyed the liberty and dignity of the individual, private property and the social order. Yet one would have to be blind not to see that such liberty, dignity, property, and social order were limited to a minority, and that the others could not lose these precious goods, since they did not possess them.

The real religious faith of the popular masses is perhaps one of the most solid stumbling blocks to the spread of Communist ideology. A striking example is Mexico. If the reaction of the Cuban masses to the expulsion of the clergy and the extortions against the Church (much less violent than in Mexico) seem rather weak, it is partially because the state of religion in Cuba was one of the most deteriorated in all of Latin America. But if there thus exists a genuine spiritual force, deeply inscribed in the popular culture, this does not mean that a minority with a true social leadership cannot seize power and actually get support. On the other hand, those who think they can use this spiritual force to avoid social reforms, will bear the true responsibility of the orientation of any future revolutions.

NOTES

[1] See R. Cereceda, *op. cit.*

[2] Orlando Fals Borda, *op. cit.*, p. 12.

[3] *The Economist,* April 22, 1961, p. 331.

[4] Harry M. Johnson, *op. cit.,* pp. 641–43.

[5] *The Economist,* April 22, 1961, p. 322.

[6] An unpublished and unsigned document entitled *An Analysis of Latin American Aspirations.* A survey conducted between February 2 and March 4, 1961, in Mexico, Guatemala City, Bogotá, Quito, Lima, Santiago, Buenos Aires, and Rio de Janeiro.

[7] Gino Germani, *op. cit.*

11

Family, Education, Culture and Religion

THE FAMILY

In speaking of the disorganization of cultural elements, we have already made allusion to the problems of population expansion and family structures.[1] There are other aspects of social change which are turning this basic social group upside down.

A fundamental characteristic of a technological civilization is the specialization of man's social activities. Whether it is a matter of economy, education, leisure, or even religion, the technical demands and the growing mobility create the need for more numerous, but univalent institutions. The basic social groups which have been multivalent, i.e., exercising several functions, now lose some of their functions. This is what has happened to the family, the village, the neighborhood, or in the religious sphere, to the parish. The family, which was almost the sole economic unit (it was both producer and consumer), which dominated the education of the children, which was the basis for political authority, which controlled leisure and cultural activities, not to mention its religious role, is now seeing these functions slip away one by one.

The patriarchal or matriarchal family, such as it still exists in most of the Latin American rural regions, is about to experience a telling crisis. Georges Hahn, Director of the International Uni-

122

versity of the Pyrenees, after studying this phenomenon in North Africa, describes it in the following way:

> The principle of the patriarchal family in a traditional society . . . is not ridiculous, but strictly logical. The oldest member is necessarily the wisest, for knowledge is not acquired by study, but by daily experience. . . . As can be expected, the mere extension of modern education is enough to shake the foundation of this type of family: the child just out of elementary school is more "learned," more experienced than the head of the family, especially in what appears to be the most important matter: the knowledge of the modern world and what makes it run. He is the one who has the theoretical knowledge of how a motor works, how a State is organized and directed, and the practical knowledge of how to drive a car and how to vote. . . .
>
> Hygiene and the modern economy undermine the patriarchal family just as much as the school. Rapidly growing in number because of a proliferation of children, which an excessive infant mortality does not seem to limit, the family group becomes almost impossible to govern or feed. To the most vigorous male members of the group, escape appears not only possible, but practical and necessary. If the one who leaves remains single, he only partially dissociates himself from the group: he sends material help to the family, and this enhances his prestige and authority, to the detriment of the elder; what is more, he brings back ideas from the exterior world which further help to destroy tradition. If, on the other hand, the one who leaves marries, he establishes an independent household and is definitively lost to the patriarchal family, in fact, he founds a new institution, destined to replace it.[2]

Transformation does not automatically mean progress. It is indispensable if the family is to adapt to the present type of society; but, all things being considered, the new structure of the family is not socially less good than the former, perhaps even the contrary is true. But in the process of social change, what an upheaval has taken place! The fact that most of the other social and economic institutions are not keeping pace with this change, makes the family's situation quite dramatic.

It finds itself in a state of intense disorganization. Not only are its functions changing before its relations to the new institutions have been established, but its internal roles are changing, dislocating the internal hierarchical mechanism and provoking a conflict of generations, which is accentuated by a conflict with civilization. Further disorganization results from the sub-standard living conditions of the city slums or rural regions.

The abrupt passage from one way of life to another, without time for the behavior patterns to adapt, is the basic cause of cultural disorganization. It is in this framework that one must view the climate of sexual liberty which prevails, especially in the cities. We are not referring here to the decadence of a certain segment of urban society, but to the popular masses. It must be remembered that the urban immigrants come from a social system where high fertility was normal, and they now find themselves obliged to limit this fertility, so that marriage is delayed and numerous psychological frustrations drive them to seek compensations.

The family will be in a state of normlessness for many years to come. To accelerate the social and cultural reintegration of this group, so vital to the basic equilibrium of the individual, one of the most important tasks will be to organize every type of social service that can work together with the schools and personally with the members of the family, especially the mother, to help the family group perform its functions during the period of disequilibrium.

EDUCATION

Education forms the basis of any social or cultural reintegration. Whether it is a question of innovating structural changes or making them possible by adapting the mental and behavior patterns of the people, in a word, their culture—it is always to education that one must appeal.

Education cannot be achieved through the schools alone. In a certain sense, it is a never-ending task; for since society is in a rapid and thorough state of change, the institutions are generally behind, and substitutes must continually be found. Thus in the modern world, mass media play an increasingly important supplementary role in education, especially by enabling more of the population to participate in the global culture. In Latin America, mass media, such as the press, motion pictures, and the radio, are having a growing influence in reducing the cultural marginality of the masses. (Appendix Table VI shows the proportion of daily newspapers in different countries.)

The social structures themselves play a part in the educational process. Changes in the family group, urbanization, the birth of new functions and institutions in the rural world, cause mental and behavior patterns to adapt to new points of reference. The place of pre-eminence, however, must always be given to the educational institutions. In a changing civilization, it is indeed the schools that perform the indispensable function of systematically synthesizing the social attitudes with philosophical, scientific and technical knowledge.

Basic Education

Basic education, strictly speaking, includes elementary education, but we are using the term here to refer only to adult instruction. The specific task of such a program is to adapt the adults to the new realities resulting from social change. Its purpose is not to confer new knowledge as much as it is to change attitudes.

Many techniques have been developed for this purpose, but we do not have the space to enumerate them here. We shall simply mention some of the organizations which have initiated basic education programs in Latin America: the ILO in the Andes Mission, UNESCO, the Organization of American States, some governments, several universities, Protestant missionary groups, unions, cooperatives, Catholic Action groups and many other organizations of the Catholic Church. So immense is the task, that there is a place for every program.

There is a specific need for the utilization of all available means of communication. Radio renders a great service in this regard, particularly in the rural areas.[3]

A change of attitude toward the most common, everyday problems involves a change of values. The standards of living are almost immediately influenced. For example, once the peasant is convinced of the value of certain agricultural or breeding techniques, he will adopt them. The same is true in areas of: hygiene (the use of soap); the most simple furniture (the use of beds, instead of sleeping on the floor, the construction of tables, chairs, shelves); the house (separate living quarters for men and animals, the installation of windows in houses that did not have them because of the mountain cold); food (the eating of vegetables); community organization (improvement of roads, construction of a school, of an assembly place), etc.

It is along these lines that a basic education must be approached. It naturally supposes a sound knowledge of the local customs and mentalities, but also the necessary means to implement the program. If radio is used, for example, the broadcasts must be supported by an effective organization: auxiliaries who can give explanations, booklets, specialists, and training centers for the elite of the peasant youth, who could become a permanent factor of social fermentation, and a new leadership capable of responding to social change.

The Educational System

The preparation to confront the structures and the values of society is accomplished largely through the instrumentality of the schoolroom.[4] It is here that a man acquires both the knowledge which "equips" him for his social obligations, and the values which enable him to accept reality, to understand it, and to make the necessary adaptations to future changes.

Since the educational system is a social institution, it generally lags behind social realities, especially when they are in a state of rapid change. This is inevitable. But the consequences will not be serious if the gap is kept small. The rapid changes in Latin America have as their starting point a society whose cultural values were transmitted through the traditional channels of the patriarchal family and rural structures; and as their terminus, a society whose channels of transmission have become quite different, both because of the changes in social structure and because of the growing complexity of this society. One of these new channels is the schoolroom. This is an important development, for the schools have a basic part to play in creating a culture.

The masses have been quick to comprehend the importance of schooling. They have understood, unconsciously perhaps, but quite forcefully, that to make any progress on the road to emancipation they must learn to read and seek an education. In this context, education has a much more powerful significance than in a developed society. In any educational system, the orientation of the teacher is of such obvious importance, that it is not surprising to see the Communists already infiltrating the teacher-training schools.

Elementary and Secondary Education

The rate of illiteracy is still very high in Latin America, although some countries do constitute definite exception. The over-all estimate of the number of illiterates on the continent in 1960 was about 40 per cent. Twenty years earlier, the figure was over 50 per cent.

For effective operation, the elementary school system needs more buildings and more trained teachers. But the educational budgets of most states are too anemic to meet the challenge. Certain Latin American countries still allocate more of the national budget to military programs than to education. This reflects an attitude that is disfunctional, to say the least, in the over-all development of the country.

The subject of secondary education must be viewed in a somewhat different light. There can be no question of considering it as a social right, at least not while the present illiteracy ratio prevails. This level of education is important, however, in the process of social change, both because of the type of youth it influences and the type of instruction that is imparted.

The total per capita figures of those attending secondary schools in Latin America are the lowest in the world, except for Africa. The world figure, based on 10,000 inhabitants, is 244; in Latin America it is 166 (1960 estimates).

This, once more, is a reflection of the general characteristics of Latin American society. For a very long time (and the situation has not radically changed in many countries) secondary education was reserved to the dominant social classes. Furthermore, the schools are almost exclusively located in the cities, for they suppose a certain level of cultural life, and in Latin America this seldom exists outside the urban areas. These cities, moreover, are so grouped into concentrated areas that the rest of the territory has become an economic, social and cultural desert.

Thus bound to the traditional social structures, the educational institutions tend to be identified with the social classes they serve. They are utilized by these classes as a cultural instrument which enables them to maintain a certain monopoly and to transmit certain values. Hence there is a social segregation within the system and a fierce opposition to the democratization of secondary education. Consequently, the educational institutions, most of the time unwittingly, prolong social structures and cultural values that are perfectly disfunctional in the present evolution. The remedy consists in creating an awareness of the social evolution in progress, and in opening the secondary schools to new social classes, notably the middle categories.

It would be hardly possible to pass over the activity of the Catholic Church in the educational field. At the present time, Catholic institutions represent about 40 per cent of the secondary school enrollment in Latin America, and in some countries, as high as 60 per cent and 80 per cent. There is a teaching force of 17,000 priests, full-time or part-time, not to mention a great number of Brothers, Sisters, and laymen. The Church has been establishing schools since colonial times. She has had her share of opposition, as is evidenced by the expulsion of the Jesuits in the second half of the eighteenth century, and the unnumbered confiscations of her property throughout the nineteenth and twentieth centuries.

The real objective of the Church's efforts has been the training of an elite. The whole problem today, however, resides in the definition of "elite." Due to the social change now in progress, the very concept of elite is rapidly altering. There is a nominal elite, which still enjoys, during this period of transition, important political, economic and cultural powers, but which has ceased to be a dynamic force in the development of the country.

It is in this perspective that Catholic secondary education has been accused of being limited to one class. This is not, to any degree, intentional. But as a matter of fact, an important part of this educational system has been utilized by the dominant classes as a means of prolonging their own existence. In this sense, Catholic education has, to a great extent, been a cultural service to one social class. Very often a considerable portion of those who have passed through this school system, after receiving its cultural values, waste no time in making a distinction between those values that are functional for their integration into social life and those values that are not. Among the latter are often religious values.

For the last several decades, however, Catholic secondary education has been developing in a different direction. Many of the schools established in the past 30 years have been oriented equally to the new classes. One religious order, the Salesians, has created an impressive number of technical schools. In short, Catholic secondary education is a typical example of how an institution is transformed during a period of social change. All institutions offer resistance and are somewhat out of tune with reality; and the more tightly they are integrated to a system that is itself rigid, the more difficult it is for them to alter. Some needs are best satisfied by creating parallel institutions. This is what has been done in Catholic secondary education.

We should inject here the note that Protestant institutions, by the very fact that most of them were founded after the Second World War, have more directly reached the middle classes.

An educational institution must be judged on the quality and content of its courses. Here again the situation in Latin America is not well balanced. In almost all the countries, the university officials complain about the inferiority of secondary education. Some universities have already revamped their program, adding one or two years of transitional courses to make up for the deficiencies of the lower levels.

Furthermore, the proportion of students taking the professional and technical courses is very low. Only in Argentina does the number surpass those who take the program of general studies; and this is indicative of Argentina's lead in the training of technicians and specialized workers. In contrast, the proportion of these students in other countries is often less than half of those in the general education program, and in Brazil the percentage is only 20 per cent (1958). Here, then, is another weakness that must be corrected if the needs of development are to be met. Certain countries, like Colombia, have begun to establish institutions for accelerated technical training.

Higher Education

Higher education in Latin America has experienced a phenomenal development. In less than twenty years the number of university students has quadrupled. But there are, to be sure, considerable structural weaknesses, such as the absence of a solid secondary level on which to build, and the lack of adequately prepared teachers, or teachers who can work full-time. In addition, the construction of new campuses has often been inspired by national pride rather than by a well-conceived plan based on the needs of the country. In fact, certain dictators have constructed housing simply as an attempt to neutralize the student population.

The Latin American universities do not merely exercise academic functions as their European or North American counterparts. It is, at first, astonishing to see the students so involved in political life. Most of the revolutions, or revolutionary attempts, originate in the universities, and the students have almost become a new "order" in the socio-political structure of the continent. This phenomenon, to be understood, must be placed in its social context.

The university plays a triple role in Latin America, and this is in addition to its proper academic function: it serves as a means of social ascension, an instrument of social consciousness and an innovator in society.

For a long time, and even today in some countries, for a member of the middle class to rise socially, he had to be accepted into the groups in power or into the civil administration. For members of the lower classes, social ascension required success in small-scale commercial activity, usually itinerant. These two types of activity were clearly parasitic.

In view of the rigidity of established society, the only possibilities of social ascension lie in the exercise of the new functions in administration, commerce, industry, and education. As society continues on its course toward a new integration, these functions multiply, and society itself becomes more fluid. Several regions of the continent are already at an advanced stage: the area around the mouth of the Rio de la Plata, the São Paulo region, a part of Chile, and the majority of the large cities and industrial regions.

But today the new functions in society demand a better preparation and a social status that is already somewhat elevated. This is where the university graduate is at an advantage, for in spite of the deficiencies of higher education, he does emerge with a greater competency and prestige. He thus finds it easier to climb the social ladder. This new role of the university is functional, therefore, in relation to change.

Although this social role is positive, it cannot cover up the serious faults in the academic area. Unless the universities build up their intellectual requirements for both teachers and students, they will quickly lose their prestige.

The second social role of the university consists in its encouragement of social and national consciousness. Student opposition to the traditional classes is heightened by the hard life at the university (most of them must work their way through) and by their desire to climb socially. The very fact that the university is in itself a means of ascension makes their social awareness even more acute. The student in turn ferments the social consciousness of the lower classes, either because he comes from these classes, or because of his occasional, and in some places, frequent participation in political and ideological movements. In moments of crisis, he takes a definite position and becomes a catalytic factor.

The student plays a similar role in respect to national consciousness although to a lesser extent, it seems, than in Africa or Asia. But national consciousness is older in the Latin American countries, and the recent social movements have utilized nationalism to give added drive to their momentum. The ideological force of nationalism is powerful. It is a decisive factor in making even radical change acceptable, for it provides an apparent goal, namely, the strengthening of the nation, especially in its relationship to other nations.

Since in Latin America the economic and political influence of the United States has been so prevailing and only recently (and timidly) oriented toward a social dynamism, anti-Americanism is an easy and effective tool for strengthening the objectives both of nationalism and social change. This was the obvious tactic of Perón and Fidel Castro.

Whatever direction the revolutionary elite work toward, they have a tendency . . . to interpret the aspirations of the masses in terms of national interest. Whereas in Europe during the nineteenth century, the nation was considered by the leftist movements as the "land of the bourgeoisie," in Latin America (as in all the other ex-colonial countries) the unique and authentic expression of the national interest is "the people," while the bourgeoisie and oligarchies are considered as defenders of foreign interests.[5]

The third supplementary role played by the university is that of social and cultural innovator. Society is rapidly passing from a feudal-type structure with its two distinct social categories, to one more and more diversified, industrial, and technological. It is understandable that the university graduates who assume the positions of responsibility in the new structures should do battle with the old. They are in touch with the new world, its aspirations, its ideologies and its techniques. They are consequently cultural agents of innovation in a society which, until recently, experienced very little innovation, a society that needs an enormous capacity for adaptation.

This triple role of the university provides an explanation as to why Marxism has such an influence among university students. It is not simply a fad. Compared to the ineffective social theories of the traditional classes, Marxism appears as the ideology best adapted to social change. It proposes a logical and complete transformation, and thus is a powerfully explosive force for innovation.

Furthermore, it opposes those very structures that are the obstacles to social ascendancy, and it injects the necessary dose of heroism by the clandestine character of many of its activities. It channels the aspirations for social ascension and orients them toward a collective ascension, thus providing the students with a quasi-messianic mission. Lastly, to nationalism it adds a social aspect and an international dimension.

We shall not describe all the forms which Communist activity has taken on the university level. Suffice it to say that it consists essentially in creating cells of militant party members, infiltrating regional and national student movements, utilizing national and international events to maintain an atmosphere of tension, putting inexpensive scientific, economic and social literature on the market, infiltrating the faculty, and finally, offering scholarships for study in Prague, Moscow, East Berlin, Belgrade, Peking, and Havana.

The most effective way to compete with these activities is to orient the students toward social action, work out non-Marxist models of social reform, and make available inexpensive studies on social, economic and political subjects.

Various types of social action are possible: community organization and development in the urban and rural areas, evening courses for adults, contact with the workers and peasants through the press, and work with the youth in the poorer neighborhoods. All this in no way excludes study groups in political and social problems, or even active involvement in certain major events in the national life. It is worthy of note that where social initiatives do exist, they are often on the part of Catholic Action groups, or under the inspiration of a few priests whose apostolate is to work among the students.

The problem of presenting models of social reform is not, of course, limited to the university level. The problem assumes a major importance when one considers the dearth of coherent and concrete solutions which the Western world offers for social change. This lack only gives added force to the solutions proposed by the Marxists. But concrete solutions do exist. They have already been partially realized in several places in the fields of agrarian reform, unionism, housing, farmers' organizations, basic education, and political life.

A coherent doctrine exists also. It has been elaborated by the Christian churches, either within the Catholic Church, by *Mater et Magistra* and *Pacem in Terris,* or within the World Council of Churches. There is a doctrine, and also occasional concrete realizations. But what is needed is a link between them, a whole series of model programs, applied under diverse circumstances of time and place, which would show that the doctrine is not a mere collection of unapplied or inapplicable principles, and that the concrete realizations are not mere accidents, attributable to an exceptional personality.

Finally, publications in the pure and applied sciences practically ignore socio-economic questions. The ones that are relevant are either Marxist and generously made available along with their scholarships, or else they are expensive and contain models applicable only to developed countries under a liberal capitalistic system.

Educational Planning

The progress of education will largely depend on the effectiveness of the planning to be undertaken in the years to come. The 1962 UNESCO conference at Santiago, on Education and Development in Latin America, underlined its necessity and decided to create an educational planning section within the organization for general planning for Latin America.

Proceeding a step further, the same conference determined the key points for aid by the Alliance for Progress: certain university departments, the teacher-training schools, technical schools, and certain forms of basic education.

For a while the Alliance for Progress gave little attention to private initiatives in the social and educational field. Its program was essentially intergovernmental. Another reason for this lack of attention was the fact that the majority of these private initiatives were sponsored by the Catholic Church. Projecting the American pattern of Church–State relations onto the Latin American scene, the Alliance extended help almost exclusively to public institutions. At present, however, the necessity of mobilizing all dynamic forces for the social change, and the recognition of the possible role of the Church in Latin America (cf. the many statements of Vice President Humphrey in this regard) are changing past trends.

Education planning in the private sector, therefore, is equally imperative, both on the national level, and on a continental scale.[6]

CULTURAL VALUES

It is, of course, impossible in a few paragraphs to treat adequately the cultural values in Latin America. But we shall offer a few observations.

At the very origin of basic personality, there is a series of fundamental values which deeply impregnate the mind and mentality of a group. These are transmitted from generation to generation and manifest a remarkable continuity through social transformation. They are, moreover, often linked with moral values, and even religious values.

Latin America includes the cultural elements of the Indians, the Negroes, the strapping Basques of Costa Rica and the province of Antioquia in Colombia, the Germanic races in southern Brazil, not to mention the new syntheses between the divers southern elements which form, for example, the peoples of Cuba and Argentina. Because of this great ethnic diversity, we can single out only a few general traits that are fairly widespread throughout the continent.

All the cultural traits are ambivalent. They can be functional or disfunctional in relation to a given social situation. We shall judge them in relation to social change and development. Cultural values are indeed the motive forces of a new equilibrium, and it would be a perfect illusion to think that structural transformations alone will solve the problem. It is enough to observe how the Communist regimes organize their propaganda to create new values which will be socially functional. In Cuba, for example, the year 1963 was a year of organization, and special campaigns were conducted to emphasize to the people the importance of increased productivity. As a result, campaigns were organized to select "the factory or store of the month" or even "worker of the vanguard."

It would be completely erroneous to accord a negative moral value to the cultural traits, except for very particular cases where they contradict moral values, either absolutely or relative to a particular set of circumstances. On the other hand, it must be pointed out that many aspects of the Latin American cultures are inoperative in relation to development. We limit our observations to four themes and around these try to synthesize some of the major aspects of the Latin American mentality.

The Values of the Mind and the Disdain for the Real

The Latin mind, more so than the Anglo-Saxon, has always been attracted by spiritual values, in every aspect from intellectual speculation to mysticism. The religious divisions between Catholicism and Protestantism are quite deeply rooted in these cultural factors, which in turn are strengthened by the accent placed by these groups on one or another aspect of the Christian message. Is it not remarkable, for example, to see that in all those countries where both religions exist, the proportion of Catholic students is higher in the juridical and literary fields, while the number of Protestant students exceed in the scientific and technical fields?

Furthermore, in those areas that are uniformly of Latin stock, the disproportion between the number of students in the speculative sciences and positive sciences is enormous. This quite naturally poses a serious problem regarding development and helps explain the startling fact that in many countries industry is in the hands of foreigners or immigrants of the second or third generation.

The speculative tendency is expressed in many ways and is often accompanied by a contempt for reality. For centuries, and especially since the *Leyes de Indias*, legislation has been a magnificent juridical apparatus of implacable logic, but often destined merely to satisfy the intellectual appetites of the doctors of law.

When it is time to organize, the speculative mind of the Latin American is always ready. No one makes more logical and decorative organizational charts, but these most often remain on paper. It is the same with planning, so needed today, which becomes for many an exercise in style. In this regard, they are past masters.

The reasons for such a state of affairs are too numerous to give here. The absence of a democratic tradition is probably both a cause and an effect. It nevertheless poses a real problem when it comes down to meeting the needs of development and social reintegration. Too often the most well-conceived plans and the purest intentions never cross the frontiers of the mind into concrete realization.

On the other hand, the consequences of this primacy of mind over matter are not unfavorable in every respect. An integral development does suppose the development of spiritual values. Does not the specific contribution of the Latin world to technology consist in its power to spiritualize it, if only aesthetically? Consider, for example, what Latin America has brought to modern architecture. The possibilities of a Latin American contribution to technological civilization is, therefore, very great and very real.

The term "spiritual value" is ambiguous and can be applied to various realities. In fact, many do not hesitate to pervert its meaning and utilize it in a puerile anti-Communist campaign to defend the most flagrant social injustices.

We shall treat later of the values that are properly religious. But at this point we must at least mention their importance in the process of cultural reintegration. Christianity can channel in one direction or another the values of a population grappling with social change.

Generosity and Improvisation

It has often been said that the Latin American has his heart in his hand, but has more heart than head. This is true in many respects. He is always ready to join a good cause; he is affable, hospitable, full of excellent intentions—but for how long?

The positive value of his generosity goes further than one might think, sometimes to heroism. This corresponds to the eternal youth of these races and is one of the principal forces in the many revolutionary movements. However, improvisation, lack of perseverance and, in the last analysis, lack of responsibility too often counterbalance this magnificent generosity. These traits must be taken into account if we are to avoid hasty, or even unjust judgments. They are essentially cultural traits.

In an article entitled "El Latino-americano y el Tiempo," Fr. Rafael Carias, S.J., explains how these character traits are linked not only with a somewhat southern temperament, but with a philosophic conception of time.[7] According to the author, a perception of time as an immediate moment, unconnected with the future, geocentric or cyclic, is at the origin of some very basic attitudes of the Latin American. Their opportunism, and the fact that they avoid making decisions or have little sense of responsibility for the consequences, all have deep roots in their vision of how life runs its course. Time for them is a simple repetition of the present moment, and not a continuous journey toward progress, where each step conditions the next. In his article the author gives a few examples of the consequences: the sizeable number of university dropouts, instability in the professional careers, the reluctance to be married in the Church, the many promises which are unkept—without the least regret. In this category one could add, among other things, the many buildings and public works which are abandoned before completion.

Unconcerned with anthropological problems, his time is concentrated on the *recurring* moment, cutting off a view of the future, thus making impossible a true sense of the future, of destiny or of responsibility. To this can be traced his volubility, his opportunism, the impermanent character of his attitude and habitat, and especially his inconstancy, which unconsciously motivates him to avoid definitive commitments with supreme values.[8]

This analysis, a bit extreme perhaps, has the merit of clarity. It ends, by the way, with the judgment that this is a period of transition and not necessarily a pessimistic indication of the future.

As an epilogue to these judgments, we might cite the observations of certain Soviet experts. In their opinion, the people of Cuba are really not cut out for a socialist revolution, for this demands a perseverance and a sense of responsibility that seem to be beyond their capabilities.

Personalism and Caudillismo

Personalism is also ambivalent. In analyzing some aspects of the basic mentality of the Latin American, what stands out is not so much his conviction of the intrinsic value of the human person, as his conviction of the primacy of the individual over the group. (The former conviction does exist in theory, however, to the degree that his Catholicism is taken as the norm.)

This personalism is a positive value insofar as one man can give precise orientation at all the levels of society, or insofar as individual initiatives can influence any development. But its disfunctional aspects are made more prevalent by the characteristics we have previously described.

Such personalism, especially in a society whose social and political structures are so weak, turns quickly to anarchy or *caudillismo*. This despotism comes out on every level, from the local *patriarca* to the Brazilian *coronel* or the national dictator.

As a result, the group is put in the hands of the leader, and this is contrary to a true social participation. Moreover, such an attitude makes any real teamwork quite difficult.

Messianism and Inertia

Quite related to the trait we have just described, messianism is brought about by the projection of individual aspirations into a single charismatic personality. Perón and Castro offer recent examples. These messiahs can cause great popular movements. But if they are equal to the task of inspiring a people to revolution, they find it much more difficult to furnish sufficient motivations for a long-term effort.

This indicates a certain vitality and dynamism in the masses, which in many respects is admirable; but on the other side of the coin is their inertia. This inertia is especially evident in the rural populations, who lived so long in a condition of marginality, that any change was *a priori* excluded. The ability to bear suffering, misery and hunger, without any apparent reaction, is bound up with the social structures themselves, and only their transformation will bring a gradual change of attitude. The typical fatalism of the underdeveloped rural masses is particularly striking among the Indians, but it is present under many forms in the Brazilian peasant of the sertão, in the gaucho of the Argentine pampas, or among the mestizos of Colombia or Central America.

The only conclusion that these observations permit is that a social reintegration will only be possible through a gigantic effort in the cultural sphere. The two go hand in hand. On the one hand, the cultural integration of the masses must be encouraged by an intense cultural activity and broader opportunities for social participation. On the other hand, an elite must be trained for more sustained and responsible efforts. Since both aspects involve a fundamental view of the world, religion can be a significant factor.

THE RELIGIOUS SPHERE

In the socio-cultural reintegration in Latin America, religion assumes a considerable importance. Certain values put forward by the religious groups can be either functional or disfunctional in relation to development. We shall pursue this point in Part III so that it can be integrated into a global picture of the Catholic Church. We would only mention here that the Church's role is bound to be determining, since she embraces in one way or another 95 per cent of the population. Her cultural influence alone is significant.

It is clearly apparent that the action which the Church is initiating on the Latin American continent has a very broad significance, and in fact is a sign that the Church is really a universal Church. The cooperation between the Church of Latin America, Europe, and North America is a recent but important development, for the outlook of these Churches has been thereby transformed. Furthermore, Latin America is the only rapidly developing continent where Christians are in the majority, and this implies a very great responsibility toward the whole underdeveloped population.

In the following pages we shall also have a few words to say concerning the other religious groups in Latin America, in particular Protestantism. The existence of these groups should not be dismissed because of their small numbers. The ecumenical significance of their presence must not be overlooked.[9]

Our only purpose in the following chapters is to furnish a framework for reference. We hope that from the multitude of facts and figures, a more precise and comprehensive picture of the continent will emerge.

NOTES

[1] See B. Corredor, *La Familia en América Latina* (Fribourg: FERES, 1962), and V. Piñeda, *La Familia en Colombia* (Fribourg: FERES, 1962).

[2] Georges Hahn, "Bref aperçu des problèmes modernes de la famille musulmane," *L'Afrique et l'Asie*, 1961, p. 21.

[3] See S. Torres and B. Corredor, *op. cit.*

[4] See the various books on education in the Latin American countries, published by FERES between 1961 and 1964.

[5] Gino Germani, *op. cit.*

[6] The International Office of Catholic Education has undertaken this work in conjunction with the CIEC (The Inter-American Confederation of Catholic Education).

[7] Rafael Caria, S.J., "El Latino-americano y el Tiempo," *SIC* (1962), pp. 482–85.

[8] *Ibid.*, p. 485.

[9] In this regard see: Prudencio Damboriena, Manuel L. Avellan and Enrique Dussel, *El protestantismo en América Latina. Efectivos, métodos, motivaciones* (Fribourg: FERES, 1963), 2 vols.

III

The Latin American Church
in the Social Change

12

The Population Explosion and Religious Institutions

THE NUMBER OF INHABITANTS PER PRIEST

The first consequence of the demographic evolution to the Church is the very high number of inhabitants per priest. The situation is not exactly new. The first crisis occurred at the end of the eighteenth century, when the Jesuits were expelled from the Portuguese and Spanish colonies. Independence brought a second crisis, which especially affected the religious orders, the seminaries and the hierarchy (certain countries were twenty-five years without a bishop). The liberal anti-clerical regimes of the nineteenth century merely prolonged the crisis by not allowing the Church to develop her structures: dioceses, religious congregations, seminaries, and schools. This explains why in 1912 the number of inhabitants per priest was already as high as 4,480.

In the second quarter of the twentieth century the relations between the Church and the State began to normalize in most countries, and Church structures were once again able to develop. But just when the situation began to improve, the rapid population growth came along. Thus in 1945 there were, on the average, 5,770 inhabitants per priest, with, of course, great differences from one country to the next.

Between 1945 and 1960 this proportion diminished somewhat (5,400 inhabitants per priest), but the improvement was due, in great measure, to outside help. A certain number of missionaries came to Latin America from Asia, and later the Holy See's call for priests from Europe and North America bore its fruits.

TABLE 5
Number of Inhabitants per Priest in Latin America between 1912 and 1960

Year	1912	1945	1950	1955	1960
Inhabitants per priest	4,480	5,770	5,720	5,530	5,410

But the present situation remains very difficult, especially when one recalls that Latin America is passing through a period of transition which demands that pastoral activity be not merely normal, but dynamic.

A more detailed analysis of the figures available shows that the increase of religious priests has been much more pronounced than that of the diocesan clergy. This presents serious pastoral problems whenever well-coordinated general efforts are required.

TABLE 6
Relative Number of Diocesan and Religious Priests in Latin America between 1912 and 1960

Year	Diocesan Priests	Religious Priests	Total
1912	11,776	4,578	16,354
1945	12,992	11,389	24,381
1950	14,270	13,282	27,552
1955	16,145	16,010	32,155
1960	18,451	19,185	37,636

It would be a bit presumptuous to make conjectures for the future, particularly in a domain subject to so many factors. It is legitimate, however, to make projections, that is, to prolong the present rate of growth into the future, and to discuss its validity. The projected figures can serve as a guide for forecasting a positive or negative development of the present situation.

Three different projections can be worked out: the first, based on the rate of development during the 17-year period between 1944 (date of the first available statistics) and 1960; the second, based on the period between 1950 and 1960; and the third, based on the years between 1955 and 1960. The projected results of the third period will be higher, since during these six years the increase due to the influx of foreign priests was considerable. On the other hand, however, the projection based on the entire 17-year period gives relatively low results, since the statistics for the first years are probably not quite complete. The projection worked out on the basis of 11 years (1950–1960) totals between the other two. The three sets taken together, therefore, should provide a workable gauge.

TABLE 7

Projections of the Number of Priests in Latin America
between 1960 and 2000, according to Three Hypotheses

Projection I	*1960*	*1965*	*1970*	*1975*	*2000*
(on 17 years 1944–1960)	36,730	40,950	45,220	49,390	70,490
Projection II					
(on 11 years 1950–1960)	37,538	42,603	47,668	52,733	78,058
Projection III					
(on 6 years 1955–1960)	37,988	43,848	49,708	55,568	84,868

To attain the projected results, the annual increase of priests from the years 1960 and 2000 would have to be (according to the hypothesis used) 844(I), 1,013(II), or 1,172(III). Between 1955 and 1960, the average annual increase was 1,084, thus falling between increases projected by the hypotheses II and III. Moreover, since the actual number of priests in 1960 was 37,636, the situation that year was, in fact, between those predicted by hypotheses II and III.

Translated into figures of inhabitants per priest, the projections based on hypotheses I and III give the results as seen in Table 8.

TABLE 8

Number of Inhabitants per Priest in Latin America, according
to the Projection Established between 1960 and 2000
(Hypotheses I and III) and the Average Demographic Projections
of the United Nations

	1960	1965	1970	1975	2000
Hypothesis I					
(based on 17 years)	5,333*	5,338	5,438	5,623	7,409
Hypothesis III					
(based on 6 years)		5,186	5,215	5,336	6,851

* Actual figure for 1960.

As can be seen, the figures for the periods up to 1975 indicate
a slight increase. Although the projections after this date are
extremely hypothetical, the high figures for the year 2000 are due
to the fact that the population increase will become even more
rapid. This period will necessarily feel the effects of the lower
infant-mortality rate and the greater longevity of the past two
generations.

In projecting toward the future, consideration must also be
given to the question of vocations. Unfortunately, there is only
information available concerning the diocesan clergy. It is surprising to learn that between the years 1955–1959, while the
growth index of the Latin American population passed from 100
to 113, that of the major seminarians rose from 100 to 103, and
the minor seminarians from 100 to 110.

The period under consideration is probably too short to draw
any definitive conclusions, but the general tendency shows that the
pace of population increase is not being equaled by that of vocations. This is true for Latin America as a whole, though it varies
from country to country. Only in Colombia and Ecuador have vocations kept pace with the population growth.[1]

A study made on the seminarians of Colombia and Brazil gives
some indication concerning the origin of vocations. Whereas the
urban population of Brazil (cities of 10,000 plus) represents 32.3

per cent of the country's total, 48.9 per cent of the vocations come from the cities. And in Colombia, the rates are 31.7 per cent and 42.9 per cent respectively. If, therefore, it is still the rural areas that furnish the majority of vocations, it is nevertheless certain that the percentage of rural vocations is clearly below the percentage that the rural areas represent of the total population. Furthermore, rural vocations come almost exclusively from the families of landowners, at least in Brazil, thus there are very few from the salaried farm workers (5.9 per cent of the rural vocations).

Urban society, then, seems relatively more fruitful in vocations. Is it not commonplace to consider city life as harmful to vocations, and country life, most conducive? The statistics seem to indicate the contrary. One thing evident, the social groups, whether rural or urban, that give the least number of vocations are those where illiteracy is high and living conditions, substandard. This fact is significant for it indicates the influence of the dynamism of societies on the number of vocations, and shows that the socio-cultural elevation of the marginal masses, far from hindering vocations, is a major factor in their growth.

Although not exactly related to the numerical aspect of vocations, a few observations are in order concerning the formation of the clergy, both diocesan and religious. The shortcomings are indeed serious.

The system of minor seminaries is still very prevalent. Although it is justified in certain rural regions or those particularly deficient from a socio-cultural point of view, it has many serious drawbacks. It isolates the young student at an age of 11 or 12. This cuts him off from the cultural universe of the milieu in which he is to live and is responsible both for the low percentage of those who persevere (less than 5%) and for certain crises which occur after ordination. Several experiments are now underway for modifying the system, especially in the urban areas. In some cases, the minor seminaries have been converted into regular secondary schools, as in Santiago, La Paz (Bolivia), or Cucuta (Colombia).

In other places, provisions have been made for the seminarians to live in a less artificial environment, such as San Juan de las Misiones in Paraguay, or a diocese in the outskirts of Buenos Aires.

In some countries, the multiplication of small major seminaries impairs the very high quality of spiritual, theological, and simply human formation that is necessary for candidates for the priesthood. Countries like Colombia and Brazil have taken steps to combine smaller seminaries into larger ones, but institutions for religious have not yet been affected.

The demands of pastoral work, which we will speak of in later chapters, will sufficiently prove the necessity of adapting the system of seminaries. The clergy must respond to present and future needs. This is one of the reasons why pastoral institutes are indispensable.

THE SIZE OF PARISHES

The large number of inhabitants per priest automatically indicates large-sized parishes. In 1960, for the whole continent, the average geographic area of the parishes was 383 square miles, and the average number of souls 15,332. These figures have little significance unless they can be compared to the national averages and to the averages for the rural and urban sectors. But it is immediately apparent that the pastoral methods advocated in Europe or North America need serious adaptations before being applied in Latin America.

In 134 out of 348 dioceses, the average area of a parish is more than 347 square miles, and in 177 dioceses the average parish has the care of more than 15,000 people.

The number of parishioners per parish priest is important to know to get a clear picture of the situation. In many countries the average is more than 10,000, the low being 7,464 in Paraguay, and the high, 16,667 in Honduras.

The geographic size of the rural parishes is always greater than the national averages. It is regularly as large as 200 square miles in the more populated areas, and 770 square miles in the others. However, in contrast to the distribution in Europe, these parishes are larger in population than the city parishes, except for some of the larger metropolitan areas. To give only two examples: in 1956, the number of inhabitants per parish in the cities of Brazil was 11,800, while in the country parishes it was 14,000. For the Dominican Republic, the 1960 figures were 17,600 and 28,400 respectively.

The same situation exists for parish personnel. The number of souls per priest in the city parishes of Brazil in 1960 was 5,000 as against 11,400 in the country parishes, and in the Dominican Republic, the figures were 5,900 as against 19,400. Moreover, men and women religious are concentrated in the city. In Uruguay, for example, 78% of men religious and 72% of the nuns reside in Montevideo; in San José, Costa Rica, the proportions are 75% and 83%; in Quito, 45% and 43%; in Asunción, 50% and 71%; and in Caracas, 53% and 50%.

A few figures concerning the average population-size of the city parishes should give an appreciation of the problem. The following estimates were made in 1960: Bogotá — 15,000; Lima — 16,000; São Paulo — 22,000; Rio de Janeiro — 25,000; Montevideo — 25,000; Buenos Aires — 27,000; Santiago — 30,000; Mexico — 40,000; Havana — 60,000. This means that a good number of parishes have a population of 50,000, 80,000, 100,000 and in some cases even more.

It should not be forgotten that there are rarely more than three priests per parish, which should give an idea of the pastoral responsibilities of the city clergy.

The basic conclusion that can be drawn from these figures is that parish structures, both rural and urban, cannot meet the present pastoral needs. If it were merely a question of a minimal amount of ordinary pastoral duties for a stable rural society, the parishes might prove adequate. But today they are becoming purely formal structures for the mass of the population, assuring effective religious assistance for a small number of persons.

THE SACRAMENTS

Although the immense majority of Latin Americans are baptized in the Catholic Church (more than 90%), they have little opportunity of receiving the other sacraments because of the lack of priests and the inadequacy of parochial structures.

Weekly attendance at Mass is possible only to a very small minority. It has been estimated that in Peru and Venezuela only from 3 to 5% of the rural population have the advantage of weekly services. In the cities, figures for attendance at Sunday Mass range between 10 and 20%, and in some cases go below 10% (Buenos Aires between 7 and 9%). In Rio de Janeiro, for a population of about 3.5 million there are only 700 Masses celebrated on Sunday. By calculating on an average attendance of 500 per Mass, this means that only 10% of the faithful are practicing Catholics on a weekly basis.

If attendance at Mass is so low, the reception of Holy Communion is bound to have an even lower frequency. In the year 1958, in Brazil, the Eucharistic Crusade decided to discontinue its campaigns for frequent Communion for children. In several places in Colombia the clergy request the children not to receive Holy Communion on Sunday because it would be physically impossible to distribute that many Communions.

This non-reception of the sacraments therefore is not due to religious indifference (except for a fraction of the urban population) but simply to the physical impossibility of administering them in the present framework of Church structures and discipline.

We need not pursue the problem of Confession or the Sacrament of the Sick; the stark truth is, they do not exist for the majority of the Latin American population.

PROTESTANTISM

It was during the second half of the nineteenth century that Protestantism became officially organized in Latin America and established its principal churches. Until 25 years ago, however, its spread could be considered marginal. Since then, Protestantism has made relatively important progress. The statistics in Table 9 should give evidence enough. Between 1937 and 1961, the proportion of Protestants in relation to the total population of the continent increased from 0.49 per cent to 3.84 per cent.[2]

TABLE 9

Development of Protestantism in Latin America:
Number of Faithful and Ministers between 1938 and 1961

Year	Number of Faithful	Total	Number of Ministers Foreign	Native	% of Native
1938	632,563				
1949	3,171,900	10,971	3,821	7,150	65
1951	3,380,300	16,223	5,708	10,515	65
1956	4,230,400	20,660	6,361	14,299	69
1961	7,710,400	41,088	6,541	34,547	84

This growth is the result of a systematic Protestant effort throughout the continent. At the origin of this intensified evangelical activity was the difficulty experienced by the missions in the Far East. When Communism or nationalism caused the expulsion of so many of their missionaries, the Protestant churches decided to concentrate their efforts on other continents. The International Missionary Congress, at their 1938 meeting in Madras, declared Latin America the missionary territory of prime importance. This choice was justified by the many advantages it offered Protestantism: its linguistic and cultural unity, the freedom of action accorded by the majority of governments, and the effective protection provided by the consular authorities. Certainly, Latin America was Catholic, but its Catholicism was denounced as "a decadent form of Christianity." It therefore urgently needed an infusion of evangelical Christianity, which some were already referring to as a "second Reformation."

Thus it was that a good number of missionaries was sent to Latin America, along with financial resources originally earmarked for the Asian missions. Preparatory planning was undertaken by a commission of specialists, and unity of action was assured by the "Committee on Cooperation in Latin America" and the "National Christian Council."

Two phases can be distinguished in the work undertaken since these decisions. The first phase was directed to an intensive propaganda, especially in Mexico, Guatemala, Colombia, Ecuador, Haiti, and Peru. It was notably in conjunction with government campaigns against illiteracy. Illiteracy was considered one of the results of the Catholic Church's abandonment of the populations. The propaganda was both oral (lectures, radio broadcasts) and written, and disseminated simultaneously by different groups: Baptists, Presbyterians, Mennonites, etc. The second phase was more directly one of proselytizing. Its success is evidenced not only by the numerical increase in membership, but also by the organization and stabilization of institutions. Aided financially for the most part by their North American communities, the churches multiplied houses of worship (2,635 in 1916; 42,420 in 1961), created biblical schools, secondary schools, a few universities, hospitals and clinics. In addition, the churches had at their disposal an abundant library of religious books, good radio stations, and a variety of other means for missionary activity.

At the same time, efforts were directed to the formation of a native clergy whose proportion has steadily grown to 84 per cent of the ministers in 1961. This has led to the rapid establishment of national churches. Although church membership has increased, the number of faithful per minister (both ordained ministers and male and female auxiliaries) has decreased (289 in 1948, 188 in 1961). Whereas an ordained minister is responsible for an average of 482 faithful, a Catholic priest must look after 5,300.[3]

At the present time, it can be said that the Latin American

Protestant community is becoming more and more acculturated, that is, it is gradually adapting to the socio-cultural structures of the continent. But taking into account the historical complexity of the continent and the diversity of social classes, this process is far from being complete. In some countries, however, the Protestants constitute an important minority; in Chile, for example, they represent 11 per cent of the population.

Finally, it is noteworthy that numerical increase has been accompanied by an increase in church attendance: 36.5 per cent in 1957 to 48.6 per cent in 1961 (see Appendix Table VII for details). One should not lose sight of the fact, however, that these communities are relatively recent, and the history of religions frequently shows that they undergo a period of fervor when they are first implanted in a new country, especially when they oppose an established religion and take the social form of small, tightly coherent groups.

OTHER RELIGIONS:
SECTS AND SYNCRETISMS

The various Protestant churches should not be confused with the numerous sects that are active in Latin America. These are characterized by religious incoherence and sometimes attract a following by political intrigues or by the material advantages they offer. There often results a jumble of religious ideas and an extreme fanaticism fiercely directed against the Catholic Church. Many of these sects are not even recognized as Christian by the Protestant churches. Unfortunately, total statistics make no distinction and show that they share in the increase of non-Catholic religions.

Another indication that Christian religious training has been deficient is the emergence of syncretisms. They are particularly prevalent among the Negroes and Indians. Haitian voodooism, Brazilian spiritism, and other forms found in Guatemala, Bolivia and Peru, are all characterized by some kind of mixture of Christian and pre-Christian (African or Indian) elements. They are symptoms of an incomplete evangelization and a backward trend of Christianity due to a shortage of priests, an insufficient Catholic acculturalization, and other causes.

How important are these syncretisms numerically? We shall give the figures for only the two largest movements. Reliable estimates maintain that in Haiti not less than 80 per cent of the baptized Christians take part in voodoo practices. In Brazil, the 1940 and 1950 census figures showed that the number of adherents rose from 463,400 to 824,553, which represents 1.12 per cent and 1.59 per cent of the population. There is no doubt, however, that a much larger part of the population are devotees of spiritism.

Among the causes of this growth of spiritism and religious sects, two stand out rather clearly: the religious needs of the people unsatisfied by the too formal structures of Catholicism; and the psycho-social shock due to the sudden upheaval of social structures. The former seems to be the basic cause, both in the cities and in the rural areas that have been deprived of pastoral care. Several inquiries conducted in the cities of Brazil and Chile have revealed that the principal motivation for joining sects was the desire to belong to a small-sized community.[4]

THE PRESENT REACTION

The Latin American Church has not remained indifferent to this situation. We shall rapidly describe the measures that have already been taken before examining what could be planned for the future.

First of all, a look at the increase in the number of priests since the Second World War shows what efforts are being expended. From 24,381 in 1945 the figure reached 37,636 in 1960. This means an increase of 13,255 priests: 7,796 religious and 5,459 diocesan.

Unfortunately, there are no precise figures to indicate how much of this increase is due to the influx of priests from other countries, but an estimate of 50 per cent would probably be fairly safe. A study by Father A. Sireau in 1960 resulted in the following estimates: Germany — 1,480; Austria — 82; Belgium — 268; Spain — 7,352; France — 583; Italy (diocesan priests) — 470; the Netherlands — 1,208; Switzerland — 102; Canada — 312; United States — 1,106.

Almost half of the diocesan priests came from Spain and Italy. Today, however, there has been an increased number coming from Belgium, Canada, and the United States.

In recent years there has been an intensified effort to encourage vocations. It is too soon to judge the results, but they will depend very heavily on the pastoral dynamism of the Church. Moreover, the religious training in the seminaries will have to undergo profound modifications if priests are going to be prepared for the type of pastoral work that present circumstances demand.

The first real change in pastoral structures has been the multiplication of dioceses. In recent years the creation of dioceses has assumed a rapid pace. There have been almost as many new dioceses established between 1950 and 1960 as between 1900 and 1950. In Brazil, during the six-year period between 1956 and 1962, 60 dioceses were created.

The bishops in charge of the new dioceses are fully aware that the mere establishment of a diocese does not solve the problem. They still have the most elementary needs, not the least of which is priests. But they realize that theirs is the generation that must make the sacrifices. Their successors will reap the benefits of the new dynamism resulting from this decentralization of responsibilities.

Parishes have likewise multiplied. In 1960 they numbered about 12,300.[5] But if their number has increased somewhat over the past 15 years, it has not kept pace with the increase in the clergy, and even less with the population. The increase in the number of new parishes will naturally proceed more slowly, for it depends directly on the number of new priests available. Moreover, adding a priest to an existing parish is often more beneficial than creating a new parish.

Most of the new parishes have been almost exclusively limited to the cities. The revolutionary trend toward urbanization, notably in the metropolitan areas, is rather recent; except for the case of Buenos Aires, it dates only from the 1940's. In most of the cities, the first great wave of rural immigrants was not matched by an increase in the number of parishes. As early as 1910 the average population of a parish in Buenos Aires had reached 49,550; in 1909 in Montevideo it was 44,180; in Havana (1931), 39,000; in Rio de Janeiro (1900), 31,435; in Mexico City (1910), 34,321; and in São Paulo (1905), 25,000.

New parishes were established quite rapidly, but the continued rapid increase in the urban population has periodically neutralized any progress, especially in the suburbs. Even though the multiplication of parishes has not yet resolved the problem of Christianizing the new urban populations, it does give evidence of the dynamic efforts that are being exerted.

Finally, in certain countries, such as Brazil, a relatively large proportion of the rural parishes (as much as 30% in some areas) do not have a resident priest and must depend on a pastor from a neighboring parish to give them occasional assistance.

To offset some of these problems, for some years now, and in most countries, there have been important initiatives in the training of catechists. CELAM has given much attention to this work. To aid the many diocesan and national offices of catechesis, the Latin American Catechetical Training Center was founded in Santiago in 1961.

NOTES

[1] See the studies of FERES on vocations in Colombia, *El problema sacerdotal en Colombia* (Fribourg: FERES, 1963), by Gustavo Perez, and in Brazil, *O Problema sacerdotal no Brazil* (Fribourg: FERES, 1965), by Gustavo Perez and Afonso Gregory.

[2] See P. Damboriena, *op. cit.*

[3] *Bilan du monde* (Tournai: Casterman, 1964), Vol. I, 2nd ed.

[4] See Procopio Camargo de Periera, *Aspectos sociologicos del espiritismo en São Paulo* (Fribourg: FERES, 1962).

[5] This is the figure for diocesan parishes and does not include vicariates and prefectures apostolic.

13

Socio-Cultural Change and Religious Life

So far we have dealt mainly with the quantitative aspects of social change in Latin America, that is, the consequences of the great population increase. We have already mentioned a series of qualitative elements, for the two cannot be categorically separated, but we shall now take a closer look at them, especially the ones which result from the changes taking place in social life, culture and values. These deeply affect the life of the Church.

Considering the history of the Church in Latin America, the crises it has undergone since the end of the eighteenth century, its long-standing shortage of priests, the influence of freemasonry and positivism during the nineteenth and early twentieth centuries, the vigorous secularism in many sectors of social life, and the recent Marxist infiltrations, it is truly amazing that the Latin American people have conserved their Catholicism to such an important degree.

Latin American Catholicism has often been described as a mere facade, or as a set of basically superstitious beliefs. Nothing could be more untrue. Granted that various forms of Catholicism on the continent are still very close to a cosmic-type religion where nature plays the prime role; granted that a long evolution will be necessary before Christianity will be lived in its universality and spiritual purity; and granted there exist some strange mixtures, genuine syncretisms, such as spiritism in Brazil, voodoo in Haiti, or certain Indian cults where the statue of the *pacha mama,* goddess of the earth, is found beside the statue of the Blessed Virgin; yet the claim is true that, except for certain urban populations, the Latin American masses has conserved the faith and a manifest attachment to Catholicism. Even in long-neglected regions this deep-rooted faith is evidenced by the impressive response of the people to any kind of dynamic evangelization.

How can this paradox be explained? In examining the human aspect of history, we do not wish to give the impression of rejecting a supernatural explanation; after all, human elements are the habitual channels of Grace. The passing-down of religious values, in spite of the lack of priests, was made possible by the very type of society in which the people lived. Until 1925, scarcely 10 to 15 per cent of the population lived in dense urban areas. Today the proportion is about 30 per cent. Until very recently, then, the immense majority of the population lived in a rural, pre-technological-type society. The very immobility of this society provided a smooth transmission of traditional values. Authority was in the hands of the older members of the group, and the patriarchal-type family played a basic role. Thus, even in the absence of priests, religious values were handed down from one generation to another, somewhat distorted at times, but with absolute regularity.

The new ideas developing in the cities, as well as the antireligious political regimes, had not, until recently, exercised much influence over the rural masses because of their marginality. But today, the social structures of the masses are rapidly losing these characteristics of immobility and marginality. In other words, the social structures which had been so convenient for transmitting religious values are undergoing profound modifications, or even disappearing entirely. Since we cannot depend much longer upon a quasi-natural transmission of values, proper and specific means must be provided, for example, an organized system of catechetical instruction.

Although the masses continue to call themselves Catholics, there is the ever-present danger that they consider their Catholicism merely as a cultural trait: one is Catholic because he is born in such and such a country, or village or family. It never occurs to people of such a mentality that they could be anything else. It would be unthinkable to be a Buddhist or a Moslem. Thus Catholicism can become a simple attribute of the natural group to which one belongs rather than a distinct and specific adherence to the Church.

For this reason we can say that the major consequence of social change might well be a reduced transmission of religious values, particularly among the masses.

Social change does not merely affect the existing structures and values, it creates new social forms (such as factories) and new social categories (such as the working class). All this is necessarily accompanied by new values, a new vision of the world, a new ethics, in a word, a new culture, incompatible with the world of yesterday. Such a development often takes place outside of, if not in opposition to, the scale of Christian values. It is true that traditional society was heterogeneous and that its structures (the system of landed property, for example) no longer answer the present-day needs of Christian morality. But it is all-important to examine the new conceptions of man which govern the present development of economic structures, the ideology which prevails in the universities and unions, as well as the values which propel the emerging middle class. In most of the key areas of social change, it is the non-Christian values that are winning out. Too often Christian values have been absent or rejected.

The history of Latin America during the nineteenth century is replete with ideologies, some anti-Christian, that have cropped up here and there on the continent. Today, however, with the mass means of communication, such ideologies are passing from a relatively limited circle to ever-broadening segments of the population. Also in the religious sphere a diversity of ideas exist, especially in those areas where Protestants represent a considerable portion of the population. And since the most remote village is now in contact with the outside world, the Latin American continent is now participating in the pluralism of the world society.

It should not be difficult to understand why, in such circumstances, a pastoral program based merely on conserving the faith is wholly inadequate. Yet time and again this is what one finds in operation. The characteristics of this conservative program are, first of all, the grouping of the masses into collective pastoral structures, and secondly, a priestly leadership based on authority. The larger the size of the pastoral structures the less personalized they become, and because of cultural transformations, they become more formal and external. Moreover, this system makes pastoral labors more burdensome and encourages manifestations of authority.

Assuring the transmission of the faith and essential Christian values must not be identified with a pastoral program of conservation. In fact, to adopt conservative pastoral methods would be to ignore deliberately the fact that there will be an increase of 400 million inhabitants in the next 35 years, that they will form a new society and a new culture, and that new methods must be utilized if Christians are to be prepared to cope with the social transformations and their apostolic mission in a new world.

Let's be concrete. The system in the rural regions (the only place where it is still possible) consists in assuring a minimum of control over religious behavior by occasional visits, while concentrating action on the center of the village. Because of the phenomenal population growth, pastors find it difficult to insist on more than external religious observances. Since the leadership is almost exclusively clerical, the work becomes all the more demanding as responsibilities multiply with the ever-increasing number of souls to care for.

Modern means of communication are sometimes used, but only to strengthen the system. A jeep can help the priest to service the parish with more apparent effectiveness. A loud-speaker on the church tower can assure a wider broadcasting of orders, even to those who are not present at Sunday Mass. Thus is avoided creating new roles in pastoral activity and developing a lay leadership.

This pastoral tradition is perfectly understandable, but nevertheless disfunctional in the present circumstances. It is not limited to Latin America. With a few cultural differentiations one still encounters similar situations on all continents.

14

The Practice of Religion

Latin America is a continent of great complexity and there has not yet been compiled a workable inventory of religious data, although the studies initiated by FERES have unearthed considerable information. Much additional study and research will be necessary, therefore, before more definitive results and conclusions can be reached.

It would be of interest, however, to scan the existing material, put it in some kind of order, and attempt an outline of a religious sociology. This would provide at least certain working hypotheses for the future, and food for thought concerning pastoral activity.[1] We synthesize our material around two major aspects: religious practices and (in the next chapter) religious motivations.

THE SACRAMENTS

Most of the Latin American countries indicate that about 90% of their population is baptized. This has been verified from many sources. Mexico and Central America have even higher ratios: 95% and 98%.[2] Other countries fall below 90% (in Cuba it is only 73%).[3] Moreover, in some coastal regions, as in Ecuador, less than half of the population is baptized.[4]

While a very high proportion of the Latin American population is baptized, certain neglected regions show a relatively high ratio

164

of non-baptized infants, and it seems that the over-all trend of the continent is slightly downward. But only reliable national statistics could verify this hypothesis. Unfortunately, present data do not give a general and uniform view; more precise studies are necessary.

The same precise information is lacking on First Communion figures, which could be very easily recorded from year to year. The figures that are available are higher than those for the annual Easter duty, but they are far below the number of baptisms, which fact suggests that a strong minority, and possibly a majority, of the population has not received formal religious instruction. In Central America in 1955, 70% of the population made their First Communion,[5] but in the Dominican Republic only 30% (of the children), in Puerto Rico—31%, in Cuba—23%.

Regarding Holy Communion, it might be well to mention that in some countries, entire regions have a strong devotion to First Friday Communion. Devotion to the Sacred Heart and First Friday practices are on the increase, in spite of the long, tedious hours of standing in line for Confession the Thursday before.

Religious marriages seem to be proportionately lower than the fulfillment of the Easter duty in several countries. In Central America 40% of the marriages are performed in the Church; other figures: 63% in Puerto Rico, 50% in the Dominican Republic, and only 28% in Cuba. In Mexico the percentage depends upon the number of priests in the area. These figures are substantiated by the number of illegitimate children in these countries. In Cuba 40% of the children are illegitimate, in Puerto Rico — 36%, in the Dominican Republic — 60%, and in Jamaica — 63%. It is known that in several regions of Venezuela, illegitimate children account for 80% of the births. In Bogotá, a very cursory survey of the parishes on the southern end of town disclosed that from 10% to 30% of the parents were not legally married.

Concerning Confirmation, the Sacrament of the Sick, and Confession, we have only sporadic information. The figures for Confessions seem to follow those for Communions. The Confirmation figures for Mexico show great variation from one region to another, the minimum for a diocese being 25%, with an over-all average of 75%. In Cuba, for the same period (1955), 25% of the population was confirmed, while in the Dominican Republic, 80%, and in Puerto Rico, 92%. Information on the Sacrament of the Sick is even more rare: five Mexican dioceses give figures below 25%, two dioceses between 25% and 30%, one diocese 65%, and ten dioceses higher than 75%.

SUNDAY MASS

The *Herder Korrespondenz* relates that the conference of Latin American bishops in June, 1958, concluded that Sunday observance on the continent amounted to 3.5% of the men and 9.5% of the women. We presume these figures concern the adult population.[6]

A report on Argentina, Chile, Paraguay and Uruguay indicates that the proportion of practicing Catholics is between 15% and 30%.[7] The highest rate of religious observance is in the small cities, while the large cities and rural areas have very low percentages. Only 10% of the people in Buenos Aires attend Mass on Sunday.[8] In Paraguay, the estimates of a "reliable source" place the attendance there between 15% (Encarnación) and 25% (Villarcia). At Asunción and Concepción it is about 20%. An inquiry conducted in 1951 by the seminarians of the diocese of Melo, Uruguay (172,000 inhabitants, 1 bishop, 8 diocesan priests, and 7 religious priests) revealed that only 5% of the faithful went to Mass on Sunday.

In Chile, the research conducted by the *Oficina de Sociologia Religiosa,* which functions under the control of the Episcopacy and uses most reliable methods, furnishes the following data: Chile can be divided into three religiously different zones: the north, the south and the central region. The north and the south have Sunday observance rates that fluctuate between 8% and 12% (Arica, 6%; Inquique, 12%). Similar figures are found in the south: Valdivia, 12.3%, with great diversity among the extreme parishes. The figures for the cities of the central region are between 12% and 25%: Talca, 12%; San Felipe, 17%; Los Andes, 23.3%; Curico, 25%; with a high and low among the parishes of 28% and 3%. The parishes of Santiago have analogous percentages.

In Sucre, Bolivia, 23% of the Catholics were practicing in 1954. A similar situation existed in Cochabamba.

At Caracas, Venezuela, an extensive survey in 1954 revealed that 13% of the Catholics attend Sunday Mass. Figures for other cities were calculated the same year: Merida, 31%; Trujillo, 17%; and Valera, 14%. In 1960, in the diocese of San Cristobal —the best in Venezuela, it seems, from the point of view of religious observance—it was found that 19.9% of Catholics over 7 years of age practice their religion, but parishes vary between 38.2% and 3.5%. In the country regions of Venezuela, Sunday Mass attendance is generally below 20%, and in some extreme cases, almost nonexistent.

On Brazil we possess only fragmentary information and estimates. William J. Coleman proposes an over-all figure of 10% practicing Catholics.[9]

In Colombia, certain dioceses enjoy a much higher level of observance: the figure advanced by Coleman is 15% or more.

For Mexico, the report already cited indicates that in 12 dioceses religious observance runs between 5% and 25%; in 16 dioceses, between 30% and 60%; in 6 dioceses, between 75% and 98%; and 2 dioceses claim complete observance.

With the above general statistics as a base, we can, with great reserve and pending further study, hazard the following conclusions concerning Sunday religious observance in Latin America. In the cities, the high and low for religious observance is 5% and 30%, with an average probably not higher than 17% or 18%. There are some exceptional city parishes whose Sunday Mass attendance goes over 50%. In the rural areas where the clergy is still present, the rate can go as high as 75%, but the average seems to be about 20%. It seems useless, if not impossible, to speak about the vast territories where there are no resident priests and no regular Masses. Religious observance in these areas would naturally be very weak. The coastal regions have particularly low percentages; but it does not seem to depend solely on the presence or absence of priests. As to the Indian populations, their religious problems are related to general traits, of which we shall speak later, and particular circumstances which often date back to the religions existing before the arrival of Columbus, and which unfortunately cannot be treated within the limits of the present work.[10]

OTHER CEREMONIES AND THE MISSIONS

The surveys conducted on the subject of various devotions, pilgrimages, missions, etc., are too incomplete to draw any sure conclusions. The influence of the Basilica of Guadeloupe and other shrines of the Blessed Virgin, the throngs that take part in local processions and in the feasts of patron saints, the masses that visit churches of renown or are stirred by the missions, all this is well known outside Latin America.

But one should not let himself be misled by these phenomena. First of all, they are not universal. The missionary preachers of Ecuador have noted an almost total indifference in some coastal regions. Secondly, the results of the pilgrimages and missions are not always very durable. And thirdly, a closer look at these throngs would reveal many pertinent factors. Numerically speaking, the proportion of the population taking part in these religious devotions is steadily diminishing. Next, just what part of the population is represented in these masses? We have personally attended processions, rosaries, Benedictions of the Blessed Sacrament, where the older and feminine elements of the population made up the great majority of the congregation. The younger elements were led there by nuns or school teachers; thus their desire for a personal participation can certainly be questioned. Lastly, what are the cultural levels and personality-types of the participants? It is not sure that they would correspond to those needed by the leaders of tomorrow.

This kind of analysis must be pursued, but one thing seems certain: a hope of renewal and progress cannot be founded on the participation in these services and devotions unless the content of these services and devotions are renewed. And that will not come about automatically.

Some studies by reliable authors on popular devotion in Paraguay, Costa Rica,[11] Honduras, and Mexico show that the religious content of the external forms of worship vary to a great extent from one country to another. It seems, however, that in most cases the feasts (local feasts or family celebrations) in the popular milieux, and particularly among the Indians and mestizos, have only a weak religious significance and are rarely in accord with the moral principles of the Church. These feasts are usually an occasion for worldly entertainments, often accompanied by excessive drinking.

The faith of the Paraguayan people is vigorous and never ceases to astonish the outsider. Among the manifestations of a religious nature, especially worthy of note are the processions, in which participate a large number of faithful, perfectly disciplined and very enthusiastic.

The families have the custom of praying before and after meals and gather in the evening for the recitation of the rosary. At the end of the rosary the children ask the blessing of their parents. The same tokens of filial respect are shown to the godparents,[12] close relatives and especially to priests. Another indication of the religious nature of the people is their custom of frequently invoking Divine Providence.

It should be noted that in a surprising spirit of sacrifice the Paraguayan people accept all for the love of God. In the difficult moments of life there is a great use of the sacramentals: the imposition of ashes, the use of holy water, etc. Holy Week is observed in all parts of the country and there is a great devotion to the Way of the Cross.

In the country areas of Costa Rica, men and women assist piously at Sunday and weekday Masses. Religious pictures are hung throughout the home, although sometimes the veneration given a patron saint exceeds that given God or his Holy Mother.

Rosaries of the Infant Jesus and vigils for the dead are the most interesting manifestations of religious fervor. Entire families gather in a house to recite the rosary and alternate the mysteries with genuine folksongs.[13]

In the eyes of the outside observer, the religious part of many of the feasts seems only the crowning of a worldly ceremony at which the group re-creates and recreates. All observers are struck by the close association the popular conscience makes between ceremony and excessive drinking, particularly among the Indians. Some priests refuse to cooperate with such feasts, even though they are a considerable source of revenue. It seems to them that the gestures and ceremonies that one expects of the priest have lost all their Christian or religious meaning—if indeed they ever had this meaning. Perhaps, therefore, conclusions concerning the religion of the people should not be based on the great popularity of these feasts. We shall return to this point in the next chapter, where we shall try to determine the "quality" of this religion.

RELIGIOUS OBSERVANCE ACCORDING TO AGE, SEX, CULTURAL LEVEL AND SOCIAL CLASS

If general statistics are so rare, rarer still are specific breakdowns into age, sex, cultural level, and social classes. There are several reasons for this. First of all, there are usually no civil statistics with which religious statistics can be compared. Secondly, the *liber status animarum* is not ordinarily brought to light, and for a very good reason. Precise questionnaires are not practical because of the high rate of illiteracy, so that the only possible way of obtaining information, except concerning the educated class, is by personal interview. This is the method utilized by the University Catholic Action of Cuba,[14] but it is far from ideal. Since persons in a direct personal interview often tend to exaggerate the frequency of their religious practices, their answers will not be too reliable.

TABLE 10

Church Membership in Cuba according to Age

(survey conducted in 1957)

Age	Claimed To Be Catholic	Claimed To Be Indifferent	Claimed To Be Protestant	Other Answers
18 to 25	65%	24%	9%	2%
25 to 50	77	15	5	3
50 and older	82	10	7	1

A glance at Table 10 shows clearly that the younger generations are less and less considering themselves Catholics.

Similar tendencies are found in an inquiry made by the Institute of Sociological Investigation of the University of Chile:[15] whereas 86.9% of the total sample declared themselves Catholic, the proportion fell to 80% among those between 18 and 24 years of age.

The practice of religion, on the other hand, follows an opposite trend: it falls off with age. In the central area of Chile, 50% of the youth between 11 and 15 years of age practiced their religion; in the 16 to 20 age group the proportion lowered to 22%; and for those between 21 and 30 years old it plunged to 10%.

Religious attitudes in Costa Rica follow the same evolution that is observable in most Latin American Catholic countries, with some differences between the urban and rural populations. The piety acquired in childhood passes through a phase of systematic secularization during adolescence, and finally dissolves into agnosticism. The young students of the Catholic schools are not completely immune to this process, except the youth who take part in the Catholic Action movements.[16]

The figures by social class are equally significant. In Cuba, it is in the lower class (which represents 57% of the population) that one finds the most indifference and the least percentage of avowed Catholics. The figure for avowed Protestant membership is also important: 7%. In the upper class everyone claims to be Catholic, but this class comprises only 1% of the population.

TABLE 11

Church Membership in Cuba according to Social Class (1957)

Social Class	% of the Population	Catholics	Protestants	Indifferent	Other
Lower	57%	67%	7%	25%	1%
Lower middle	32	82	7	9	2
Upper middle	10	88	—	11	—
Upper	1	100	—	—	—

In Chile, by way of contrast, the educated and professional circles have a lower percentage of individuals who declare themselves Catholics: 74% of professional people, 67% of individuals with a college education, 87% of those who went no further than secondary school, and 90% of those who completed only their elementary education. But Sunday observance follows an inverse trend, similar to the situation in European countries: the lower classes, especially the workers, have an extremely low rate: 2 to 4%, if the figures obtained in the working-class parishes have any validity.[17]

Just as in Europe, and perhaps even more so, women are more faithful to religious duties than men. In some countries, however, particularly in the southern part of the continent, a change has recently been observable. "The increase (since 1931) in male attendance is quite worthy of note," writes Msgr. Francesco Vives.[18] Raimondo Sanchez de Lozada remarked the same development in Bolivia:

Most of the members of the leading social classes claim to be Catholic. Their religion, however, is rather sentimental and superficial. Their religious training varies in completeness, but it is better than that of the lower classes. As to the practice of religion, it was for a long time relegated to the women. But for some years now, there has been a noticeable increase in male participation. A liberal spirit dominates, however, and there is a quite pronounced tendency to reconcile religion and private interests rather than conform personal behavior to religious precepts. This tendency is a major obstacle to the rechristianization movement launched by Catholic Action. Morally speaking, these groups are quite heterogeneous. In such an atmosphere, the rate of divorce followed by a second marriage is very high. Religious training has progressed, however, and is affecting many individuals, transforming a sentimental religion into a deep conviction. One enemy of religious observance has been conquered: human respect. It is no longer uncommon today to see many men receiving Communion before work. One is no longer looked down upon for being a practicing Catholic. The number of men making their Easter duty has doubled since 1939.[19]

We have at our disposal a rather thorough study of the "young intellectual" of Colombia by the Spanish Augustinian priest, Paciano Fermoso.[20] It should be noted that the figures contained therein are not the result of direct observations, but calculated according to the responses of those questioned. We find that 43 per cent of the male students (university and secondary school combined) claim not to miss more than three Sunday Masses annually; for girl students the figure is 79 per cent. Nine per cent of the girl students and 33 per cent of the boys admit missing more than 9 Masses a year. Table 12 isolates the results for university students.

TABLE 12

Sunday Observance of University Students in Colombia,
according to Sex and Type of University (1959)

Frequency	State Universities		Private Universities	
	Male Students	Females	Male Students	Females
Never miss	15%	40%	17%	49.5%
Miss 3 times a year or less	15	28.5	19.5	24.5
Miss 4 to 8 times	22	19	20.5	16
Miss more than 8 times	48	12.5	43	10

Concerning the Easter duty, only 11 per cent of the male students and 1 per cent of the females said that they did not make it.

More than half of the students thought that their political party was more important than the Church. The number of students, especially girls, in the Catholic Action groups seems high, "but many of them, rather than concentrate their efforts on fellow students, do active work with other groups and with other social levels. In other words, they cannot be thought of as belonging to a university apostolate."[21] The author concludes on a pessimistic note: "The universities, principally co-educational institutions and institutions for men, are sadly neglected from the point of view of religion."[22]

The only other universities for which we have statistics on Sunday observance are the two universities of Caracas. In 1960 the figures were 7 per cent at the national university and 13 per cent at the Catholic university.

We have no percentages for the students in Chile, but we know that the prestige of the Christian Democrat group, animated by the university Catholic Action movement, which itself was created in 1956, has grown steadily. In 1958 the Christian Democrats came out on top in the university elections.

By way of conclusion, it seems safe to say that, at least in some countries, the newer generations are less Catholic than the old. Women and girls practice their religion more regularly than men and boys. The children practice more than the adults. It seems foreseeable that the youth of today will follow the example of their elders and partially abandon their religious duties as they grow older. Moreover, since there are less Catholics among the new generations, it seems predictable, all things being equal, that religious observance will be even lower among the adults of tomorrow, especially among the men.[23]

However, one should not be hypnotized by the statistics on religious participation. The nature and motivations of this participation are just as important as crude figures for the future of

Christianity and the Church. If it is probable that some of the percentages will descend even lower in the near future, it is also probable that the quality of Latin American Christianity will become steadily purified and less dependent on exterior circumstances. We are given to hope so by the present renewal in some countries (sometimes truly prodigious) of the apostolate and pastoral activity. This higher-quality Christianity of tomorrow can prepare a quantitative progress in the more distant future—if a truly radical solution can be found to the acute shortage of priests.

NOTES

1 This chapter and the following are a résumé of the book of Emile Pin, S.J., *Elementos para una sociologia del catolicismo latino-americano* (Bogotá: FERES, 1963).

2 Statistics taken from an anonymous report made in 1955.

3 Two independent studies agree on this point: one made in 1955 on the religious state of Cuba and other areas of the Caribbean, and an investigation conducted by the university Catholic Action group of Cuba.

4 *Report on the Recent Mission in Ecuador* (1960).

5 *Report on the Religious Situation in Latin America* (1955).

6 *Herder Korrespondenz*, No. 13 (1958–59), p. 2.

7 *Report on the Religious Situation in Argentina, Chile, Uruguay and Paraguay* (1955).

8 Results released by CISOR (The Center for Socio-Religious Investigations of Buenos Aires), based on several surveys whose total figures had already been published.

9 William J. Coleman, *Latin American Catholicism* (Maryknoll, N.Y.: Maryknoll Publications, 1958), p. 31.

10 See Emile Pin, S.J., *op. cit.* (the chapter on the Indians).

11 R. Bogarin, the chapter on Paraguay, pp. 366–67; Jaime Fonseca, the chapter on Costa Rica, pp. 159–60, in Richard Pattee, *El Catolicismo contemporaneo en Hispano-América* (Buenos Aires: Fides, 1951).

12 Sponsorship at baptism has a great significance in most of the Latin American countries and establishes important secular obligations. See D. H. Salman, "Parrainage et 'compadrazgo' " *Social Compass*, Vol. VII (1960), pp. 299–306.

13 R. Bogarin, *op. cit.*

14 A survey conducted before the Castro revolution. Results were mimeographed.

[15] See Renato Poblete, *La prática religiosa en Chile* (Fribourg: FERES, 1963).

[16] Jaime Fonseca, in Richard Pattee, *op. cit.*, p. 157.

[17] Information communicated by the *Oficina de Sociologia Religiosa*.

[18] Msgr. Francesco Vives, the chapter on Chile in Richard Pattee, *op. cit.*, p. 195.

[19] Raimondo Sanchez de Lozado, the chapter on Bolivia, in Richard Pattee, *op. cit.*, pp. 79–80.

[20] Paciano Fermoso, *Religiosidad del joven culto colombiano* (Bogotá: 1960).

[21] *Ibid.*, p. 211.

[22] *Ibid.*, p. 211. Also see the same author's article "Religiosité du jeune Colombien," in *Social Compass*, Vol. VIII, No. 1 (1961), pp. 49–60.

[23] Dardo Regules, the chapter on Uruguay, in Richard Pattee, *op. cit.*, pp. 433–34.

15

Religious Motivations

If the available data on the practice of religion in Latin America were less than satisfactory for drawing the conclusions of the preceding chapter, precise information concerning religious motivations is almost nonexistent. On this subject, therefore, we are reduced to proposing a few hypotheses suggested to us by observable characteristics.

THE SATISFACTION OF NATURAL ASPIRATIONS

All peoples experience natural aspirations (personal, family, tribal, and national) that they are not capable of satisfying by their own industry. Every man spontaneously feels the need of recourse to gods or to God. The rites which comport this recourse to the supernatural can be furnished by an established religion, nevertheless these rites are personalized by the individuals using them. This utilization may or may not correspond to the original purpose of the rites. Furthermore, it sometimes happens that established religions create rites that are specifically adapted to satisfy the natural aspirations of its members.

One of the principal characteristics of this type of religious life is that the rite is oriented to "natural" needs: the personal health of the individual or of those dear to him, his material or affective well-being, the pre-eminence of his family or clan, his concern for the deceased of his family, or the protection against cosmic forces and exterior evils. In these cases, the religious rite is not primarily oriented toward a modification of his personal moral life.

The contents of this rite, consequently, do not have to be meaningful, that is, have a direct rapport to his personal moral behavior. The rite, in and by itself, is expected to obtain a result that is believed unobtainable by personal efforts. The rite, therefore, has an intrinsic power and is pervaded with "mystery."

An extensive study would not be necessary to reveal these very traits in the popular religion of most of the Latin American countries with which we are acquainted. The same observations could probably be made in many other Catholic countries. However, we shall not attempt to establish in these pages any kind of comparisons; they would be neither scientific nor fair.

Brief studies made in Brazil, Buenos Aires, Chile, and Colombia have convinced us that the most frequent intentions in the prayers of the people are "natural" needs. A pastor in Bogotá sums up the opinion of his fellow priests (in 20 parishes of south Bogotá): "Masses are ordinarily requested for someone deceased or for the Poor Souls in general (in order to obtain through their intercession some material 'graces'). The most frequent prayers are those asking for success in temporal affairs and undertakings."

These traits, that the well-informed Christian will perhaps judge as negative, must not take away from more praiseworthy characteristics of the Latin American Catholic, notably his confident piety toward God, the Blessed Mother and the saints. But the two tendencies go hand in hand: it is precisely because God is looked upon as a very personal Father, that He is asked to provide daily needs. The Latin American people have a permanent fear of *mal suerte,*[1] and they expect religion with its rites to protect them. This explains both a certain passivity—and we shall come back to this point—and a constant prayer for divine intervention or a miracle.

It should cause little wonderment that this type of religious expectation would give rise to corresponding rites in the established churches: for example, the devotions organized around the "saints for hopeless causes." In fact, these devotions are a means of subsistence for the parishes or religious orders that organize them. Is not the success of spiritism and other cults due to this same type of religiosity? Not having to maintain the same universal standards as Catholicism, they can organize these rites in an even more "functional" way.

The second trait proper to this type of religious motivation is its unrelatedness to the ethical life of the person participating in the rite. Here again many cases could be cited. It is perhaps not exceptional for prayers to be inspired by rather dubious motives, like the young man who made a novena of Communions in honor of the Blessed Virgin for success in an adulterous love affair.

Msgr. Gustavo J. Franceschi attributed this mentality to the lack of religious instruction which characterized the colonial period. "There resulted a very sincere but ignorant religiosity, a faith mixed with superstitions, a vaporous sentimentality. This is why moral deviations were unaffected; one prayed to the Virgin, but one lived in concubinage."[2]

The third consequence of this spiritual orientation is that the rite contains scarcely any meaning in itself. Its relationship to the result is automatic, it requires no effort, no action on the part of the participant. All that matters is that the rite be well performed. A Colombian peasant who was asked how he treated his trees against insects answered that the year before he had used *rezos*,[3] but that he had bad results. The reason he gave was that the "reciter" did not know the formula very well. That particular year, however, since he could not find a good "reciter" he had to use a chemical product. We are here not very far from magic.

Even the liturgical services of the Church, as conducted in Latin America, do not seem to fall completely outside the category of rites we have been discussing. Coupled with the difficulty of the Latin language (which in these circumstances only serves to intensify the atmosphere of "mystery") is the almost total absence of attempts to give the rites a meaning. Promulgation of a ritual in the Spanish language has been long awaited. The gestures of the priest are either invisible, because of the great distance between him and the people, or they are performed with lightning rapidity. During Mass there is a continuous entrance and exodus of the congregation, children run in the aisles, babies cry, the adults carry on a conversation. The faithful rarely use a missal; they simply wait, impatiently, for the end of the ceremony, which to most of them is incomprehensible. There are even churches where several kinds of ceremonies are going on at the same time: Masses, baptisms, devotions to some saint, and all this accompanied by the distribution of Holy Communion (at the most unexpected parts of the Mass) and a sermon that has nothing to do with the Eucharistic celebration at the altar. Other variations of the liturgy are: an absolute silence, or the recitation of the rosary, or musical accompaniment which is supposed to elevate the soul, but which teaches nothing about the meaning of the prayers of the Mass.

In addition to the doctrinal objections that could be levied against this type of religious motivation and the rites which correspond to it, there can be mentioned the doubly disfunctional character they bear: they encourage the transfer to other "religions" better adapted than the Catholic Church in satisfying the natural religious aspirations, notably to spiritism.

Secondly, the maturing technical and rational mentality proper to urban civilizations will be quick to discern the vanity of these ritualistic expectations. Unfortunately, the effect will not be a purification of religious motives, but rather a reaction against a religion that will be looked upon as a collection of useless rites.

These motivations do not engender the feeling of belonging to the Church, nor do the religious services adapted to these motivations create such a feeling. The Church does not appear as a religious society to which each member is conscious of belonging, but rather as an organization which possesses sacred things, or an administration whose employees have sacred powers and to whom one goes and bargains with for obtaining specified results. The hierarchy and the priests are "sacred technicians," respected because of their contact with the world of "Power," but not necessarily loved and followed as leaders to whom one can be close in good times as well as bad.[4] Requesting a sacrament or a spiritual service from a priest is not necessarily a psycho-sociological sign of membership in the Church. Such a request might have personal motivations, or even motivations not officially approved by the religious group.

OBEDIENCE TO THE RELIGIOUS NORMS OF THE NATURAL GROUP

If the above type of Catholicism can be called "popular," we might conveniently refer to the type of Catholicism we shall now discuss as "cultural"—the word here having a broader meaning than when used by Redfield. We are speaking of a Catholicism more or less identified with the culture of the individual and which he feels obliged to adopt in order to define himself or to be faithful to the group to which he belongs. It is a label for which he feels a great need, for without it he would not be sure who he is. He accepts en bloc everything this label implies. Since the label is a result of birth and not of choice, he considers it a right and does not concern himself with its real meaning: to be a Latin American (or Argentinean, Chilean, Colombian, Mexican, as the case may be) is to be a Catholic. One does not look to the Church to define Catholicism, but to culture, tradition and custom. The priest, in this case, is not a leader of the community who must be obeyed, but a servant of both national and religious culture. His word is not valued so highly as custom; in fact, he must submit to custom if he is to be accepted. "He was good," they said of a pastor who had just died. "He knew all our customs. He never interfered; he was everybody's friend."[5]

Custom, in its religious aspects, is often reduced to a few

essential acts whose character is more cultural than properly religious, or expressed in another way, whose role is the sacralization of social events. The rites mark the principal moments of existence or turning points in life, and make them exist socially, such as baptism, First Communion (which is equivalent to an initiation), marriage, and burial. Certain practices may deepen this impression: in some countries where the Church takes care of civil functions, to be born is to be baptized; and not to be baptized is, in a certain sense, not to exist legally.

Culture can be even more demanding. It can happen, especially on the more educated levels of society, that the consciousness of being a Catholic is accompanied by the knowledge of what this label implies. The attachment to tradition is thus "imbued" with a more authentic Catholicism and the Church is given the right to define it. Nevertheless, the Church is not considered as a society to which one belongs, but rather as a public servant of the culture, somewhat subordinate to it, with scarcely any authority to modify, control or judge it.[6] The "subversive" role of the Church appears considerably reduced, and when one of its priests takes the liberty of pointing out the opposition between cultural norms and the demands of the Gospel, he is often denounced as a Protestant or a "Communist."[7] This conscious defense of culture and society, with which is combined an obedience to so-called "Catholic" cultural norms and a refusal to let the Church pass judgment on this culture, is more frequent among the upper classes, for they assimilate more thoroughly than the other classes the culture of the society in which they participate. One has only to consider the upper-class reaction to recent episcopal declarations on social problems in Colombia, Peru, Chile, Brazil, Paraguay, and Uruguay.

Submission to this religious-cultural superego is a question of survival and psychological security for the members of these classes. A spontaneous and unconscious cultural motivation, however, is to be found among the popular classes. The culture which orients the profane and religious aspects of their behavior has its source—at least its immediate source—in tradition and in the common good of the village or region. This unconscious attachment is much weaker than in the upper classes. No doubt for the less fortunate members of society, as for all men, the ethos is a necessary condition for collective survival. But any ethos, at least in its totality, has value only within a given system of social relationships, only within a specific socio-economic structure. As long as this structure cannot be modified, the ethos is imperative and each individual remains attached to it; but if men, especially the less fortunate, see the possibility of modeling a new socio-economic structure, and if this structure is presented to them in very specific details and popularized by an expertly devised propaganda, replete with illustrations[8]—as is the case with Communist propaganda—then it is quite possible that attachment to the former ethos, and more generally to the former culture, will not long endure. This explains the sudden veering of populations who were believed to be solidly rooted in their traditions.

Since the attachment to religious practices is so tightly bound up with a cultural attachment, there is a real danger that it will not survive social upheavals. In the individuals of the upper classes, such a cultural motivation might engender melancholy remembrances of the beauty of past times and the secret hope of a cultural and religious restoration, but it is doubtful that in times of persecution this motivation will raise up many defenders of religion. And since the attachment to religion is so closely allied with the attachment to culture, these defenders might very easily compromise the cause of the Church and transform it into a politico-cultural cause.[9] We have already said that the popular strata of society do not have the same reasons for defending their culture as the upper classes. It is possible, then, that the controlling classes' defense of the Church might be in the eyes of the popular masses a symbol of political conservatism, and this could provide valuable ammunition for the adversaries of the Church.

Awareness of the dangers of an imperfect type of motivation can help to re-emphasize a fundamental Christian truth: eternal salvation is accomplished not through a natural, but through a supernatural membership in the Church. In final analysis, this membership must rest on faith in the Church, the Mystical Body of Christ, distinct from all natural societies. Where attempts have been made to instill this sentiment in small groups (by Catholic Action, the Legion of Mary, Marian Congregations, neighborhood cells, etc.) it has blossomed into fidelity to a persecuted Church, even to the point of martyrdom.

"Cultural" motivation seems to us to be quite widespread in Latin America, both in its popular form and in its conscious form. Its popular form shows up in the fiestas, which we have already described,[10] and the resistance that the clergy encounters in its efforts to define a more authentic Catholicism. Some priests say that they are expelled from villages when they try to combat the drunkenness and disorders that accompany the feasts. The people treat them as Protestants, so closely is their Catholicism allied to their local customs. Other priests feel they must close their eyes and materially cooperate with public and family feasts which occasion conduct condemned by the Church. They fear that a refusal on their part would only bring about the complete abandonment of religious practices. This fear is justified, but it shows what motivations inspire these practices.[11]

Such inconsistencies are not found in the upper classes, or when they do exist they are not related to the practice of religion.[12] In these classes, cultural Catholicism is characterized by a confusion between the interests of the national community, such as they are understood by the controlling groups and by the Church. This confusion breeds a mentality that divides the world into two camps: the good people and the bad people. Evil is not conceived as something interior, born in the heart of man, but as the existence of a threatening and despicable "out-group." It is rather common for this mentality to view the problems of Latin American Catholicism in terms of purely exterior dangers: Protestantism, spiritism, Communism, secularism, etc.[13]

It should not be necessary to point out that this motivation, like all others, is not a prerogative of Latin America. But it seems to us that there are many indications of its presence, and its consequences in the exceptionally rapid changes the continent is undergoing.[14]

THE PURSUIT OF SALVATION, OR THE SPIRITUAL INTERNALIZING OF RELIGIOUS NORMS

By spiritual internalizing we mean the superior motivation that looks upon religion as an interior transformation through which eternal salvation is achieved. A man inspired with such a motivation will give himself to such religious "practices" as prayer and reception of the sacraments, and will strive to conform his behavior to the norms imposed by religion.

Within this definition, several sub-types can be distinguished, corresponding to the different schools of spirituality acceptable to Christianity. We shall analyze only two extreme types, which we shall call an individualistic religion of eternal salvation, and a communal religion of spiritual transformation.

The first type, or individualistic religion of salvation, is the least internalized of all the types we group under the general heading of spiritual internalization. Those who are inspired by this type of motivation are convinced of the truth of Christian faith, or at least convinced that Christianity represents the most probable hypothesis; they thus submit to its norms, insofar as these norms are necessary for their eternal salvation. In this type of religion, two elements play a major role: mortal sin and hell. Next in importance come Confession and certain devotions which are especially reassuring in regard to eternal salvation. A negative outlook characterizes this type of religion. It concentrates on the avoidance of sins that have been certainly catalogued as mortal. The less generous souls are content with a regular confession of the serious sins they have committed, but which they have not quite decided to avoid. This type of religion is also private, in the sense that membership in the Church is no more important than in the previous motivations analyzed. The difference lies in the kind of service expected from the "sacred employees"; in the present type it is eternal salvation, in the former types discussed, it is help in temporal affairs. This difference is reflected in the kind of esteem one holds for the priest, the legitimacy of his priesthood and his jurisdiction. Whereas priests under interdict might still exercise their ministry over persons animated with "cosmological" motivations, they stand very little chance of being accepted by persons motivated by their eternal salvation. But this attachment to the clergy and the Church does not include a feeling of membership. It simply signifies the desire to benefit from rites that are certainly efficacious. This same contrast is found among persons of the upper classes: they have the very deep awareness of their Catholic traditions and of belonging socially and culturally to a Catholic nation, but in their religious practices there is no specific sentiment of membership in the Church. They do not look upon the Church as a community of believers, but as an organization which, on the one hand, possesses the rites assuring eternal salvation, and on the other hand, sustains the socio-cultural edifice.

It would be a mistake to think that Latin America has a monopoly on this individualistic religion of eternal salvation; but there is no doubt that this form of religion does exist among the best Catholics of the continent, and that it is quite universally preached in the towns and taught in the schools. Many authors have noted that the sermons are concentrated on mortal sin, and the threat of hell recurs incessantly. Fr. Fermoso remarked about it several times in his study on the Colombian students.[15] We ourselves have personally witnessed it many times. The emphasis on these themes probably comes from the fact that the preachers have observed their effectiveness on a population that is both given to passion and penetrated with a tragic sense of existence. Time and time again observers have commented on this paradoxical combination in the Latin American character: an exuberant life filled with sentiment and passion leading at times to uncontrollable excesses, and a tragic religion, focused on death, expiation, and the fear of hell. The ceremonies and celebrations which often accompany Holy Week are a striking example.

Having analyzed the individualistic aspect of this type of religion, we would now like to call attention to a correlative often attributed to Latin countries in general and to Latin America in particular. Civil society in its economic and political aspects is poorly organized and suffers frequently from corruption, from a spirit of anarchy, in a word, from a genuine *anomie*.[16] It would certainly be imprudent to attempt to explain these failings simply by a type of religion. Both the type of religion and the form of the civil state are effects of deeper causes. Nevertheless, it must be noted that organized religion in some way remains an independent variable and can strengthen or weaken inherent tendencies. The point is, a religion too centered on the negative ideas of mortal sin and hell hardly does much to orient men toward a positive and permanent transformation of their life in its individual and social aspects. Moreover, this religious motivation, even though it has as its objective eternal salvation, that is, freedom from hell after death, does not attempt to come to grips with life here on earth, to control it, to give it a meaning. Religious sociologists have noted that when man is choked with the anguish of inevitable evils, he looks to religion to free him from these evils or, at least, to "do something about them."[17] Some religions or spiritualities will orient the action of the individual toward asceticism and thus make it effective;[18] others, on the contrary, will orient it toward the rites themselves which the individual will view as an end, even though the official significance of the rites is a transformation of life. The sacrament of Confession, wrongly understood, can so alleviate the anguish of the individual that he feels dispensed from any positive action. The same for other devotions which claim to guarantee salvation. The soul thus relieved coasts along until a new accumulation of sins creates an unbearable anguish, and again the rites remove the strain. The individual is liberated, but his life scarcely changes at all.

We do not pretend to judge such an attitude, nor to see in it any conscious duplicity or calculation. We only suggest that this type of religion ordinarily has as its correlative a certain social disorganization which at times is characterized by normlessness. These observations might perhaps explain the frequently noted paradox of a moralizing religion and a laxity in morals and social effectiveness. When one realizes the gigantic effort that charity demands in the face of contemporary social changes, one clings to the hope that this type of religious life will give way to another spirituality, even if in the past it showed itself capable of arousing those religious dispositions judged indispensable and sufficient for "assuring" eternal salvation.

The second type of spiritual internalization that we have chosen to discuss is what we call "the communal religion of spiritual transformation." In the general category of spiritual internalization this is situated at the opposite extreme from the type just described.

In the preceding type, it is true that evil is perceived as something internal, or more exactly, the "true" evil, hell, seems conditioned by moral evil, that is, mortal sin. However, insofar as hell is conceived as a punishment that is in some way exterior to sin, or insofar as sin is feared only because it leads to hell, this type of religion can not be said to consider the evil from which God delivers man as a truly interior evil of our nature, that is, as a deep-seated sin, a moral egocentrism by which man prefers himself to God or to others. It is even possible that the satisfaction that the individual derives from having "satisfied" his religious obligations will only serve to strengthen his self-sufficiency.

What characterizes, on the contrary, the type we are now describing is the consciousness that basic evil is neither cosmological nor socio-cultural, nor even hell, but interior egoism with its cortege of bad desires, and it is from this that we must ask God and his Church to deliver us. Such a perspective allows each individual to have a feeling of solidarity with all the sinners of the world and makes it impossible to divide the world into good people and bad. In such a perspective the sacraments are seen as the action of Christ, who wishes to cure our interior evil; and this action must overflow into daily life, if the sacraments are to be truly effective. In such a perspective the communal aspects of the Church are not secondary; they are the perfect answer to the evil we suffer; they not only express the death of egoism, they partially bring it about. The Church does not save us by organizing the distribution of sacraments, it is rather the sacraments which save us by giving us a share in the life of the Church. Political, social, and economic life is neither unrelated nor secondary, but the field where charity operates. Eternal salvation will follow, of course, but as the perfect revelation of an existence already transformed by Grace. This spirituality is one of permanent progress, a participation in the Church that becomes increasingly perfect, a spirituality of action. It appeases anguish by this action, but it never suppresses a certain uneasiness, because the desired goal, the perfect transformation of one's being, is never fully attained, any more than is the exterior social manifestation of this transformation, namely, justice and social equality.

This spirituality can already be found among numerous groups of Christians in Latin America, notably in the small Catholic Action groups. These small groups are not only spreading the knowledge of this spirituality, they are making its practical application possible by giving to each individual the conviction of belonging both to the world of sinful men on the road to spiritual progress, and to the Church in which this transformation takes place.[19]

In our opinion, it is only by systematically developing this communal spirituality of spiritual transformation, and the Church reorganization that it involves, that Latin America will be able to resolve—in the measure that it is still possible—the formidable difficulties that beset it, in particular, the shortage of priests, and its social and economic underdevelopment. We shall come back to this point presently, in our treatment of the final motivation capable of sustaining religious behavior: attachment to the religious group.

ATTACHMENT TO THE RELIGIOUS GROUP

The last motivation that can be the source of various religious practices is the attachment to the religious group. In this case, it is not to escape an evil fate, nor to be faithful to the cultural norms of the nation or village, nor directly to escape hell, that one baptizes his children, or goes to Sunday Mass or to Confession. It is rather because one feels he is a member of a community of believers and wishes to conform his behavior to the demands of this community. To get a better idea of the origin and consequences of this motivation, let us examine two cases.

This motivation is found quite frequently in countries where the Church is a minority. The religious group, threatened by the religion of the majority, closes its ranks and organizes against attack from without. The lukewarm souls fall away automatically, incapable as they are of resisting the psychological pressure of the majority. However, many of those who are by nature hesitant, once faced with an unequivocal choice, do take a vigorous stand rather than totally deny their convictions.[20] Each individual feels his own identity in jeopardy, and to preserve it, draws closer to the group to form a common front. This sentiment of belonging nourishes a spirit of discipline, obedience to the norms of the group, and attachment to its institutions. It is not necessarily accompanied by an internalizing of the norms themselves; what is internalized is membership, and this develops into an actual identification with the group so that, at least, it inspires a great fidelity to the group leaders. The religious leaders are not looked upon as mere "sacred employees" but as true heads to be both obeyed and protected by the group.

It would be unusual for such an attitude to develop in Latin America (at least for the reasons just mentioned), for in this case Catholics form a complete, or a very strong majority. But we mention this type of motivation by way of contrast, so that priests or Christians who are native to a country where Catholicism represents a minority might better understand the religious situation in

Latin America, in particular the attitude of the laity toward the clergy.

This distinction between the religious group and the rest of society, which is at the basis of this motivation, can also be the result of a conscious action of the Church itself. The Church can fashion its own structures, not only for its higher levels (which it always does), but even for its lower levels, the small groups where the feeling of belonging is directly instilled in the individual. Such is ordinarily not the case in Latin America. Below the parish level, the Latin American Church in centuries past had no real structures of her own. Does this mean that the laity was not integrated into primary groups where they could play a role, achieve a sense of personal responsibility, and control their religious behavior?

Certainly not. There could not have been such fidelity down through the centuries if there had not been such an elementary framework. But the microstructure in which the Christians were integrated was not the Church's own, it was borrowed from the natural and civil groups. These were the groups and leaders which assured Christian conformity in daily life. The Church's microstructure was really the social institutions: the family (patriarchal and conjugal), the local communities *(haciendas, fazendas, aldeas, fondos, veredas)*,[21] the work organizations, the schools, and the aristocratic circles. These social institutions, fully integrated as they were into the Catholic religion, not only abided by ethics and natural law as taught by the Church, but actively promoted the Church's religious norms (the sacraments, feasts, religious education) and the Church's discipline (pontifical and episcopal decrees). The structures of the Church and civil society were parallel but quite distinct on the upper echelons; on the lower levels of the parish and commune, however, the microstructures of the two were practically indivisible.

But changes have taken place. The conjugal family—and we shall examine this more closely—has lost a good deal of its control, and what control it has left is no longer used for the benefit of the Church, because the family itself is no longer integrated into other social units submitting to Church discipline. The patriarchal family has for the most part disappeared. The *hacienda,* the commune, the aristocratic councils have given way to impersonal and specialized administrations which have been secularized. This secularization is due partially to the specialization of modern administrations in which each employee performs a limited and specific job, and partially to an ideological evolution that tends toward a more complete separation of civil and religious matters. Even when civil society conforms to the ethics and morals taught by the Church, it no longer wishes to accept the responsibility of carrying out Church discipline. Natural and civil structures can no longer serve as a microstructure of the parish and of the Church. Without this borrowed microstructure, the parish finds it more difficult to transmit doctrine and duties, and to control families and individuals. The parish must now work with an unstructured mass of individuals, or a mass over whose structures it has no control. One should not then wonder at the relative powerlessness of the parishes, especially when, in addition to the above factors, one considers the population explosion, the migrations, and the shortage of priests.

The ineffectiveness of parish structures is particularly manifest in the field of religious instruction. It has long been known that the interest and attachment an individual accords to a doctrine is proportionate to his degree of affiliation to the group which promotes this doctrine. The most integrated persons are those who manifest most an identification with the thought patterns imposed by the group. The individuals who are marginal or exterior to the group might show a vague interest in its doctrine, they might claim that they "have the faith," but this declaration does not commit them to a deep knowledge and solid appreciation of the contents of this faith. The massiveness of parish structures is probably not the only explanation for religious ignorance; and to produce informed Christians, not only is a reorganization of parish structures necessary, but also a body of capable "instructors." These instructors, however, will achieve only minimal and discouraging results, unless they can count on the presence of primary groups in which the faith can be nourished and enlightened by daily contact with the faith of others. And since the Church can no longer rely on the natural and civil groups to furnish this indispensable microstructure, she must create one of her own.

The microstructure cannot be formed by the family alone. First of all, since it is integrated into larger social groups that are no longer submissive to the Church, the family itself (the conjugal family) is not always submissive to the Church. That does not mean that the religious motivations still present in many families cannot and should not be utilized. In the rural regions especially, the family has remained attached to numerous religious acts. Even today, it is the family that transmits the faith, a faith often mixed with error, yet a faith which brings the great majority of children to the baptismal font and a considerable part of the population to the confessional and Communion rail, and to the *despacho*[22] for marriages and burials. However, as we have already explained, one cannot count on these religious gestures, and the motivations which inspire them, to create the sentiment of belonging to the Church.

What must be done is to utilize the contacts occasioned by these religious gestures as a starting point for the integration of the individuals and families into a true microstructure. One institution that can powerfully aid the reintegration of Christians into a Church conceived as a society is sponsorship at baptism. Sponsorship in almost all the countries of the world has been greatly secularized. It is no longer unthinkable to designate as godparents non-practicing Catholics, freemasons, Communists, or sinners of some notoriety. For sponsorship to be truly effective in integrating the newly-baptized and newly-confirmed into the Church, it must be controlled by the Church and not by the family. It should be the religious group that designates the sponsors. In former times, since the Christian family was considered "the hub of the Church," the care of selecting sponsors was confided to it, in the hope that it would understand this task as a duty toward the Church rather than be preoccupied with its secular aspects. But today secular considerations are given more importance.

Another reason one cannot completely depend on the family, is that it has lost a large part of its traditional functions. It no longer constitutes for the individual, even for the adolescent, a milieu which controls him and on which he must totally depend. Even in the country it is no longer the single social unit in which the individual is inscribed. Independent of his family he can directly become a member of a school (especially a professional school), a university, a political party, a union, a cooperative, a sporting or recreational association, or an informal group of friends. And through these he participates much more directly in the life of society than through his family. No longer is the family the indispensable means for the adult or the adolescent (except the adolescents of particularly powerful families) to integrate into society. This independence from the family is further increased by the multiplication of the means of transportation and communication. If the Church would rely solely on the family to control individuals and their activities, she would run the risk of herself controlling a structure half-emptied of its functions and influence.

All this explains how the social changes of past centuries have little by little deprived the Latin American Church of the microstructure in which it was able to contain its faithful. It also makes somewhat understandable the at least apparent absence in many of the faithful today of the spirit of membership in the Church, as well as the fact that the practice of religion does not ordinarily seem motivated by an attachment to the religious group, to its leaders, and to its norms.

This absence of attachment does not imply the abandonment of religious practices. As we have seen, these can be inspired by other motivations. But it does signify that in the eyes of the faithful the Church is not a body, a community, and its ministers are not leaders of the community. The system formed by the Church and those who "use" it, is what sociologists would call a "simple system of relations with others" (G. Gurvitch). In itself, such a system of relations is incapable of engendering a feeling of membership, hence of fidelity and loyalty, in the strict sense of the words.

Certain indications lead us to believe that many parishes in Latin America, as well as many parishes in other traditionally Catholic countries, are more "systems of relations with others" than groups united by a common interest.[23]

Attachment to the religious group is not, however, completely absent in Latin America. It can be found in the groups formed by Catholic Action and by other movements which are striving to integrate the faithful by giving them a role to play, thus making them feel co-responsible for the life and progress of the Church. Only more extensive studies could give an exact idea of the relative number of faithful animated by such a motivation. Nor is it possible to know with scientific certitude which motivations habitually co-exist in an individual. We said at the beginning of this chapter that the extreme types of motivation seem to be mutually exclusive. This should be verified. It should be further verified if the "communal religion of spiritual transformation" and the "attachment to the religious group" (consciously structured) are habitually concomitant. Perhaps this concomitance is not coincidental, if it is true that Christianity is essentially a transformation of the soul through participation in the Mystical Body of Christ.

Let us recall once more that in the absence of precise psychosociological studies, we have had to limit ourselves to a series of hypotheses. These hypotheses seemed to us capable of explaining the few facts we have been able to gather, but they can in no way be considered a substitute for further serious investigation. Perhaps they can furnish a theoretical framework, a point of departure.

NOTES

[1] The word literally means "bad luck," but also can be interpreted as "evil fate."

[2] Msgr. Gustavo J. Franceschi, the chapter on Argentina, in Richard Pattee, *op. cit.,* p. 19.

[3] Prayer formulas.

[4] Raimondo Sanchez de Lozada, *op. cit.,* p. 79.

[5] From an unpublished report on the religion of the Bolivians (p. 18).

[6] This is an attitude that is by no means limited to Latin America. See Will Herberg, *Protestant, Catholic, Jew* (New York: Doubleday, 1955), especially chapters 7 and 9.

[7] It is often difficult to form an exact and adequate idea of Communism in Latin America because of the facility with which the tag "Communist" can be affixed to anyone wishing to reform society.

[8] The Chinese Communists distribute throughout all of Latin America an illustrated magazine which purports to show the beauty of family life in Communist China. Countless photos depict scenes of everyday life, simple people in an intimate and modern background. Everything is pervaded with the happiness of families and individuals perfectly integrated into an equalitarian Communist society.

[9] See Sanchez de Lozada, *op. cit.,* p. 66. The latter thinks it safe to say that certain Bolivian capitalists tried to utilize Catholic Action in the battle against Communism, not to defend the Church, but to protect their assets. A similar ambiguity can also be noted in the opposition to the Castro regime.

[10] The American anthropologist Ralph Beals says concerning the Indians and Ladinos (mestizos) of Mexico: "The Ladino is in part taking an active participation in his religious ceremonials for the purpose of the salvation of his own eternal soul. The Indian isn't; he is taking part in religious ceremonies to assure the continuance of the group, etc. He's not worried about his soul. I would say that the Catholic ideology plays a minor role." A discussion in: Sol Tax, *et al., Heritage of Conquest* (Glencoe, Ill.: Free Press, 1952), p. 218.

[11] In the report already cited, *Problèmes d'apostolat dans un diocèse brésilien*, the reasons for the adaptation of religion to culture are clearly presented. In spite of faults and weaknesses—and what form of Christianity is immune from them?—this adaptation has kept Christian faith alive in Brazil for more than four centuries and still constitutes a very strong line of defense against the invasion of foreign ideologies. It gives the country a culture, goals and a certain style of living. "The greater part of the Brazilian Church is still organized according to traditional structures. Ninety per cent of the people know no other form of religion and most of the clergy is adapted to it. The Brazilian priests in general are perfectly adapted,

and what the European priests consider faults are usually merely variations. The priests give many blessings and accept their role of thaumaturge. They are representatives of a social class. They have a fondness for decorum and eloquence. Their preaching aims to strengthen and solidify popular religion. The principal theme of their sermons is the blessing of God and the saints, and the ways to obtain it. There are many polemics against non-practicing Catholics, backsliders and heretics. One is astonished, at times, to see the seminarians' unconcern for learning theology. On the other hand, this theology would serve them little, for once in the parishes they will adopt and perpetuate the popular beliefs. The priests do not teach religion systematically. They do not teach catechism, not through negligence, but through custom. Religious instruction is not part of the traditions. The people have no desire for it. They do not see the need for it, any more than for education in general. They have no regard for school. They go as little as possible and use the best means available to avoid it. The priests interfere in neither the moral nor social life of the people. They do not concern themselves with a personal religion. This can be said in the main for the whole local clergy. But in general, the priests are devout, zealous, pious, and faithful to their duties."

This description is partially valid for Brazil, but could not be extended to all of Latin America. It does, however, give a good idea of "cultural" Catholicism and how the clergy can adapt to it. We shall raise only one question concerning these evaluations: Is it in any way certain that this traditional religion will be capable of resisting the foreign ideologies for a long time? It succeeded in the past, thanks to the permanence of the social structure; but the economic and social changes which are about to take place, the imbalances between regions, the increase of propaganda, the example of Cuba, the vicissitudes of Brazilian politics, all seem to favor internal changes in the country's Catholicism, and the Brazilian episcopacy has on several occasions shown itself quite aware of this development. Speaking more specifically of the Indians of Bolivia, who represent a type of religion even further removed from the official norms of Catholicism, the already mentioned report, *La religion des Boliviens* (p. 23), states: "Many Indians possess a deep, unshakable faith, even though it is beclouded with a host of superstitions and beliefs in the *pachamamma* and the magical power of the *coca* and *brujos*. In numberless villages which have not seen a priest for years, the 'teacher' continues to lead the prayers every day in Lent; the prayers sometime contain serious mistakes, but at least the people still pray. However, to take the attitude that nothing should be changed because the Indians are incapable of living an authentic religion and their faith endures in spite of its impurities, would be to let them advance on the road to unbelief and scepticism. Moreover, it seems quite unrealistic to hope that the minds of high school and university students, as well as the young industrial workers, are not troubled by questions and doubts. Their faith some day will be in grave danger, if Catholicism remains in their eyes a religion of Masses *'al Niñito'* (for the little Infant Jesus), of statues, sometimes confused with the saints themselves, of *responsos* (absolutions), of processions and the revelries which accompany them. On the other hand, it seems that the younger generations, even the former camp miners, have a real appreciation of the living liturgy, the Bible and Catholic Action."

[12] In the upper classes, by way of contrast, there is a noticeable tension between two ethical norms, especially in regard to sexual behavior: the ethical norm of the natural group is quite indulgent toward an aggressive masculine behavior, while the norm preached by the religious group is strict and punitive. Some resolve this tension by a complete submission to the religious norm, but most have recourse to a slightly ritualistic use of Confession, or give up the practice of religion entirely.

[13] See the first conclusion of the address of Dr. Horacio Terra to the Inter-American Conference of Catholic Action (Chimbote, Peru, 1953): *No hacer el Juicio Final en el tiempo dividiendo el mundo entre "reprobos" y "santos."* This division of the world into two camps, that is, the "in-group" to which one belongs and the evil "out-group" of non-Catholics, can lead to a complete break with a contemporary intellectual culture which is dismissed because it is not understood. We read in the report on Brazil already quoted: "The superiority complex of the clergy inhibits them from examining other positions; they thus underestimate other intellectual forces. They will not engage in discussion; they simply make haughty affirmations. It is ordinary policy not to admit the good faith of Protestants, positivists and freemasons. . . . In this context, the study of theology can remain very superficial. They have their manuals and stereotyped courses. As to secular culture, they hardly know it exists. It is generally limited to a knowledge of the poets . . . and the classical novelists of the last century. The contemporary writers, sociologists and novelists . . . are completely unknown to the clergy and to Catholic circles in general." (p. 53)

[14] We feel obliged to make clear that our remarks are not to be taken as moral judgments. The conditions we have been describing are the fruit of circumstances and difficulties which those charged with today's leadership did not create and are doing their best to cope with, according to the dictates of their conscience. We are only trying, through the insights provided by the historical evolutions which have accompanied the industrialization, urbanization and illiteracy of other countries, to measure the chances that the various forms of religion encountered in Latin America have of perpetuating themselves. We have the firm hope that Christianity will remain the religion of Latin America, but we are also convinced that its permanence will depend upon a more rapid process of internal transformation. True, this process has already begun, but we would at times like to see it more consciously, more rapidly, more universally carried out. Latin America is often referred to as a Catholic continent. This is not simply a myth. There is an undeniable reality involved. But what reality? As we

have tried to show, there are different ways of being a Catholic. All do not offer the same guarantees for the future of the Church. Certain forms have already demonstrated that they were incapable of defending the Church in the past; they might be just as incapable in the future. The Church could see its organization disappear in a matter of weeks without the population, ever-faithful to their Catholic traditions, offering the slightest opposition. It is important, therefore, to know what type of Catholicism exists in each country before there can be established a more authentic Christianity which will be not only more resistant, but more resolutely dynamic.

[15] Paciano Fermoso, *op. cit.*

[16] *Anomie,* according to Durkheim, is the state of society which exists when the former traditional values and norms of conduct are no longer understood, hence, rejected by a part or the whole of the population without, however, new norms being adopted. It is a society partially or totally "without laws." Emile Durkheim, *Suicide* (Glencoe, Ill.: Free Press, 1951).

[17] See, on this point, Talcott Parsons, *Religious Perspectives of College Teaching in Sociology and Special Psychology* (Edward W. Hazen Foundation), pp. 12–13.

[18] See the celebrated work of Max Weber, *The Protestant Ethic and the Spirit of Capitalism* (New York: Scribner, 1948).

[19] "By reviewing our religious values, they are trying to create an awareness of the advantages and dangers of our position as a traditionally Catholic country and of the necessity of revitalizing the faith so that it might effectively influence our collective and individual life. One of the most important fruits of Catholic Action is the existence of a Christian youth in our Republic and of authentically Christian families. There is no denying that the work ahead is enormous, but it is evident that the influence of this elite group on social life is beginning to show by the respect for religious conscience in public life and by the desire to see established a state of justice, inspired by the social doctrine of the Church." Cesar Arrospide de la Flor, the chapter on Peru, in Richard Pattee, *op. cit.,* pp. 384–85.

[20] The Catholics of Cuba are precisely in this situation.

[21] These were basic units of the rural world, large estates (*hacienda* in Spanish and *fazenda* in Portuguese), or small social units corresponding to very small villages (about 15 to 50 families).

[22] The parish office.

[23] See Emile Pin, "Can the Urban Parish Be a Community?" *Gregorianum,* No. 41 (1960), pp. 394–423, and reprinted in *Social Compass,* VI (1961), pp. 503–34.

16

The Present
and Future of the Church

In this chapter we shall depart from simple description and attempt to discern certain trends and even propose alternatives. Our opinion that these trends and alternatives exist is the result of serious reflection given to four years of research in Latin America and to the social and pastoral experiments initiated on the continent.

The evolution that has taken place in Latin America in just a few years' time is truly astonishing. In less than ten years, the great number of initiatives undertaken have actually transformed the face of the Church. True, in most cases it has been the result of the decisions and actions of a relatively small number of personalities or groups of laymen, priests or bishops, but their initiatives must certainly be viewed as "prophetic."

In some countries, the effects are already being felt in the social structures, and there has issued a well-planned pastoral activity. In other countries, developments have not yet reached that stage, but an awareness is in the process of being created. These changes have been observed by those within the Church as well as by outsiders. The attitude of the Latin American episcopate at the first session of the Vatican Council II was for many a surprise. Was it not Hans Küng who wrote: "More than one of us Europeans must revise his judgment on the Church, and particularly on the South American Church"?[1]

The testimony of non-Catholics can likewise be cited. A change of attitude is discernible among the young generation of Latin American intellectuals who are outside the Church because of their affiliation to a non-Communist Marxism or to other Christian faiths. In Brazil, one of them remarked: "You would never imagine how much the Church's image has changed for us in the last five years." He was alluding both to the universal Church under John XXIII and to the Church of Brazil, where in spite of obstacles to an "enlightenment" certain personalities and certain collective decisions have dissociated the Church from the feudal regime and from domestic and international capitalism.

The evolution observable in the past decade can be analyzed into three general stages, which, however, co-exist in time and among the various sectors of activity. The first stage is a consciousness of the real situation. The Church is gradually growing out of an attitude which consists in viewing everything ideally, without making any distinction between how things should be and how they really are.

The very fact that the Church has been integrated into the culture of Latin America makes this awareness very difficult. For a long time, and even today, many were under the impression that the future of Latin American Catholicism was rooted in its past; thus the many and insistent references to the "glorious tradition." *"Todos somos católicos"* ("We are all Catholics") was the leitmotif. The signs of change were either denied or interpreted otherwise. An archbishop of a large metropolitan area, who, after listening to the chaplain of the Young Christian Workers describe the social, moral and religious state of the working youth, answered: "Yes, that might be true, but deep down they are all Catholics. All I have to do is wave the banner of Our Lady and I have all the people behind me." This is what one priest, well acquainted with the Church on the five continents, called "blindfolded Christianity."

The same attitude was evidenced by the Roman curias. Only recently a Latin American bishop, having conducted an investigation on the religious and moral state of his diocese, was energetically taken to task. He had not even published the report, but simply submitted it to a Roman examining board. The Roman administration insisted that the observations concerning the religious state of Latin American people could not be interpreted in the same way as the situation in Europe. This is correct; but in reality it signifies a refusal to accept even the idea that a process of de-Christianization might be in progress.

This stage of awareness is a very difficult one, both from an intellectual and pastoral point of view. One must be understanding and adopt an attitude of respect in face of the dissension it provokes. Such a respect is even more necessary on the part of outsiders. There is nothing so disagreeable as to hear people make hasty judgments. They are often almost completely ignorant of the historical background of the continent; and worse yet, they judge the problems of the Church in Latin America in relation to the situation of the Church in their own country, unconsciously using the latter as the norm. Not only do they provoke a just anger, their criticisms have the opposite effect of burying Latin Americans more deeply in a defensive attitude. This attitude becomes even further entrenched when many Latin American bishops, priests, and laymen who have had occasion to visit and view directly the Church of North America or Europe return not always completely edified. Such was the case with a vicar-general of a particularly dynamic diocese who expressed his deep disappointment over the pastoral sluggishness he found in most of the parishes he visited in Belgium, the Netherlands, and Germany. Or the priest who returned from several weeks in the United States extremely disconcerted over the superiority complex and the reactionary attitude concerning a theological, liturgical and social renewal.

The result of this awareness is a certain confusion. All at once one is confronted with a situation whose existence was not even suspected. There is good reason to be alarmed, but a feeling of powerlessness develops. The dimensions of the newly discovered problems are terrifying, yet there are few concrete points of reference to aid in finding solutions.

A second stage issues from this awareness. The newly discovered problems must be acted upon. For a time, the only concrete points of reference are the experiments attempted abroad, principally in Europe, in those countries where they have long been searching formulas for both missionary activity and a deepening of the faith of Christians who must live in a pluralist world. We are specifically referring to France, Belgium and Germany.

Some methods were also imported from Spain, Italy, Ireland, and the United States, but more perhaps from the initiative of the priests and laymen of these countries than from the desire of the Latin Americans themselves. Whenever these methods of action were rigid and geared to the cultural environment or religious situation of the country in which they were originally developed, they bore little fruit when transplanted to Latin America. There either resulted an ideological and institutional rupture with the original proponents of the methods, or a fanaticism which only served to accentuate the incongruity between the methods and the real problems they were supposed to solve.

On the other hand, whenever these imported methods contained the possibilities of adaptation, they led quite rapidly to a third stage. This third stage consists in the acclimatization of the social, cultural or apostolic initiatives, in other words, they become truly indigenous in character and relevant to the particular situation in Latin America and more precisely in the country, region and neighborhood where they are applied. This does not necessarily imply that there is a rupture with the exterior, or that non-Latin Americans do not play an important role.

We can distinguish two aspects of this stage. First the movements or institutions from abroad undergo a process of "autochthony." We cite two examples. The Young Christian Workers movement in several Latin American countries, notably in Cuba before the Castro regime, succeeded in identifying itself with the youth of the sub-proletarian level and formed militant workers who are today active in the dynamic union organizations. And the Better World movement, founded by Father Lombardi in Italy, realized a transformation in Brazil which answered the pastoral needs of the country as a whole, and inspired pastoral planning on a national level and in the regional secretariats, principally in the Northeast.[2]

But there is another aspect to the third stage: original initiatives not based on models from other countries. They are very numerous today in the social and pastoral domains. To mention but a few examples: the radio schools, originally established in Colombia[3] but today spread throughout all of Latin America and even in certain African and Asian countries; the organisms for the redistribution of marginal urban populations, such as *Techo*[4] in Santiago; the institutes for rural training in Chile;[5] or finally the *juntas veredales* of the Colombian villages, associations of peasants for community development, an indirect product of the *Acción Cultural Popular* (the radio schools of Sutatenza).

In the pastoral sphere, let us mention in passing: the first experiments in religious services conducted by laymen in the North of Argentina;[6] the canonical establishment of general pastoral principles for the 35 parishes in the southern section of Bogotá (working-class and sub-proletarian neighborhoods); the new system of seminaries in Paraguay and at San Isidro on the outskirts of Buenos Aires; the community pastoral method of the diocese of Natal, Brazil;[7] and the small informal teams of laymen created in Cuba for a deeper appreciation of religion and apostolic activity.

On the social level, there is a great variety of activities that are common to most countries of the world, but which are worth mentioning in regard to Latin America: the cooperatives, such as those in Mexico; the labor unions[8] strongly developed as of late by Christians in the urban and rural regions;[9] the centers for social studies and their publications; the various national movements of Christian employers, etc.

To return to pastoral activity, there are a host of experiments that should be cited: the liturgical renewal in the parishes of Buenos Aires, Santiago, Bogotá, São Paulo, Panama, and in a very special way in Cuba; the remarkable efforts of the Benedictines in Cuernavaca (Mexico); the new sacred art exemplified by the cathedral of Brasilia (a new construction) and Cuernavaca (a renovation); the university apostolate conducted by priests working at the Central University of Caracas or by the students in the university parish in Mexico; the toddling but dynamic YCW movement in Brazil and Chile; the priest-workers in Buenos Aires; the priest missionary group of Valparaiso; the organization of diocesan pastoral planning in Temuco and Valdivia (Chile), Reconquista (Argentina), Cajamarca (Peru), and in many other dioceses; the elaboration of a pastoral method specifically adapted to the cultural, moral and religious level of the Indians in Riobamba (Ecuador);[10] the abolishing of "payment" for the sacraments in San Isidro (Argentina) and Girardot (Colombia); the adoption of the "clergymen" in Brazil; the organization of religious statistics by the Missionary Sisters of Jesus Crucified, etc., etc. Volumes could be written about these experiments. There remains much to be done, but it can be said that the Latin American Church is presently undergoing a transformation that has rarely been equaled in history.

NOTES

[1] Hans Küng, *The Council in Action: Theological Reflections on the Second Vatican Council* (New York: Sheed and Ward, 1963), p. 77.

[2] Conferência Nacional dos Bispos do Brasil, *Plano de Emergência para a Igreja do Brasil* (Rio de Janeiro: Ed. Dom Bosco, 1962).

[3] See François Houtart and Gustavo Perez, *Acción Cultural Popular. Principios teológicos y sociólogicos* (Bogotá: Ed. Acción Cultural Popular, 1960).

[4] Literally, "roof."

[5] See Oscar Dominguez, *El campesino chileno y la Acción católica rural* (Fribourg: FERES, 1961).

[6] *Celebración dominical donde no hay sacerdote a cargo de un delegado del Sr. Obispo* (Buenos Aires: Ed. Pastorales de Goya, 1962).

[7] *Planejamento Apostólico* (Arquidiocese de Natal, 1963).

[8] See Juan Arcos, *El sindicalismo en América Latina* (Fribourg: FERES, 1963).

[9] The rural syndicates of northeastern Brazil are a striking example. In less than three years (1960–1963) they numbered 350,000 members and formed the strongest pressure group in that region of the country. They were organized by laymen but under the initiative of the bishops.

[10] See Jorge Mencías, *Riobamba (Ecuador). Estudio de elevación sociocultural del indio* (Fribourg: FERES, 1961).

17

The Church
in a Changing World

The bulk of this chapter will concern the need for social action, and the next chapter, the need for pastoral action. At times we shall allude to a specific experiment, but only by way of illustration, and not intimating that other similar experiments do not exist. Such is the dynamism of the evolution of Latin America, that before these pages are in print, new forms of action will certainly have been initiated.

Before treating the different types of social action that have been realized or promoted by the Church, we would like to say a word about the perspective in which they should be viewed.

EVANGELIZATION AND
PRE-EVANGELIZATION

The task of the Church is to spread the Gospel, and this is the world's most basic need.[1] Yet we do not hesitate to begin this chapter, dedicated to the action of the Church, by a consideration of social action. At first this might seem contradictory, but we believe that the social dynamism of Christians, both priests and laymen, will be the sign of the Gospel for men in a changing world, just as Christ's solicitude for the sick and the poor was the sign of His mission to the men of His time. Men are concrete. They are not convinced by reasoning but by acts.

If words should not be feared, they should at least be explained. We do not speak of pre-evangelization as a stage separate from evangelization, as if one could proceed without the other. Rather, they are distinct approaches, inspired by a single basic attitude. We shall give two precise meanings to this idea, which is basic to our view of the Church's task in a changing continent. In both instances it concerns a sign of evangelization: a sign of presence in the world, and a sign of charity.

The Sign of Presence in the World

The first sign of evangelization is the approach to man through his fundamental preoccupations; for we know he accomplishes his divine mission only by performing his daily human tasks.

Today this approach supposes an involvement in every phase of humanity's evolution from scientific research to its technical applications, and especially the organization of the world on bases that are functional to its present expansion. This is principally the work of the laity, but not exclusively. Suffice it to recall the stir caused by the treatment of temporal problems in the encyclical *Pacem in Terris.*

Such an attitude demands that we discard the very narrow outlook which considers the problems of humanity from a strictly "ecclesiastical" point of view. We must not attempt to force the world into the molds of our mind, our organizations and our internal preoccupations; we must go out and meet it. Msgr. Helder Camara, Archbishop of Recife, on one occasion formulated this truth in a striking way, as he is wont to do: "The number one problem of Latin America: the lack of priests? No. Development."

So often we trick ourselves into believing that we are attacking the basic problems of humanity, when in reality we are revolving in an entirely different orbit. We are nowhere near the beginning of evangelization until we go out and meet our fellow man in his individual and collective preoccupations.

The Sign of Charity

In a world that has become conscious of the disequilibrium caused by development, the sign of the Church of Christ, visible to the world, will be her social concern and social action. These today must be collective and apply to social awareness as well as to social organization.

The Church is a community of faith, of worship, and of charity; but to be perceived in the first two aspects, it must express itself in the third. How is the Gospel recognized? "The blind see, the deaf hear, and the poor receive the good news."

It is really a sign of the love of Christ. That is why pre-evangelization and evangelization are inseparable. But for this charity to be a sign to the modern world, it must be directed to the true problems and use the appropriate means, which today are more and more collective in nature. It is no longer enough to build schools and hospitals; we must understand the new forms of development, enter into an effective planning which will force us to break through our "parochialism" and our "congregationalism," work out unheard-of collaborations with Christians of other faiths or with non-Christians, and promote social transformations which can fearlessly be called revolutionary.

The sign of the Church in the underdeveloped world will be her efficacious love of men who desire to elevate themselves. But we would like to make clear from the outset that this action must not become an expression of power. And this is not always easy to get across. How many priests, and even laymen, give way to the temptation of establishing the Kingdom of God by human means, and of utilizing individual or collective social action as an instrument of pressure or power. Automatically such an action loses its value as a sign of evangelization. In this case, pre-evangelization becomes an action for itself, emptied of all evangelical values. Only those who participate in the spiritual Kingdom can work at an authentic pre-evangelization. It is first of all a spiritual attitude.

To establish contact with men living in a society that, because it is badly organized, is incapable of assuring their sustenance and their participation in economic, social and cultural resources, means to fight alongside these men for a transformation of this society. But frequently the obstacles are so great and so many that only a radical and rapid transformation will satisfy the double pressure of a population increase and a deepening social consciousness. Let us state it clearly, it involves a revolution, but a revolution that does not necessarily imply the use of violence.

What will be the most perceptible sign of the Church of Christ to these men? The renewal of sacred art or the use of their own language in the Mass? (And we purposely cite measures we consider very important.) No. It will be her participation in the "social revolution," that is, in the profound transformation of the structures of a society that is unjust because it does not assure the existence and well-being of its members.

In the northeast of Brazil, the peasant masses live like animals; their average life span barely reaches 30 years; more than half of their children die before reaching one year of age. They suffer from endemic hunger often on lands that are fertile but badly utilized by the rich landowners. These masses who have neither the right to possess, nor the right to educate, nor the right to vote, what do they expect of the Church of Christ? The distribution of powdered eggs? Better education for their employer's daughter? Lace for Monsignor's surplices? Or even, the construction of a cathedral?

If we cite this last case, it is because an archbishop of this region, Eugenio Sales, formerly from Natal, without the least hesitation stopped construction of the cathedral. He did not lack appreciation of its symbolic values to a Christian community; but he wished to give a perceptible sign of the charity of Christ by

training laymen, who organized the peasants through rural syndicates, by extending the radio schools, by multiplying cooperatives,
by organizing intensive training programs, and by deepening social consciousness. We can still hear one of the men, with wrinkled
face, not very talkative, a true rural type, declare at one of the
village meetings: "Without the Church what would we be?"

As can be seen, this attitude and action must be common to
both clergy and laity. Neither pre-evangelization nor evangelization can separate the fundamental union between these two elements of the Church. It is not correct to say that temporal matters
should be reserved to the laity and spiritual matters to the priests:
for each, in his own way, has a role to play in both stages. If
the Latin American bishops and priests were solely preoccupied
with the renewal of the liturgy and of sacred art, how could we
have a laity truly involved in development and deeply integrated
into the Church? And conversely, how could we meet the needs
of evangelization, if laymen were not associated with the growth
of the Eucharistic community in its form of faith and worship?

Although pre-evangelization and evangelization must not be
confused, and although it must be well understood that, even
for Christians, the building of an earthly city is not evangelization,
there can be no doubt that the laymen of Latin America must be
oriented first toward development. It would be erroneous, both in
relation to the purpose of the orientation itself and to the pedagogy
to follow, to group the laymen among Catholic organizations, either
with the idea of later sending them on to other activity, or for
the purpose of initiating them directly into purely religious activity.

Indeed, we must first start with basic realities. We live in a
society whose upheaval is so complete that every element of collective life is being affected by social change. And this change is so
swift that certain institutions can no longer fulfill their normal
functions. Various explanations of this can be advanced. Either
these institutions have been slow in adapting (for example, the
juridical and economic institutions of the rural world), or they
have not abandoned completely antiquated methods (state admin-

istrations), or they have not undertaken new functions (the schools). All this only accentuates the disequilibrium and contributes to the social disorder into which most of the social groups have been plunged. The effect on human beings is often tragic. Here is where competent Christians can pour forth their charity by contributing to development at whatever level. Beautifying churches, erecting a statue to the Sacred Heart, that can come later (in view of the present situation) as well as systematically straightening out marriages, or blessing the fields and houses.

As to pedagogy, experience teaches two things. First, the best method of participating in the concrete problems of our fellow man is not learned in books nor at school, but by lending a hand. The rest will come afterwards, as an indispensable complement. Second, it is rare that a small group, artificially formed, initiates by itself any effective action. It runs the risk of going around in circles, bogging down, attacking problems which are figments of its imagination, or attacking real problems from such a particular angle that they will never be effectively handled.

Other serious deviations are possible when one first organizes Christians into Catholic Action groups, for example, the direct engagement of these groups in a purely secular activity in labor or politics. Is this not the case with the Young Christian Students movement in Brazil? Such an attitude is understandable, however, for it is a protest against secular ineffectiveness.

But of course, to accomplish a true pre-evangelization, the laity must be assisted in their efforts by the Church. In other words, their integration into the Eucharistic community must be assured and continually deepened. This demands the pastoral action of which we shall later speak. The Christians engaged in the social revolution must be integrated into an adult faith and a community of worship which is more than a display of lace, accompanied by mysterious rites.

A Church that would not take into view the whole condition of the men to be evangelized, would be no more than a giant sect making propaganda.

THE FORMS OF SOCIAL INVOLVEMENT

Effective presence in the world and social preoccupation can be manifested in many ways and at many levels. We here attempt to group them into various categories, though the list can in no way be thought of as exhaustive.

First of all, there is the *spiritual aspect,* which is far from being negligible. Indeed, pre-evangelization flows directly from a spiritual attitude capable of giving unity to the life of Christians and orienting them toward the development of the world in which they live. The vision of the world which we have heretofore been describing looks upon the material universe merely as an instrument of a spiritual society, if not a reality simply tolerated, or worse yet, condemned by Christ.

Such a conception forgets that God (and not the Devil) gave us the mission of developing the earth, and that Christ condemned sin, not the material world. This conception gave birth to a special type of spirituality, which Fr. Vekemans, S.J., once labeled "the spirituality of underdevelopment." One of its results was the training of a remarkably pious laity impregnated with high religious values, but almost completely out of contact with the secular world, having no awareness of the aspirations of the men around them or of the social injustice in which they were often participating.

Then there is *intellectual action.* It will depend mainly on the guidance given by the hierarchy on the problems of development; although the action of the laity in this domain is to be of great importance. This action will consist in the development, teaching and diffusion of an intellectually coherent system. So rarely does one encounter effective and global solutions outside of Communism. Is there a way out of the dilemma: underdevelopment with liberty or development without liberty? An interesting remark can be related to this subject. In June 1963, a Chilean Communist official, who was in Havana for a Latin American youth meeting, declared to a Cuban director of the National

Institute of Agrarian Reform, who had asked him about the chances for a Communist victory in the presidential elections of 1964: "We have given up hopes for a victory; the Christians have organized. They are presenting about the same program we are, but without blood and with liberty. How can we fight against that?" Granted such programs must prove they can really work, but proposing a coherent doctrine is already a step in the right direction.

The most essential factor of intellectual action, however, is the attitude of the hierarchy. Their word engages the Church even more visibly in the struggle and offers a guarantee to the action of lay Christians. For it is clear that the laity commit themselves to the social revolution not merely out of personal convictions but under the inspiration of their faith. Declarations of the hierarchy are all the more important since their silence is interpreted, and even exploited, as signifying their approval of the existing order.

We could cite many such declarations both of individual bishops and, what is of even greater value, of national episcopates. Among the great pastoral letters we would like to attach particular significance to the one issued by the Colombian bishops in 1960 concerning the agrarian reform. Not only did it emphasize the urgency of concrete measures, but it gave implicit approval to the project prepared by a national commission, and at a time when certain groups were utilizing religious arguments to combat it. What caused this document to attract even greater attention was the fact that it appeared at the very moment the twenty-one republics of America were meeting in Bogotá, which was preparatory to the conference at Punta del Este, from which was to issue the Alliance for Progress.

It would certainly be unfair to leave unmentioned the letters and declarations of the episcopates of Peru, Paraguay, and Ecuador, as well as certain bishops of Uruguay, Venezuela, Mexico, and Central America. But we would like to concentrate on two documents that unmistakably caused the greatest stir: the letter of the bishops of Chile in 1962, and the declaration of the Central Commission of the Conference of the Bishops of Brazil in 1963.

The first caused a considerable reaction in Chile and became the object of violent attacks, mostly indirect. Its fame soon reached international proportions. In July 1963, the then Senator Hubert Humphrey, a foreign policy specialist, presented the pastoral letter to the U. S. Senate and asked that it be printed in the *Congressional Record* as a model of orientation for the social transformations in Latin America.

This letter contains a rapid description of the socio-economic situation of Chile, and proposals for orienting social, economic and political action.[2] It begins with a general introduction, where one reads: "In the crucial period in which we live, there are powerful entities that propose solutions, but there are groups that do not believe them possible and who desire to maintain the status quo."

The Bishops then consider the matter of structural reforms. After describing, with the support of statistics, the uneven distribution of the revenue, the housing situation, unemployment, inadequate salaries, and the weak school system, they give closer attention to each problem, starting with that of revenue. To help resolve it "the Christian must favor those institutions that demand social action, and if the problem directly concerns him, he should participate in this social action. He must also support institutional changes, such as an authentic agrarian reform, a reform in business enterprise, a fiscal reform, an administrative reform, and other similar reforms."

But it is not sufficient to clear away the obstacles to development. The Christian must become boldly involved, principally by improving his technical competences and making his goods useful to the community: "this is why it would be anti-Christian in the present circumstances to let one's goods remain unproductive or to invest them abroad. It would also be anti-Christian to consecrate them to the production of articles or services that satisfy the fictitious needs of a small minority of the population, while the basic necessities of our national community are ignored."

The document also treats of Communism, not only to recall its condemnation by the Church, but to point out the causes of its success: the abuses of the liberal economy, the weakness and inaction of governments in the face of the intolerable injustices of the social situation, the clever Communist propaganda, and the lack of unity among those who combat it.

As to the Brazilian document,[3] published April 30, 1963, and signed by the three cardinals and three archbishops who made up the Central Commission of the Conference, it also caused a great reverberation. Its tone was perhaps more formal than the Chilean letter, but it attacked the most crucial problems of Brazilian society. Some of the large conservative newspapers which at that very moment were publishing the encyclical *Pacem in Terris,* with rather detailed commentaries, refused to publish the text of the episcopal declaration. To have it printed, the Secretariat had to pay the regular advertisement fees. There were also some bishops who publicly declined to support the document, but this was hardly surprising. For these same bishops—at least two of them—had the previous year published a book entitled, *Agrarian Reform, A Question of Conscience,* attacking the very principle of the reform and presenting the right of private property, and the right of property owners to direct society, as natural rights of divine origin.

The partisans of these ideas, including some bishops who were adversely influenced by elements of the existing social regime, were naturally to react before passages like:

No one can believe that the social order in which we live [the situation in Brazil] is the one proposed by the new encyclical[4] as the unshakable foundation of peace. Our social order is still burdened by the heavy weight of a capitalist tradition which has dominated the West these past centuries. It is a system in which money and economic power are the underlying determinants in all economic, political and social decisions. It is an order in which a minority has access to culture, a high standard of living, health, comfort and luxury, and in which the majority, having no way of obtaining these goods, are by that very fact deprived from exercising many of man's basic and natural rights, as enunciated in *Pacem in Terris*: the right to existence, the right to a decent standard of living, the respect of his dignity and freedom, the right to participate in the benefits of culture, finally, the right relative to his life in society.

After describing the existing negative atitudes of the rich "who do all in their power to maintain the status quo," of the opportunist reformers, of the sterile agitators and totalitarian extremists, the message speaks of the transformations "which appear the most urgent and which touch directly on the crucial human problems." First, the agrarian reform:

No one can be unaware of the situation of millions of our brothers who live in the country, unable to participate in the benefits of our development, in conditions of utter poverty which are an insult to human dignity. . . . To satisfy such an urgent need [the possibility of acquiring land][5] expropriation in the interest of society contains nothing contrary to the social doctrine of the Church.

Then the document mentions the reform of the system of business enterprise, whose objective will be "to convert the profit system into a service capable of answering the real needs of the national community." Next comes the fiscal reform: "A revision of our policy must aim to give a more effectively progressive character to the tax on revenue, at the same time establishing forceful measures capable of suppressing the various forms of tax evasion and fiscal fraud." While on this subject, the text recalls the duties regarding investment: "It would be a grave fault against justice and a deeply anti-Christian gesture to keep unproductive capital or to send it elsewhere for the purpose of speculation." Finally, the various aspects of an administrative reform are treated: the commonweal, greater effectiveness, better organization, the fight against corruption, and the electoral system, "so that adequate measures might be taken to increase the number of citizens who can effectively participate in political life."[6]

The message ends by taking a position for the presence of the Church in the transformations of the world, indicating the reasons for its importance and the respective responsibilities of priests and laymen.

One fact is certain. It cannot be sincerely claimed that the Church in Latin America is a reactionary force. The renewal is not complete, of course, and there are still Christians—even members of the hierarchy—attached to feudal social forms; but on the whole, the partisans of social change represent the dynamic element of the Church.

One aspect of social action, however, might raise questions. Must the Church necessarily take sides in these problems? To dissociate the Church from one social system simply to integrate it into another, is this not really putting it back in the same situation, that is, making it the function of a system? And what about the accusations of opportunism that will certainly be levied? Is it not true that since the Church pursues a supernatural end, which transcends all particular forms of society, it should not be utilized to strengthen one type of society or to cause the disintegration of another?

The history of Latin America offers enough examples of how the Church was utilized, from the conquest to the absolutism of the Bourbons, or of Pombal, not to mention the present forms of utilization, more subtle, perhaps, but no less insidious, such as the sanctimonious anti-Communism of certain groups. And it might very well be that the Church will one day be "utilized" by the progressive forces.

But the Church is not a purely spiritual reality. It is composed of flesh-and-blood Christians who live in a society and whose scale of values and behavior have an influence on the social system. In the sociological meaning of the word "function," that is, consequence and not end or objective, the Church is necessarily functional or disfunctional in a social system.[7] In Latin America, where 95 per cent of the population is baptized, the Church's influence is particularly great. And if the Church takes a position in the questions we have been discussing, it is not because of a preference for this or that political or social regime, but for the purpose of satisfying the need of justice for all men at a given moment in history. Today, since it has become technically possible to conquer infant mortality, to give all men a share in material and cultural wealth and in political life, any regime that does not assure such possibilities has become unjust, even if it was not so formerly.

Not to take a position means to favor the status quo, that is, injustice.[8] It becomes evident how important it is for the Church to be able to analyze objectively the evolution of the society in which it is engrained. Certain extreme "spiritualists" refuse to become involved. Not realizing the consequences of their attitude, they develop the unrealistic spirituality mentioned above, which can be qualified as "angelism."

Educative action is one contribution the Church can make beyond mere orientation. In addition to her function of orienting the scales of individual and collective values, the Church can be considered sociologically as an "agency of education." This task touches not only the supernatural, but the whole man. Today, the duty to develop one's competency and to assimilate technological values appears as a duty of charity. This is true for the Andean peasant who must learn the methods to combat soil erosion, as well as for civil administrators or businessmen.

Educative action, therefore, is something continuous, not merely the creation of Catholic schools. No doubt the school system is very important to development, but it is not the only form of education. There are two other sectors that are equally, if not more, important. First of all, adult education for the popular masses, sometimes called basic education. The principal method employed in Latin America is the radio schools, which we have already mentioned. They view the problem as a transformation of values and mentalities.

The second important sector is the training of leaders through intensive courses, study sessions, workshops, and publications. All social categories are included: professional people, labor personnel, young workers, politicians. Activity in this field has multiplied, due in great measure to the efforts of specialized Catholic Action groups and training centers specifically adapted to the needs of labor and political life.

Although the school system has been the traditional sector of the Church's educative action in Latin America, its size on the elementary level is not very impressive, representing scarcely 10 per cent of the total number of elementary schools. Catholic secondary education, on the contrary, is quite important, since it accounts for 50 per cent or more of the schools in countries such as Brazil and Colombia. In general, however, the growth rate of public schools surpasses that of the Catholic school system. As for higher education, Catholic universities represent a minority of 10 to 15 per cent, in spite of the 28 Catholic universities, and the one hundred autonomous university departments in Brazil.

Unfortunately, Catholic education in Latin America does not give much emphasis to social values. In fact, its network of institutions can often be considered a negative factor in social change. Technical schools are not highly developed, although they have increased in number over the past few years. Catholic education on the continent is one of the weakest sectors of Church action because of its conservatism, individualism and refusal to adapt. Here and there one finds praiseworthy efforts toward renewal, but they remain isolated. We are probably headed toward a crisis, at the precise moment when education has been recognized as an integral part of development and has become the object of serious planning. It would be dangerous for the Church to defend indefensible structures under pretext of guarding its rights in education.

Another type of initiative needed is *action on the social, economic, political, and cultural structures.* A society is not transformed by episcopal declarations alone, nor merely under the effect of educative action; men must work on its structures. They must work for a multiplication of goods and services and for their just distribution; they must organize pressure groups to clear away obstacles; they must develop activity in the political domain.

Here we touch on a field of action quite proper to laymen. It is not suitable for the clergy to engage in forms of direct action that sometimes involve a violent struggle. As much as possible their intervention in these matters must be limited to education, orientation, informing the action with doctrine. Concrete action in the political or labor field usually presents numerous alternatives of relative value, whereas the priest must appear as the minister of transcendent values, which is not to say he is unconcerned about material things, and as the servant of peace, which is not to say one who compromises.

This kind of action can take place at all levels, from small structures in the village to international organisms. It can be applied to student groups, worker groups, educational institutions, recreational organizations, etc. There are few adult laymen who, formed by their participation in the Eucharistic community, can not be oriented toward these sectors of action.

Exemplative action consists in performing certain acts which by themselves do not produce great results, but which have a symbolic value. One example is the Latin American bishop who effected an agrarian reform on the lands belonging to the diocese in Talca, Chile—Bishop Manuel Larrain, current president of CELAM.

The manifestation of a true poverty enters into the category of exemplative action. It will be all the more striking since for building the terrestrial city in Latin America we have only the poorest instruments at our disposal.

The Church has a long way to go in this regard. As far as individual members of the hierarchy are concerned, considerable progress has been made; there are practically no rich prelates. But on the collective level and regarding the exterior signs of wealth, not much has been accomplished.

In former times these exterior signs were able to be considered a testimony to the importance attributed to the sacred character of persons or rites, and they are still so considered among primitive populations. But today these signs appear linked with a feudalistic spirit or a desire to overwhelm by prestige or power. This is probably a universal phenomenon, but in Latin America it takes on a greater importance, since these exterior signs are often exuberant—and to be perfectly frank, childish—and also since the social change is so violent.

The true signs of the evangelization of the poor are not the make and model of the bishop's car, nor the mansion he constructs on the hilltop, but the wooden cross he adopts as his episcopal symbol, or the humble residence he establishes among the poor, converting his mansion into a center for training working-class leaders.[9]

Supplementary action involves the Church's taking charge of secular activity because of the absence of any other organized body capable of doing it. There are situations where, for historical reasons or because of present circumstances, the Church must take initiatives that are no longer accepted in a technologically developed society. This is a delicate matter, for it is difficult to know just when such an initiative should be undertaken, be it in the area of labor, cooperatives or education. Furthermore, the long tradition of the Church's domination of society risks getting the initiative off on the wrong foot.[10] The Church's image is also endangered far outside the immediate area of activity, and since highly developed communications have practically eliminated geographic isolation, any action must be considered in relation to the impression it will create on the rest of the world.

In several Latin American countries supplementary action is absolutely necessary, especially in certain rural regions and among the Indians. But certain conditions must be observed. The following seem indispensable. First of all, it must be demanded by the common good. Next, it must be transitory. As soon as it becomes institutionalized to any important degree and becomes a power, it must be put in the hands of a private or public organism which is not directly dependent on the hierarchy of the Church. Next, a lay structure must be formed as rapidly as possible. And as a final condition, the initiative must not be looked upon as an instrument of power over men and society, nor even a mere instrument of the apostolate. In short, it must be an impulsion of charity, but with the objective of fulfilling the specific need which inspired the action.

THE CHURCH AS A DISFUNCTIONAL FACTOR IN DEVELOPMENT

In speaking of the forms of social action, we have several times made allusion to the negative aspects of certain policies and actions of the Church. At this point we merely wish to restate the problem and give a few examples. The disfunctions are certainly not willed, and most of the time they are not even perceived as such. They often result from the mere fact that society changes. In sociology this is the typical example of the gap between social realities and social institutions.

We have already made reference to the disfunctional aspects of certain spiritual motivations. But in addition, Christianity in Latin America has experienced a whole sequence of events, from the legal prohibition of Protestantism in the mission territories of Colombia, to the assumption of civil power by the Church in some countries, not to mention the epic (and useless) struggles against legal divorce, and the union of Church and State in countries like Argentina and Ecuador.

We shall limit ourselves, however, to one particular case, since it involves a large number of priests and nuns, and because it risks being one of the major obstacles to positive action by the Church. We are referring to Catholic education. We consider it here only with respect to its positive or negative value to evangelization, without questioning either the right[11] of the Church to engage in this kind of activity, or the good faith and devotion of those who consecrate themselves to it.

Created as a service to the whole of society, to educate the elite in a feudal system, these institutions played a positive role. In the countries where education has been democratized, the school system has become a service to the Christian community. It has, to be sure, its advantages and disadvantages, but it stands as a proof of the Church's interest in the education of all men.

Its significance is quite different, however, in regions where education is merely on the road to democratization. There, especially because it is not subsidized by the State, the Catholic school system is a service not to the Christian community, but to those, Christians or not, who can pay. This is the ordinary situation for Catholic secondary and higher education in Latin America. There are laudable exceptions on the university level and in the area of technical schools and teacher colleges, but this has been made possible, for the most part, through subsidies granted by the State.

Regarding the education of girls, we are aware of objectively scandalous practices of social segregation and, in some instances, even racial segregation (of the Negroes in Brazil and the Indians in Peru). Moreover, the girls often complete their training with an almost total ignorance of the society in which they live. This education is a service to a specific class; for to be accepted in certain circles, one must have graduated from such and such an institution. We are firmly convinced that it would be better to suppress Catholic education than to let it continue in such conditions.

As to the Catholic universities, beside the fact that their excessive multiplication limits them to an intellectual standing of second or third rank (except for two or three outstanding schools), in the eyes of most of the students of the state universities they are simply a means for the power classes to survive the social revolution. Too often such universities appear as centers of conservatism and social reaction, whereas their sole justification should be their participation in development, by struggling against structural and cultural obstacles, and by introducing new forms and new values.

The national and continental associations of Catholic education have so far merely reflected the same spirit. They are more pre-occupied with the defense of their rights, or with classical culture, or with anti-Communist declarations than with the process of social reintegration. However, in some of these organizations (in Chile, for example), an awareness is beginning to dawn, and the idea of educational planning is gradually taking root.

PROTESTANT EFFORTS IN SOCIAL ACTION

Protestants constitute a small minority of the total population; their social action, therefore, will be quite different. The numerous sects, by the way, are little interested in global social phenomena.

As with Catholic social action, Protestant initiatives operate on several levels. Many of the small groups organized by the churches or sects have, at least virtually, a function in social integration. This point has been well demonstrated by many studies. Protes-tantism, especially the traditional churches, has often played a positive role in the "rationalization" of social values, concerning itself with economic, administrative, scientific, and even political responsibilities.[12] Also fairly well known is the influence of numer-ous Protestant missions on the improvement of literacy and the suppression of alcoholism among the Indians.

Besides a considerable number of hospitals and schools, includ-ing some colleges, that are run by the Protestant communities, we would like to cite the accomplishments in the fields of ethnology and social thought. Concerning this last point, mention must be made of the initiatives undertaken by the Department on Church and Society, of the World Council of Churches. Of special note is the 1961 conference in Huampani, Peru, on the theme of social change[13] and the 1963 conference on "Christians and the Revolu-tion in Latin America." The documents published at these two meetings contain bold and concrete suggestions to incite Chris-tians to become active elements of social transformation. The parallelism between their conclusions and those of the Catholic documents is striking and shows the areas where a practical unity can be realized.

NOTES

[1] The major part of this section is taken from François Houtart's *Les tâches de l'Eglise dans les régions de besoin,* a paper delivered to the Congress Pro Mundi Vita (Essen, Sept. 1963).

[2] See *El Deber social en la hora presente.* Pastoral Letter of the Bishops of Chile (Sept. 18, 1962).

[3] *"Pacem in Terris* et la réalité brésilienne. Message de la commission centrale de la Conférence des Evêques du Brésil," *La Documentation Catholique,* LX, No. 1403 (July 7, 1963), column 899–906.

[4] *Pacem in Terris.*

[5] Editor's note.

[6] Illiterates do not have the right to vote.

[7] See François Houtart, "Les variables qui affectent le rôle intégrateur de la religion," *Social Compass* (1960) No. 1, pp. 21–38.

[8] "Silence on our part would constitute culpable neglect." Letter of the Bishops of Chile, *op. cit.*

[9] These two cases actually happened.

[10] Actions and declarations are sometimes misunderstood. Even the letter of the bishops of Chile, as straightforward as it is, sometimes uses a vocabulary that is ambiguous and which could give the unpleasant impression of an exhibition of power.

[11] This is a word that repeatedly occurs in ecclesiastical documents, and which should be used much less frequently.

[12] See E. Willems, *Uma Vila Brasileira* (São Paulo: Difusão Européia do livro, 1961).

[13] Latin American Commissions on Church and Society (Montevideo) and the Department on Church and Society of the World Council of Churches: *Christians and Social Change in Latin America* (Geneva, 1961).

18

The Pastoral Renewal

We begin this chapter with a review of the difficulties that the pastoral renewal of Latin America is encountering, first in the types of religious attitudes of the various segments of the population, then in the deficiencies of the traditional pastoral methods themselves. In our discussion of these matters we shall be as frank as the renewal has been forceful. It is still in an embryonic stage, but its dynamism and diffusion augur a rich future of pastoral maturity. One thing is certain, the experiments in Latin America are among the most advanced in the Church today. But first, a brief description of the obstacles will give a greater appreciation of the renewal.

THE DEFICIENCIES OF RELIGIOUS LIFE

In the *rural world*, besides the already mentioned deficiencies due, for the most part, to the lack of priests, there is a much deeper religious deficiency even where the priest is present: a naturalist religiosity, inspired by biological and cosmological motivations, and a naturalist vision of the relationships between God and the world. There have been few systematic efforts in instruction and liturgy to transform it. The present rites, feasts, devotions, and processions often only encourage this type of piety. It is a religion of Divine Providence, without concern for the moral life,

227

and incapable of inspiring action for transforming the world. God is conceived as already present; one simply asks His assistance in daily life. This providentialism contributes indirectly to social immobility and would justify the accusation of the atheist revolutionaries, that religion performs an anti-social function.

The great *unintegrated urban masses,* who have not yet been assimilated into the culture of industrial life, are very close to the rural masses in mentality. They are inspired by the same type of piety. The difficulties presented by urban life often make the "remedies" offered by Catholicism unequal to the task. The size of the parishes, the urgent need of small groups to be socially recognized, the absence of effective social cures, etc., all make these people an easy prey for superstitious cults in which the presence of mysterious forces can be sensibly experienced. These urban masses are not Communist, but they can easily rally behind a revolutionary leader; they have nothing to lose and everything to gain.

Many from the *transformed urban masses* have rejected Catholicism in favor of syncretism, sects, or else religious indifferentism. Intent on participating, by force if possible, in the economic development of their country, they reject a religion which in their eyes is incapable of inspiring such action. With the exception of a few favored regions or some countries having specialized Catholic Action movements (of very limited size, it must be admitted), this segment of the population has been often sadly neglected.

A strong religious spirit can be found among *university students,* but also an opposition to the Church which at times extends to hostility and open combat. They see the Church as one of the institutional elements of a society past, and an obstacle to the concrete forms of development, which for them are revolutionary.

The religion of the *upper classes* can be characterized as ritualistic and other-worldly. It coexists with a theoretical and practical refusal of social improvement, one manifestation of which is the use they make of their capital. Some upper-class families remain attached to a feudalistic vision of society and assume that nothing can be done about the fundamental inequality between men. These same families see Communism in every desire for social equality and every vindicative action of labor unions. Even priests and bishops are accused of being Communists. Accompanying these attitudes, and with complete compatibility, is a personal devotion to generous almsgiving and charitable works for the protection and well-being of the poor masses. But these charitable actions are an integral part of a basically unequal society and are rejected by those who desire a new society in which everyone will be protected from the humiliation of begging alms.

PASTORAL DEFICIENCIES

It must also be recognized that pastoral activity has been burdened, and still is burdened by important faults and failings. These deficiencies are by no means the exclusive property of Latin American Catholicism, but they are quite prevalent on this continent. We list some of the traits below.

Conservative and defensive pastoral activity. This is based on the conviction that we are dealing with a Catholic population that must be conserved in the faith and defended against exterior attacks. This conviction leads to a rigidly structured and static type of pastoral activity based more on authority than on loyalty. It also inspires repeated condemnation of anything in society that changes, for this endangers the existing faith. There are several consequences to this attitude. It is almost unthinkable to question the quality of this faith, to ask if what is being conserved and defended is truly a living faith. Furthermore, there is an absence of a true missionary spirit, and a marked unconcern for the new sectors of society, attention being concentrated on the traditional sectors.

Sacrament-centered pastoral activity without adequate catechesis. This situation is partially explainable by the lack of priests. The sacraments we have reference to are principally baptism and matrimony; these are the ones received by most of the population. What really results is a sacramentalization without evangelization. And it can very easily fall into a ritualism without any internal meaning.

Pastoral emphasis on devotions. For the simple populations, devotions eventually become the essence of religion. Little by little the religion of these people is emptied of the central mystery of Christianity, the paschal mystery. This type of religion is equally devoid of reference to concrete action in earthly life, except, as all too often happens, to the biological or cosmological elements. And since the devotions are often a source of income for the Church, they further risk deviating motivations.

Individualized and casuistic morality. Teaching and moral instruction are centered on a code, which is often reduced to a few obligations and a few taboos (principally in sexual matters). A social morality is little taught, which partially explains the failure to instill true Christian principles in the traditional elite.

A spirituality centered on the Sorrowful Mysteries and on mysticism. It is obvious that cultural factors have strongly influenced this tradition. It is perfectly legitimate that a culture emphasize a particular aspect of Christianity, but a problem arises when such an emphasis becomes too exclusive. There results a spirituality whose vision of Christianity is unbalanced. This is particularly undesirable when the accents placed on certain aspects run counter to the type of spirituality needed by the men of today.

Priestly authoritarianism. In the rural regions mostly, the priest was, and in many cases still is, the leader of the community. His pastoral labors, instead of being a service, frequently become a symbol of power. The priest is still often viewed in this light. His pastoral attitude, consequently, becomes authoritarian, and this extends to his activities outside the pastoral domain. Too frequently a responsible group of laymen never develops because the priest considers himself more a boss than an educator who must form his people.

Utilization of social and political power. Since the priest is often the leader of the community, and since the Church has traditionally played an important role in the nation, recourse to social and legal pressures to assure orthodoxy is not at all uncommon.

Triumphalism. This term, which has become classic since the first session of Vatican II, defines rather well a whole category of attitudes: the Church can never be wrong; mistakes are always the fault of others. This attitude also refuses to view objectively the reality of situations. If unpleasant facts are unavoidably evident, they are attributed to slight weaknesses, or are rationalized away, or are carefully covered over so that the "enemy" cannot take advantage of them. This allows "triumphant" declarations and attitudes to continue. There is, moreover, a whole series of related attitudes which find expression, for example, in the exterior signs of prestige, either carried over from a feudal society or newly created.

Condemnation of everything that is not Catholic. Distinction is not always made between "un-Catholic" and bad faith. There results an attitude of moral condemnation of persons who are of another religion, another philosophy, or even another political tendency. This attitude was all too evident in the past in the type of accusations leveled against freemasonry, and today against Marxism and Communism.

Commercialism. Throughout the universal Church, pastoral activities are, for the most part, financed by a system of donations. This supposes informed Christians who understand that the donation given when a spiritual act is performed is not payment for the service. But in Latin America, a false interpretation became almost inevitable in a civilization where commercial exchanges became much too numerous and where solid religious instruction was lacking. Complicating matters is the financial "exploitation" of certain devotions, developed especially by some of the religious orders.

Lack of continuity and coordination in pastoral activity. There have already been efforts to solve this problem, but they have not been followed through either because they did not give immediate

results, or because they were too scattered to effect a real coordination of global activity. One factor is the individualism of many
religious congregations who find it difficult to adopt outlooks other
than their own and to integrate into diocesan pastoral systems.

The priest's lack of human culture. At a time when society is in
full transformation, this deficiency of the priest is particularly re-
gretted by those who participate or aspire to participate in the
change. The priest is either uninterested in these matters, or he is
ignorant of the great problems which face humanity today.

The non-integration of nuns. For many reasons, religious
women have not participated in general pastoral activity, except
very recently and on a very reduced scale. Their principal field
has been the education of upper-class children.

THE NEED FOR PASTORAL
DECENTRALIZATION

By pastoral activity we mean all action of the Church designed
to lead men to, and advance them along the path of salvation. It
includes every effort to facilitate Christian conversion; it exploits
the individual and sociological circumstances which condition it;
and attempts to immerse the people of God ever more deeply in
Christ. It is therefore a pedagogy. As such, it utilizes everything
that enables it to better understand and direct the forces which
weigh on individual lives; in this sense it embraces pre-evangelization as well as evangelization.

Since conversion to the Kingdom of God is never either definitive or perfect on this earth, pastoral activity is committed to work
toward continual improvement, so that the Gospel will bear greater
fruit in the community as well as in the individual, in social structures as well as in Church structures.

Pastoral activity, therefore, is a function of the hierarchical
Church. The civil order is not its proper end, but it must concern
itself with the civil order for two reasons: it forms a favorable
or unfavorable climate for the budding and development of a

living faith, a faith that is lived in the community; secondly, the civil order is the substance in which the ferment introduced by Christ must unfold and find expression.

To the quantitative aspect of social change, that is, to the problems caused in the parishes by the population explosion, only a decentralization of pastoral activity offers a solution.

Since pastoral activity strives to form the Mystical Body, it is quite concerned with facilitating entry into Christ's Church. The theological foundation for this type of activity is the missionary character of the Church. This must grow as humanity grows. Experience has taught that a pre-evangelization must precede or accompany evangelization, but it must be remembered that the betterment of the conditions of human life is undertaken for the purpose of permitting or facilitating evangelization properly speaking, that is, announcing the Word of God.

But pastoral activity also strives to mature the Mystical Body, that is, not merely to extend it quantitatively, but to promote the theological development proper to Christian life. Since this theological life must never cease to grow, the Church cannot be satisfied with a pastoral method that merely conserves or defends the faith. It must be essentially dynamic, ever striving for improvement in a world where sin and error are always present. Finally, pastoral activity strives for the fecundity of the faith and of the personal and communal charity of the faithful. Indeed, being a realistic pedagogy, it cannot leave the faithful short of their goal.

When describing the quantitative effects of social change on the Latin American Church, we already noted the formalism of pastoral structures due to the excessive number of parishioners per priest. This situation has a much greater urgency in today's changing society than it had when social structures and values remained practically stable.

It has always been traditional in the Church to proceed to a decentralization of pastoral structures as soon as these no longer met certain norms. Whenever this measure was not taken, a rapid trend of de-Christianization was observable. This is what happened in the industrial societies of Europe, when in addition to the powerful anti-religious ideologies, the lack of adequate pastoral structures became a decisive factor. By way of contrast, in the United States, parish structures kept pace, in an extraordinary way, with the rhythm of population expansion, and this explains in great measure the dynamism of the Church in this country.[1] Faced with the rapid demographic evolution of the Latin American continent, a phenomenon without parallel in the history of mankind, the decentralization of pastoral action appears as the fundamental lesson to be learned from the history of other continents.

Since a sufficient number of priests to accomplish a decentralization on a grand scale is not possible in the foreseeable future, at least not for another two generations, and since this relatively short lapse of time will be decisive for the Church in Latin America, there is only one obvious solution: the utilization of the laity in pastoral work.

But before speaking of the laity, let us examine the role which religious Brothers and Sisters can play.

The number of religious Brothers in Latin America is relatively high, and contrary to trends in Europe, it is increasing. Between 1956 and 1960, the number went approximately from 8,500 to 12,800. The majority are engaged in teaching or work in the monasteries. It is difficult to foresee any other major short-term utilization of these religious. However, those who have adequate religious training could be admitted to the diaconate and thus furnish help in the distribution of the sacraments.

In the general panorama of the Latin American Church, the women religious represent the segment that has experienced the most rapid increase. Their numbers have grown more rapidly than the population. According to relatively precise statistics, they numbered 80,580 in 1956, and 100,200 in 1960; this means there is a nun for every 2,003 inhabitants in Latin America. One can hope that this rate of increase will continue for several years.

It should be noted, however, that a very high proportion of

these religious are engaged in education, and that the majority reside in the cities. Out of 7,810 religious houses for women, nearly 500 are houses of formation, and more than 3,500 are educational institutions. Regarding these institutions, let us simply remark in passing that there is still much to be done in the democratizing of education.

That the majority of religious live in the cities can be partially explained by the educational work in which they are engaged, but also by the poor condition of pastoral activity in the country. What Mother Superior would dare send Sisters into localities where they could attend Mass and receive Holy Communion only once every fifteen days, or once a month, or even less frequently?

It is certain, as numerous experiences have shown, that nuns can play an extraordinary role in a true effort for pastoral decentralization. In addition to the helpful tasks they can perform in community development of city neighborhoods and rural groups, there is the direct aid they can bring to pastoral action. They can train catechists and supervise their work, they can prepare the people for the reception of sacraments: baptism, holy communion, matrimony and the sacrament of the sick. They can initiate laymen to certain pastoral roles, which we will discuss later, and they can prepare the Christian communities for participation in the liturgy by explaining its meaning, teaching them the singing, etc.[2]

This naturally supposes an orientation and religious training quite different from what is ordinarily given. It does not seem impossible however, at least in a certain number of open-minded congregations. In order for this new pastoral activity of nuns to extend to the rural regions, however, certain permissions will have to be given them, for example, administering holy communion to themselves (this practice is now permissible in some mission territories of Brazil).

In spite of the role that religious Brothers and Sisters can play, it seems evident that the decentralization of pastoral action cannot be realized without confiding to the laity certain religious tasks for the benefit of the Christian community, especially in the rural regions. We shall list these tasks in the following paragraphs. The reading of the Gospel and catechetical instruction have already been entrusted to a great number of laymen. Prayer meetings conducted by them could be multiplied, and they could even be given the responsibility of distributing certain sacraments.

Why not, then, immediately propose the diaconate? This indeed seems to be the logical solution toward which we must work. But perhaps Latin America is not psychologically ready to accept such a solution. A period of transition would, of course, be necessary. During this period, certain laymen, judiciously chosen and supervised by the bishop, could receive a temporary mandate, renewable annually, permitting them to perform certain religious acts. Their ordination to the diaconate a few years later would cause no wonderment.

One of the great merits of Catholic Action in Latin America has been the formation of laymen capable of worthily fulfilling such a vocation. In every diocese there are many such men, heads of stable families, leading a deeply religious life, who would answer the call. Far from hindering vocations to the priesthood, we would see them flourish in such families.

THE DECENTRALIZATION OF CATECHESIS

The Church lives as a community of faith. We shall return to the qualitative aspects of this sector of pastoral action. But first, we would like to point out the importance of a decentralization of catechesis, which would extend religious instruction not only to small cells in the parochial centers, but to the scattered populations in the rural regions or the crowded urban masses.

During the past few years, an important movement for the training of catechists has been taking shape in most countries. CELAM has made great efforts in this direction. After the establishment of many diocesan and national offices of catechesis, the Latin American Center of Catechetical Training was created in Santiago in 1961. The turning point has been reached, and it can be said that the movement is today spreading throughout the continent. Much progress has to be made, however, in the quality of catechetical instruction. In this regard, the collaboration of the European centers of catechesis, such as the Catechetical Institute of Paris or the Lumen Vitae, has been most helpful.

THE DECENTRALIZATION OF WORSHIP

In Latin America, whenever the priest is absent, there is ordinarily no gathering of the Christian community. This was not always so. In many localities, the first missionaries would appoint community leaders. This office, not sufficiently supervised and often endowed with secular privileges, either fell into disuse or was suppressed because of abuses. In other regions of the world, the Church has given laymen the responsibility of leading the prayer of the community, and with much success. Such is the case in the Philippines and in many Asian and African countries where great distances and the shortage of priests make weekly services impossible.

The decentralization in the transmission of the authentic Christian message should normally be accompanied by a decentralization in ritual worship. Every community of believers should express its faith by worship in common. The absence of the priest must not prevent the faithful, whatever their number, from uniting for Sunday services. Such a gathering is in itself a communal sanctification of Sunday, but it also performs an important pastoral function by developing the consciousness of belonging to the Church, and by continuing Christian formation through the Word of God and the liturgy.

It is urgent that all the countries of Latin America understand that it is not enough to deplore the lack of priests, or to inaugurate pastoral systems (doomed from the outset) which have been worked out in countries provided with an adequate number of priests.

The apostolate of competent laymen, who are increasingly in

demand, will have to be extended far beyond the field of catechesis. Rituals for Sunday services without priests will have to be
worked out, and lay leaders will have to be instructed. For this
reason, concern should be given to establishing in the immediate
future the necessary centers for pastoral liturgy.

The center of Christian cult is the Eucharistic celebration. All
other forms of worship should refer to it in some way or another.
Baptism, for example, is the entrance into a community that is
called to celebrate and live by the Eucharist.

The absence of priests does not prevent the sacramental celebration of the Eucharist; nor does it prevent community services
from being focused on the Eucharist. It is up to the hierarchy to
grant this priest-less religious gathering the true status of liturgy
by approving a certain number of rites and by according a new
type of Church mandate to the person presiding (be he a deacon,
a religious or a simple layman).

At first, it might appear unusual that more initiative has not been
taken in this matter. It is understandable, however, in the context
of the Latin American Church, which has not been really mis-
sion-minded. Even in Cuba, where after the expulsions of 1961
there remained only about 200 priests, lay-directed religious services did not develop spontaneously as they did in Africa and Asia.
On these continents, other dynamic pastoral experiments are being
tried. Though they are only in a very early stage, it can be hoped
that they will develop and spread to all countries.

One thing is certain: this participation in worship is one of the
basic elements of integration into the Eucharistic community and,
therefore, of major importance in the work of evangelization.

THE DECENTRALIZATION OF
SACRAMENTAL LIFE

If Church discipline offers no obstacle to the organization of
community prayer directed by a layman, or catechetical instruction by a layman, such is not the case with the distribution of
certain sacraments.

Statistics show that there has been an increase in sacramental life, but it is not sure whether it is ahead or behind the population increase. Improvement depends on two factors. First of all, the decentralization of pastoral structures (parishes) and a multiplication of priests. Only in the measure that these elements increase faster than the population can we legitimately suppose an increase in sacramental life. But we have already noted that the rate of increase in the number of priests only very slightly surpasses the rate of the population growth, and there is no improvement foreseeable in the near future. As far as the parishes are concerned, the situation has improved relatively, but only in the cities. In these matters, therefore, we have evidently reached a stalemate.

The second factor in the increase of sacramental life is evolution of Church law. One tangible proof that this is decisive has been the effect of the relaxation of the Eucharistic fast. In the diocese of San Cristobal, Venezuela, for example, the average number of annual Communions per person in 1940 was 1.18. It fell to 0.89 in 1951, probably because of the rapid population increase due to the lowering of the infant mortality rate (infants, who could not receive Communion, assumed a greater proportion of the population). Since 1952 the average has suddenly increased, reaching 2.65 in 1959. This phenomenon, due to the changes in Church law concerning the fast, proves that the population itself is quite accessible to religious values (whether it was the same persons who received Communion more often, or a greater number of communicants) and that other disciplinary reforms would probably produce similar results, at least with the present generation.

The decentralization of sacramental life, nonetheless, poses delicate theological problems. It is not enough to say that the sacraments were instituted for men; it must also be remembered that the sacraments suppose faith.

The guiding principle in the service of souls seems to be: to work toward a more authentic administration of the sacramental signs and a more serious preparation of the faithful. The spirit of such a renovation is opposed to the now-prevalent preoccupation with a simple material increase in the number of sacraments administered. This principle in no way implies the refusal of the sacraments to those who have the right, nor does it obscure the truth that the sacraments are essentially for the supernatural progress of men. One should therefore guard against any arbitrary or exaggerated severity in the present context. Canon law by itself, or even as the major factor, cannot in a realistic way solve the problems of Latin America. Nor is it less a fact that certain structures of the Church are fixed, above all the relationship of Word and Sacrament. The degrading of the sacramental celebration into a magic rite is not an imaginary danger, any more than is the lack of Christian understanding of the sacraments. Not to try to remedy these weak points of Latin American Catholicism would be to encourage the propagation of sects, spiritism and other forms of syncretism.

THE TRANSMISSION OF FAITH
AND THE PARTICIPATION IN
THE EUCHARISTIC COMMUNITY

We now speak of the pastoral orientations made necessary by the effects of the qualitative aspects of social change.

Since the new society does not offer the traditional channels of transmission for religious values, the Church must create her own channels. Thus the prime importance of catechesis. To replace the natural channels of transmission, a systematic program is necessary. The Church is undergoing a general evolution, and Latin America is fortunate enough to be able to enter into it while there is still time.

The problems of a systematic catechesis are not simply organizational. There is the major question of content. Much reflection must be given this problem, so that the masses, while living a spirituality very close to natural religion, are not given a simple paraphrasing of a manual of scholastic theology. It would pass completely over their heads.

The mass media of communication can be most helpful in catechesis. Broadcasting a sermon or telecasting a Mass are only the most obvious possibilities; there are many others: radio plays, television series, rallies in the stadiums, etc.

But the transmission of religious values is not always accomplished directly. As a new society and a new culture develop, Christian action consists in collaborating with their growth, integrating a human development into them, and presenting to the men who are participating in them the message of Christ, that is, the free choice of salvation. In the development of society and culture there are key points, certain sectors of society that are of paramount importance because they shape not only the structures of tomorrow's society, but its values as well. In Latin America these key points are the universities (especially the state universities), the labor movements, and the emerging peasant organizations.

An intensive action, utilizing all available means and men, must be directed to these sectors, even if it means that other areas must be neglected. The task is so great that choices must be made. The choices must be judicious; they must correspond not to personal preferences but to real needs. It is more vital, for example, to assign a priest as a chaplain to students in a state university than it is to erect a new parish.

This naturally demands a vision and a pastoral planning that is not limited to the confines of a single parish, or even of a single diocese. The pastoral plans worked out by certain Latin American episcopates, after consultation with theologians and sociologists, are examples of collective thinking applied to decision making and to the determination of urgencies.

It should be unnecessary to point out that we are dealing mainly with the action of the laity, a laity engaged in the social and cultural revolution and integrated into the Eucharistic community. But there must be movements and specialized groups; otherwise there can be no valid solution to the specific problems of laymen engaged in secular tasks.

There do exist models of action in all sectors, among the

workers, the peasants, the university students, and professional people. We cannot overemphasize the role played by the Young Christian Workers (YCW) in Latin America, not only as an influence on the working youth, but as a stimulant for other social groups.

Models do not yet exist in all Latin American countries, but for many movements and organizations a continental structure has been established and this enables them to communicate and diffuse ideas and experiments, whose importance has not yet been appreciated. It can be said that after a period of excessive dependence on European and North American formulas, the continent has today at its disposal a sufficient number of indigenous experiments capable of effectively resolving its own problems.

Another important aspect is participation in the Eucharistic community. When there is a perfect equation between membership in a natural group (family, village, nation) and membership in a religious group, there is the evident danger that religion can become a simple function of society. When society changes (for example, from a rural society to an urban society) membership in a religious group can become a mere cultural trait. One of the principal objectives of dynamic pastoral action will be to develop the feeling of belonging to the Church, and to present the Church as a group with its own proper existence.

Indeed, supernatural membership in the Mystical Body of Christ is effected by baptism, but this is not adequate to create a feeling of belonging, a living consciousness of being a part of a visible social body. The feeling of membership will be created only by a real participation, either of a popular type (rather than discourage processions or pilgrimages, their content and expression should be renewed) or of a more highly developed type (liturgical renewal, the lay apostolate). In all these areas, pastoral decentralization is most important.

The liturgical renewal has its place in the deepening of participation in the Eucharistic community. All the sacraments are oriented toward the Eucharist; and the Mass is its actualization. The present experience of the Church in Cuba shows both the importance of the liturgy as a cohesive element of the community, and the feasibility of accomplishing such a renewal among the Latin American populations.

Besides being an active participation in worship, the liturgy must have a constant relationship to the whole Eucharist, that is, the Mystical Body of Christ, whose growth begins with the announcement of salvation, and whose expression of communal charity continues in the temporal action of Christians.

PASTORAL TRAINING

Need we really insist on this point? To whom is it not clear that one of the most imperative needs in the present circumstances is pastoral orientation and training? The work of pre-evangelization, naturally, comes first in Latin America, and it will be effected mostly by the laity; but it is inseparable from the work of evangelization.

A correct vision of the activity in these two domains is a necessary condition for any action of the Church. Only an evangelization that has been renewed with a true "missionary" spirit and oriented toward developing in Christians a deeper involvement in a community of faith, worship and charity, can be operative in the present situation of the continent. The facts speak for themselves, or rather it is the Spirit of God speaking to us through the facts. Furthermore, any real development of the laity can be held back by a clergy with shortsighted vision.

While awaiting a more radical reform of the seminaries, pastoral institutes seem to provide a valid answer to this need. Although they are still in an embryonic stage, CELAM has already decided to establish a Latin American institute for the purpose of providing the necessary updating of the clergy. We have no doubts that this task is more urgent than many others, including the construction of seminaries. What good is the mere multiplication of number, if perspectives are not re-focused to see the real needs of our time?

Several dioceses have recently initiated extremely well-planned pastoral workshops. It is a beginning, but it has already shown its usefulness by truly extraordinary results.

Such programs would also be most beneficial to foreign priests coming to Latin America. An almost exclusive concern with increased numbers is presently causing serious confusion in the pastoral orientation of priests from other countries: each one is too inclined to apply, without any modification, the pastoral methods adapted to his own socio-cultural and ecclesiastical environment, without taking into account the new realities with which he is faced. Canon Boulard, after a stay in a large South American city, told how alarmed he was with the pastoral confusion. Side by side were Spanish, French, American and Canadian parishes, with all their individual pastoral and cultural characteristics. How can we develop a unified pastoral action, so necessary in such a disorganized situation? Preliminary training in a pastoral institute could help these priests better adapt their apostolic labors.

NOTES

[1] See François Houtart, *Aspects sociologiques du catholicisme américain* (Paris: Ed. Ouvrières, 1957).

[2] An interesting experiment is now underway in the diocese of Natal, Brazil: nuns have been put in charge of a parish.

19

International Cooperation

We are firmly convinced that the problem of Latin America holds priority in the universal Church. This is not based on personal sentiment, but on observable fact. For world peace, the development of Latin America is not only important, it is one of the conditions. All Christians can contribute.

Latin America contains one-third of the world's Catholics, and in the year 2000 the figure will be one-half. This continent represents a very great reserve of apostolic energy for the evangelization of the world, if the present crises can be surmounted. We are not trying to say that Latin America is superior to other continents—this would not be in the spirit of Christ; but for the next five or ten years, it must have priority. After that, perhaps, the needs of other continents will take precedence.

Latin America stands in great need of aid. But aid given indiscriminately can be harmful. It must be directed to real needs, with a knowledge of their causes. We trust that the preceding chapters have sufficiently shown that the continent is undergoing profound transformations. To determine its real needs and to orient the action of the Church, a knowledge of these transformations is essential.

Another great danger is paternalism. It vitiates the human and spiritual value of any aid, which must be a common project of the initiators of the aid and the Latin Americans who are responsible for development. Not only are the rich susceptible to paternalism, but also organizations, religious orders, episcopates, and central administrations of the Church. This also places strict obligations on the Latin American leaders. They must plan their action well and work out a scale of priorities. This task calls for mutual collaboration.

The aid given must be well coordinated. In this regard, three pitfalls must be avoided. On the one hand, there must not be a complete dispersion, each bishop sending priests or money to localities where he happened to meet a friend, or religious orders choosing their field of apostolate on the basis of a chance voyage. On the other hand, there must not be an excessive centralization, which would kill all local initiative, and work against the very objectives pursued. Finally, it would be futile to create coordinating bodies without giving them the technical means to coordinate, that is, the knowledge of the facts and the possibilities of organic consultation with those charged with responsibility.

Let us realize that the countries who send aid will profit by it as much as, if not more than the countries who receive it. In addition to the supernatural merits gained, a rich flow of exchange is set in motion. Priests, Brothers, Sisters, and laymen visit the continent and return. They bring back fresh air, they enliven enthusiasm, they propose truly Catholic objectives to their local parishes or organizations. Written communications are established; magazines, radio and television programs are organized. Bishops or other representatives of Latin America come for lectures and make contacts. In short, local, diocesan and national communities began to live their Christianity more intensely.[1]

Those who return from a sojourn in Latin America no longer hold to their preconceived notions of pastoral and apostolic action. Their whole outlook is revised. The dioceses and religious congregations that send personnel can effect internal reforms which would have been otherwise impossible.

GENERAL PRINCIPLES

In order to state the question of international cooperation more clearly we present four general principles which are the result of the workshop conducted in Rio de Janeiro in 1962 under the initiative of the Conferences of the Religious of the United States and Canada, as well as numerous consultations.

Selectivity

A choice must be made. Just place your finger at random on any section of a map of Latin America and you will be pointing to an area that needs priests and financial help for social and religious action. Although the aid which is given or which can be given by Europe and North America represents only a small contribution in relation to the size of the problem to be solved, like a lever, which when well placed can lift enormous weights, it can be significant, provided it is well oriented.

One example should suffice. If we wished to solve the problem of priest shortage without the principle of selectivity, we would have to send 180,000 priests to Latin America. But in 14 years Spain has sent 600 diocesan priests, Belgium in 8 years has sent 70, the United States in 5 years, about 100, and Canada even less. No doubt these numbers will increase, but not in the proportion needed: by 1975, for example, 210,000 would have to be sent to equal the average number of priests in Europe and North America.

Selectivity supposes the working out of a hierarchy of choices. First consideration should be given to the relative importance of the different types of action, then to the circle of influence each activity would have, preference being given to those that would benefit the continent, then the country, the region, and finally the immediate locality.

Pastoral Planning

This should be a condition placed on aid given for any type of action whatsoever. Until each episcopate, each diocese, each religious group or each movement will have worked out its long-term and short-term plans, priority should be given to those that already have, for they offer the possibility of an effective integration into maturely considered activities whose relative immediacy has been established.[2]

Subsidiary Action

Where it is possible, foreign personnel should relieve Latin American priests, religious and laymen for more important action. It is very difficult for outsiders to take immediate charge of key posts; on the other hand, many Latin Americans, particularly adapted for these responsibilities, are necessarily retained in other positions because there are no available replacements. Such would be the case, for example, with a parish priest who had the particular aptitude to be the national chaplain of a movement, or to work with university students, or to teach in the seminary. It would be easier for personnel coming in from other countries to work in the parish than to take charge of specialized posts.

On the other hand, specialized personnel who can be spared in Europe and North America, or who can be rapidly trained, will always be welcomed. As many should come as possible. This arrangement, however, would have to be part of an over-all pastoral plan.

Training

The necessity of training cannot be minimized. Indeed, international cooperation cannot be set up along the lines of evangelizing "noble savages." Many of the incoming personnel will be working in a cultural milieu superior to the one from which they came. We have already stated that the object of exterior aid is to enable the Latin American Church to effect a "second evangelization," that of a new society and new culture. Moreover, the principle of selectivity in tasks supposes a principle of selectivity in personnel.

What is the program of such training? First of all, there is the language. This is most important, as everyone will agree. Next, there is the replacement in the individual of one culture by another. Without the capacity to absorb the characteristics of a new culture with its different values, hence, different outlooks on social life, institutions and pastoral methods, the candidate's progress promises to be rather painful from the very beginning. This is especially true of persons from countries which have a long cultural tradition, or which play an important role in world affairs.[3]

The third concern is theological training. There must be a serious introduction to a pastoral theology as well as to a theology of temporal matters. Indeed, everyone, priest and layman alike, will be confronted with new and unexpected pastoral and temporal decisions. (The preceding chapters should have removed any doubts on this score.)

Finally, it is becoming more and more evident that not only must the candidate be provided with vital information about the social, economic, and religious aspects of Latin America; he must also be trained to work in teams, and in the special circumstances that exist on the continent.

Concerning the sectors of action that must receive aid, we have three general considerations to propose. First of all, the situation which faces us is very complex and in a state of perpetual change. It demands a greater knowledge of and a greater reflection on the sectors of activity to be pursued. Most necessary, therefore, are centers of socio-religious research, and theological study of the pastoral and social realities of Latin America. Aid to these two projects should be of highest priority.

Secondly, since the transformation of Latin American society is so swift, the major work to be accomplished is that of training, and this includes all categories: priests, religious and laymen. Pastoral institutes, catechetical centers and Catholic Action teams should have priority over others.

Finally, in view of the rapidity of the population expansion, there can be no question of following a policy of creating additional institutions to keep pace with the expansion. Only when new institutions are indispensable for training at a certain level, should they be established. For example, rather than start primary schools, effort must be concentrated on the teacher-training schools.

Without losing sight of a principle we have already stated, namely, that all sectors of action must be integrated into an overall pastoral planning, we think it useful to indicate those sectors in which aid is desirable. We treat first pastoral action, then social and cultural action.

PASTORAL ACTION

There is, first of all, an *intensive action* on the key points. This can be broken down in three ways: according to the social groups, the geographical areas, or the types of action. As to the social groups, let us mention the university students, the workers and the peasants. What is principally involved here is the training of lay personnel. Among the most important geographical areas are the large cities, the new zones of colonization, and the regions of general pastoral work. The basic types of pastoral work include catechesis, liturgical renewal, the family, the youth, and vocations. We placed these types of pastoral work in the order of their urgency; this, of course, can be modified by particular circumstances. If we place vocations after the other sectors, it is because they largely depend on the other sectors. It would be fallacious to think that the problem of vocations can be solved without strengthening all pastoral activity.

Then there is *extensive action,* of which two categories are necessary. First, everything that can further the decentralization of pastoral action, and the training of persons among the clergy and laity to bring it about. Second, the utilization of the means of mass communication (press, radio, television) for religious purposes. Let us be quick to point out, however, that support should not be given indiscriminately to every initiative in this field. We are referring particularly to certain Catholic newspapers which defend reactionary social policies and which hence represent a counter-force.

SOCIAL AND CULTURAL ACTION

The principal fields of social action are: the organization of the peasant world, the political organizations, and the cooperatives. A word of caution seems necessary. It is not for the Church to create these organizations; it would only prolong a situation that has already cost dearly: Church domination over society. Nor is it a question of creating Catholic organizations to match the secular ones; this would only lead to a Catholic ghetto. What must be done is to orient and train laymen to organize the various sectors of social life according to Christian principles. The struggle in which we are engaged is an ideological one. It is not simply a technological, economic or cultural question.

On the other hand, it is not enough to present right principles, to elaborate an excellent doctrine, without concretely aiding the Christian laymen to translate into facts their ideas on the organization of society.

If in extreme cases—and they exist—the Church as an institution must intervene at any level, let us never forget that it must be with the idea of temporarily supplying a need and not of a permanent substitution.

Finally, we are not taken in by easy solutions which water down the real problems, with an attitude limited to "doing what is possible." The exceptional situations that face us in Latin America demand that we do the impossible. As an example of an easy solution, take the proposal to create cooperatives. It is a good proposal in itself, but at times it lacks realism. The organization of the peasant world is more urgent; once this is accomplished then cooperatives can be effectively created. Premature concern for cooperatives could drain energies toward individual projects, thus hindering a more general social promotion.

As to cultural action, it is particularly urgent in the following fields: illiteracy, teacher-training schools and technical schools (industrial and administrative).

Having indicated the various sectors of action that need help, a few words are in order about the help itself, namely, personnel and materials.

All priests, diocesan and religious, are welcome in Latin America, provided that they can understand the apostolic necessities of the continent, that is, involvement in the pastoral renewal. To send any other kind of priests would be doing more harm than good.

The action of religious Brothers is generally centered around teaching. They can render great services in new sectors or in the teacher-training schools. They themselves must be well trained in social matters, otherwise education will continue to be reserved to the richer classes.

Various tasks await the women religious. They can help toward the decentralization of pastoral action by assuming catechetical instruction, by preparing the laity, especially lay women, by engaging in social action of various kinds, and by putting into practice the new ideas in the education of girls. It is better that nuns do not come to Latin America at all, if they merely intend to work at improving the English or French of the young girls of high society.

Laymen can fit into various fields of pastoral and social action, especially those sectors that are not particularly suitable for priests or religious. But let us not create any illusions, there is no place in Latin America for a great number of laymen from abroad. There are really three categories of persons preferred: specialists in the educational, technological, economic or social sectors; directors of apostolic or social movements who might help their sister organizations in Latin America; and laymen who are willing to work in teams at the grass-roots level, in very trying conditions, and especially in the rural regions.

Besides personnel, Latin America also needs material aid. Several countries have already made great efforts in this regard. The same principles, mentioned above, must be applied to the orientation of this aid. As soon as a responsible coordinating organization can be created, an important part of the funds should be reserved to projects worked out by this organization. Any aid that is distributed without basic planning disappears like water in sand.

It has often been said that Latin America has more need of material means than of personnel, and in most cases this is correct. Does this mean that there is no money in Latin America? On the contrary, there is a good deal of money, but it is in the hands of those who have the least understanding of the present needs. The few who do are truly exceptional cases. Shall we penalize those who are sacrificing themselves in working toward a social and pastoral renovation, by denying material aid with the argument that there is already plenty of money in Latin America? As a matter of fact, it is generally invested in Europe or the United States. Or shall we ask them to await the conversion of the rich, or a revolution? The key sectors of pastoral and social action must be aided substantially and quickly; and the aid must be controlled by mutual accord. It can be in the form of machinery for the technical schools and universities, or agricultural tools, etc. Scholarships for Latin American students and social leaders are also important. In this matter we must be selective, avoid favoritism, and organize the necessary preparations so that the student might be effectively introduced to the intellectual, social and spiritual aspects of his studies. A new form of scholarship aid consists in making it possible for persons from other continents to come to Latin America for study sessions, meetings, or personal contact. Investment in human contacts is often more profitable than investment in bricks.

NOTES

[1] In this connection, we wish to cite for special mention the Latin America Bureau of the National Catholic Welfare Conference (NCWC), directed by Father John J. Considine, M.M. This bureau has made a great contribution in its efforts to increase cooperation between the Church in the United States and in Latin America. A similar contribution has also been made by the meetings of CICOP (Catholic Inter-American Cooperation Program), where many North and Latin Americans have met to discuss joint undertakings.

[2] See the discourse of John XXIII to CELAM (1958) in which he enunciates the principles: study the situation in Latin America, elaborate and plan, courageously carry out the decisions.

[3] The two main institutions for such training are the Centers of Intercultural Formation in Cuernavaca, Mexico, and Petropolis, Brazil, initiated by one of the most active people in the field of cooperation with Latin America, Msgr. Ivan Illich.

20

Conclusions

As we conclude this analysis and these reflections on a continent so important to the future of the world, we would like to say how ungratifying is the work that has been undertaken. The size of the problems, their rapid evolution, the new perspectives opening up, all this leaves one unsatisfied when he realizes how rich the life of this continent really is. Yet once you begin working, you are completely taken with your subject, you can never forget it. Latin America conquers those whom it attracts.

Development is the basic perspective in which all the problems of the continent must be viewed. Development involves gradually growing out of a colonial-type economy, based on the exportation of raw materials and agricultural goods. Only an international economic policy of price stabilization can create the basic condition for an "ungluing" of the present economies. Foreign aid, even if it is increased, will only be a palliative unless it is used to build indigenous economic structures.

But there is more to the problem than international obstacles. An internal revolution is indispensable in order to transform the feudal structures of the rural world and transform the urban masses into a true people, who participate in the economic, social, political, and cultural life of the nation. A simple evolution of the present regimes is not sufficient. Latin America no longer can afford the time for evolution. There is only one choice: revolution, that is, a radical transformation of some kind or other. The continent can choose a Marxist revolution. Or it can choose development through participation of the popular masses, economic planning, the initiative of willing intermediary groups, and an effective and massive foreign aid. History will tell which path is taken.

We must not expect miracles. Revolution implies a difficult period, even a temporary regression in certain sectors. The present failure of the Cuban experiment must not be judged now, but ten years from now. Even if we cannot accept its basic ideology, nor some of its methods, it is undeniable that Cuba is the only Latin American country which has undergone a total transformation. The methods used, plus the blockade they provoked, can only mean severe times in the immediate future. If the methods of the Cuban revolution cannot serve as a model to us, at least its objectives can.

Development supposes a veritable mobilization of all potentialities. Economic planners too often underestimate the contribution the populations can make to development. Experiments in Latin America show how basic this contribution is as a driving force. No doubt this is not enough; but if these efforts are not encouraged and integrated, only a system imposed from the outside will be able to realize progress.

This is where the spiritual realities of the continent can play an important positive role. Some will wonder what the Church can do for development. She can be a powerful factor of restraint or incentive. In Latin America, Catholicism, since it embraces more than 90 per cent of the inhabitants, carries a very heavy responsibility.

But signs of dynamism are multiplying. Christians are awakening. Many are beginning to discover in their faith the indispensable motivations for their contribution to development. Laymen, priests, and bishops have, each in his own sphere, undertaken initiatives which at times are gigantic. Whenever this spirit of faith slackens, especially in the powerful oligarchic classes, the profound motivation of Christianity is no longer in play. This motivation is also obscured in those men of the Church whose preoccupations are centered on the purely internal problems of the Church or are in reference to an integration into a society that has long since vanished. But the progressive forces are winning out in Latin American Catholicism (and the Vatican Council has shown this), even if a few centers of resistance are still powerful. The Church can be an inspirational force in development.

Her task is not primarily temporal. Yet it is striking how wholly dependent is the pastoral renewal on its perception and orientation of social change, for it is dealing with a new society and a new culture, hence must effect a second evangelization.

All Christians, Protestant and Orthodox minorities included, must do their part in guiding the development of Latin America. This task will be a true touchstone that will reveal to the world whether Christians really are the heralds of an undying message which will enable the men of today to perceive the truth.

During this, Latin America's hour, the Church is living an important period in her history, a period which will profoundly affect her universal mission.

Appendix

I

Percentage of People Employed in Agriculture in Several Countries

	Percentage of Population Employed	Percentage of National Income	
Argentina	25.2	20	(1961)
Brazil	50.5	27	(1959)
Chile	29.6	14	(1960)
Colombia	53.9	34	(1960)
Costa Rica	54.7	37	(1961)
Ecuador	53.2	37	(1961)
Honduras	83.1	44	(1960)
Panama	49.8	24	(1960)
Paraguay	53.8	38	(1961)
Peru	62.5	25	(1959)
Venezuela	41.3	6	(1959)

II
Consumer Price Index (1958=100)* and Exchange Rates
(in U.S. Dollars)†

Argentina	309 (1961)	Buenos Aires	192 (official rate)
Bolivia	144	La Paz	99 (selling rate)
Brazil	256	São Paulo	259 (free rate)
Chile	167	Santiago	164 (free rate)
Colombia	121	Bogotá	106 (free rate)
Costa Rica	103	San José	118 (principal export rate)
Dominican Republic	93	Santo Domingo	100
Ecuador	106	Quito	137 (free rate)
El Salvador	97	San Salvador	100 (selling rate)
Guatemala	98	Guatemala City	100
Haiti	90 (1960)	Port-au-Prince	100
Honduras	101 (1961)	Tagucigalpa	100
Mexico	109	Mexico City	100 (official rate)
Nicaragua	95	Managua	100 (free rate)
Panama	100 (1959)	Panama City	—
Peru	128 (1961)	Lima	109
Paraguay	152	Asunción	113 (import rate)
Puerto Rico	108	San Juan	—
Uruguay	237	Montevideo	317
Venezuela	106	Caracas	136 (free rate)

* UN, *Statistical Yearbook 1962* (New York, 1963), pp. 480–486, Table 161.

† *Ibid.*, pp. 510–519, Table 167.

III
Crude Marriage Rates, 1954–1962 (per 1,000 population)*

	1954	1955	1956	1957	1958	1959	1960	1961	1962
Argentina	7.7	7.5	7.4	7.4	7.2	7.1	6.8	—	—
Bolivia	7.6	5.4	6.2	4.2	4.8	5.3	4.8	4.9	—
Chile	8.3	8.9	8.4	7.6	7.2	7.4	7.1	7.3	—
Colombia	6.0	5.9	5.9	5.9	5.8	5.9	6.0	6.1	—
Costa Rica	7.6	7.4	7.1	6.9	7.3	7.2	7.7	7.1	—
Dominican Republic	6.7	4.1	3.1	3.7	4.2	4.1	3.6	—	—
Ecuador	6.8	6.1	6.1	6.1	7.5	6.1	—	—	—
El Salvador	4.0	3.7	3.8	4.0	3.6	6.8	3.6	3.3	—
Guatemala	4.1	3.7	4.8	4.9	4.7	5.3	4.4	4.1	3.6
Honduras	4.6	3.6	4.3	3.9	4.0	9.6	3.9	3.3	—
Mexico	7.1	7.1	7.2	6.7	6.9	7.0	6.8	6.3	—
Nicaragua	4.0	3.8	3.5	3.7	3.8	3.8	7.0	3.3	—
Panama	3.8	3.3	3.4	3.4	5.7	15.0	3.5	3.0	—
Paraguay	5.0	4.4	4.6	5.0	4.9	5.0	4.4	—	—
Peru	4.3	4.7	4.7	4.3	4.6	4.6	4.5	2.9	—
Puerto Rico	8.8	8.4	8.4	8.5	8.7	8.7	8.5	8.8	—
Uruguay	8.1	8.1	7.6	7.7	7.6	7.5	—	—	—
Venezuela	5.5	4.9	5.6	5.2	5.1	5.3	5.1	5.0	—

* UN, *Demographic Yearbook 1962* (New York, 1963), pp. 586–587.

IV

Population (1965–1980): Midyear Estimates and Projections
(in thousands) *

	1965	1970	1975	1980
Argentina	22,909	24,937	27,068	29,334
Bolivia	4,136	4,658	5,277	6,000
Brazil	81,300	93,752	107,863	123,566
Chile	8,567	9,636	10,872	12,300
Colombia	17,787	20,514	23,774	27,691
Costa Rica	1,467	1,769	2,110	2,491
Cuba	7,523	8,307	9,146	10,034
Dominican Republic	3,588	4,277	5,124	6,174
Ecuador	5,036	5,909	6,933	8,080
El Salvador	2,859	3,346	3,917	4,585
Guatemala	4,343	5,053	5,906	6,942
Haiti	4,645	5,255	6,001	6,912
Honduras	2,315	2,750	3,266	3,879
Mexico	42,681	50,733	60,554	72,659
Nicaragua	1,754	2,083	2,474	2,938
Panama	1,209	1,387	1,591	1,823
Paraguay	2,007	2,296	2,645	3,065
Peru	11,533	13,200	15,069	17,130
Uruguay	2,647	2,802	2,960	3,126
Venezuela	8,722	10,399	12,434	14,827
Total	237,028	273,063	314,984	363,556

* UN, *Statistical Bulletin for Latin America,* Vol. I, No. 1 (1964).

V

Daily Newspapers (number, estimated circulation and copies
per 1,000 population)*

Argentina (1959)	135	Haiti (1960)	11
Bolivia	34	Honduras (1959)	25
Brazil (1960)	54	Mexico (1961)	83
Chile (1961)	134	Nicaragua (1959)	66
Colombia	56	Panama	104
Costa Rica	94	Paraguay	37
Cuba (1956)	129	Peru (1957)	76
Dominican Republic (1960)	27	Puerto Rico (1961)	61
Ecuador (1961)	56	Uruguay (1960)	260
El Salvador (1960)	45	Venezuela	96
Guatemala (1961)	23	United States	326

* UN, *Statistical Yearbook 1962*, pp. 649–650, Table 181.

VI
Protestantism in Latin America (1961)*

Country	Churches	Membership	Clergy Foreign	Native
Argentina	2,067	414,323	245	732
Bolivia	544	46,663	200	253
Brazil	20,990	4,071,643	687	8,403
Colombia	1,618	92,728	96	236
Costa Rica	290	22,902	51	109
Cuba	1,416	264,927	112	527
Chile	2,490	834,839	119	277
Dominican Republic	611	19,289	95	116
Ecuador	186	11,499	77	34
El Salvador	1,144	57,691	14	197
Guatemala	1,553	149,081	44	265
Haiti	2,418	327,140	75	78
Honduras	438	34,488	39	117
Mexico	3,515	897,227	77	789
Nicaragua	297	37,666	20	28
Panama	358	41,778	58	219
Paraguay	270	36,560	99	258
Peru	1,178	94,053	168	258
Puerto Rico	934	174,707	29	203
Uruguay	243	42,594	38	93
Venezuela	60	26,042	133	82
Total	42,420	7,710,412	2,556	13,526

* Prudencio Damboriena, S.J., *El Protestantismo en América Latina* (Fribourg: FERES, 1963) Vol. 2, p. 18. (Reprinted from Kenneth Grubb, H. W. Coxill, World Dominion Press, London.)